The Bhagavadgita
A Simple Translation

By Jayaram V

Published by
Pure Life Vision LLC
New Albany, Ohio

The Bhagavadgita A Simple Translation

Published and Distributed Worldwide by Pure Life Vision LLC., USA.
www.PureLifeVision.com
First edition 2011

Publisher Cataloging-in-Publication Data

V, Jayaram
The Bhagavadgita Simple Translation
p. cm
Includes Translation of : The Bhagavadgita
ISBN- 13: 978-1-935760-17-7
ISBN -10: 1935760173
1. Bhagavadgita-Commentaries. 2. Religious life – Hinduism 3. Hinduism - Sacred Writings 4. Hinduism – Theology
I. Bhagavadgita. English. II. Title

BL1138.62.V2 2011
294.5/924— dc22 2011913517

Printed in the United States of America
10 9 8 7 6 5 4 3 2 1
First Edition

The Bhagavadgita

A Simple Translation

by

Jayaram V

ALSO BY JAYARAM V

1. Think Success: A Collection of Writings on Success and Achievement through Positive Thinking, Volume I
2. Think Success: A Collection of Writings on Success and Achievement through Positive Thinking, Volume II
3. Think Success: A Collection of Writings on Success and Achievement through Positive Thinking, Combined Volume
4. The Awakened Life: A Collection of Writings on Spiritual Life
5. Brahman
6. Essays on the Bhagavadgita
7. The Bhagavadgita: Complete Translation

FORTHCOMING

1. Introduction to Hinduism
2. The Yogasutras of Patanjali
3. Selected Upanishads: Translation and Notes

Contents

Author's Note 3
1 – Arjuna's Yoga of Sorrow 7
2 – The Yoga of Knowledge 24
3 – The Yoga of Action 52
4 – The Yoga of Knowledge with Renunciation of Action 69
5 – The Yoga of Renunciation of Action 85
6 – The Yoga of Self-absorption 97
7 – The Yoga of Knowledge and Wisdom 116
8 – The Yoga of Imperishable Brahman 128
9 – The Yoga of Sovereign Knowledge and Mystery 140
10 – The Yoga of Divine Manifestations 154
11- The Yoga of the Vision of the Universal Form 170
12 – The Yoga of Devotion 194
13 – The Yoga of the Field and the Knower of the Field 202
14 – The Yoga of the Division of the Triple Gunas 216
15 – The Yoga of the Supreme Person 227
16 – The Division of the Divine and Demonic Properties 236
17 – The Yoga of the Threefold Division of Qualities 246
18 – The Yoga of Liberation by Renunciation 257
The Greatness of the Bhagavadgita 286

Author's Note

According to the Bhagavadgita, a person should not renounce his actions or avoid his obligatory duties.

None can avoid karma by inaction. However, one can escape from it by performing one's actions selflessly, with detachment, relinquishing doership, ownership and the desire for the fruit of such actions. Whoever pursues the path of liberation must cultivate devotion to God, offering Him all his actions and acknowledging Him as the real doer. He should also live virtuously, cultivating purity and sameness towards the pairs of opposites.

He should also aware that death and modifications are for the mind and the body, but not for the Self which is eternal and inexhaustible and which is his real identity. Centered in this identity, he should remain absorbed in the contemplation of God and do his duty. Actions performed in this manner do not lead to bondage. Always engaged in actions in this manner, taking shelter in God, and earning His grace, finally a devotee attains the eternal, imperishable Abode of Brahman.

In short, this is the essence of the Bhagavadgita. Lord Krishna declared that this knowledge should never be spoken to one who was not austere, who was without devotion, who had no genuine interest in listening to the discourse and who spoke ill of God. However, whosoever with supreme adoration to Him taught this knowledge to His devotees he would attain Him without any doubt.

This edition of the Bhagavadgita contains a simple word-to-word translation. The complete translation with commentary is also available. Interested readers may refer to it to understand the true meaning of the verses and their relevance to the present day life.

Jayaram V

Translation

1 – Arjuna's Yoga of Sorrow

Sloka 1

dhṛtarāṣṭra uvāca
dharmakṣetre kurukṣetre samavetā yuyutsavaḥ
māmakāḥ pāṇḍavāś caiva kim akurvata sañjaya

dhṛtarāṣṭra = dhrtarashtra; uvāca = said; dharmakṣetre =in sacred field, in the field of righteousness; kurukṣetre = kuruksetra; samavetā = gathered, assembled; yuyutsavaḥ = raring to fight; māmakāḥ = my sons; pāṇḍavāś = Pandavas; ca = and; eva = certainly; kim = what; akurvata = doing; sañjaya = O Sanjaya.

Said Dhritarashtra, "In the sacred field of Kurukshetra, O Sanjaya, what my sons and Pandavas are doing, assembled together and raring to fight? "

Sloka 2

sañjaya uvāca
dṛṣṭvā tu pāṇḍavānīkaṃ vyūḍhaṃ duryodhanas tadā
ācāryam upasaṅgamya rājā vacanam abravīt

sañjaya = Sanjaya; uvāca = said; dṛṣṭvā = having seen; tu = but; pāṇḍavānīkaṃ = Pandava's army; vyūḍhaṃ = battle formation; duryodhanas = Duryodhana; tadā = then ācāryam = teacher; upasaṅgamya = went near; rājā = king; vacanam = words; abravīt = spoke.

Said Sanjaya, "Having seen the numerous battle formations of the Pandava's army, king Duryodhana then went near his teacher (Dronacharya) and spoke (these) words.

Sloka 3

paśyaitāṃ pāṇḍuputrāṇām ācārya mahatīṃ camūm
vyūḍhāṃ drupadaputreṇa tava śiṣyeṇa dhīmatā

paśya = look; etāṃ = the; pāṇḍuputrāṇām = Pandavas; the sons of Pandu; ācārya = teacher; mahatīṃ = great; camūm = military might;

vyūḍhāṃ = formation; drupadaputreṇa = by the sons of Drupada; tava = your; śiṣyeṇa = disciple; dhīmatā = intelligent.

"O great teacher, look at the military might of the army of the Pandavas, arraigned by your intelligent disciple and son of Drupada.

Sloka 4

atra śūrā maheṣvāsā bhīmārjunasamā yudhi
yuyudhāno virāṭaśca drupadaś ca mahārathaḥ

atra = here; śūrā = heroes; maha = great; iṣvāsā = archers; bhīmārjuna = Bhima and Arjuna; samā = equal to yudhi = in fighting; yuyudhāna = Yuyudhana; virāṭaśca = virata also drupadaśca = Drupada also; mahā = great rathaḥ = charioteer.

"Here in this army are great heroes and archers, equal to Arjuna and Bhima in fighting, also like Yuyudhna, Virata and the great charioteer, Drupada.

Sloka 5

dhṛṣṭaketuś cekitānaḥ kāśirājaś ca vīryavān
purujit kuntibhojaś ca śaibyaś ca narapuṅgavaḥ

dhṛṣṭaketuś = Dhristaketu; cekitānaḥ = Cekitana kāśirājah = king of Kasi; ca = also; vīryavān = heroic; purujit = Purujit; kuntibhojah = Kuntibhoja; ca = and śaibyah = Saibya; ca = also; narapuṅgavaḥ = Notable among men.

"And there are great fighters like Dhristaketu, Cekitanu, king of Kasi, the heroic Purujit, Kuntibhoja and Saibya and those the notable among men.

Sloka 6

yudhāmanyuś ca vikrānta uttamaujāś ca vīryavān
saubhadro draupadeyāś ca sarva eva mahārathāḥ

yudhāmanyuh = Yudhamanyu; ca = and; vikrānta = mighty; uttamaujāh = Uttamauja; ca = and; vīryavān = very powerful;

saubhadro = son of Saubhadra; draupadeyāh = the sons of Draupadi; ca = and; sarva = all; eva = certainly; maharathāḥ = great charioteers.

"There are also Yudhamanyu, the mighty Uttamauja, the sons of Subhadra and Draupadi, who are all certainly great charioteers.

Sloka 7

asmākaṃ tu viśiṣṭā ye tān nibodha dvijottama
nāyakā mama sainyasya saṃjñārthaṃ tān bravīmi te

asmakam = our; tu = but; visistah = especially powerful; ye = those; tan = them; nibodha = just take note; be informed; dvija-uttama = the best of the twice born; nayakah = leaders; mama = my; sainyasya = of the army; samjna-artham = for identification; tan = them; bravimi = I am speaking; te = your.

"O Superior among the twice born, let me tell you about the most distinguished leaders of my own army, so that you will be able to locate them and remember them during the war.

Sloka 8

bhavān bhīṣmaś ca karṇaś ca kṛpaś ca samitiñjayaḥ
aśvatthāmā vikarṇaś ca saumadattis tathaiva ca

bhavan = your self; bhismah = Bhisma; ca = also; karnah = Karna; ca = and; krpah = Krpa; ca = and; samitim-jayah = always victorious; asvatthama = Asvatthama; vikarnah = Vikarna; ca = as well as; saumadattih = the son of Somadatta; tatha = and as; eva = certainly; ca = and.

"You, Bhishma, Karna, Kripa, Aswaththama, Vikarna and Somadatta's son, who are always victorious in battle.

Sloka 9

anye ca bahavaḥ śūrā madarthe tyaktajīvitāḥ
nānāśastrapraharaṇāḥ sarve yuddhaviśāradāḥ

anye = others; ca = also; bahavah = many; surah = heroes; mad-arthe = for my sake; tyakta-jivitah = sacrifice their lives; nana = many; sastra =

weapons; praharanah = equipped with; sarve = all of them; yuddha = battle; visaradah = excellent or outstanding.

"Also many other heroes, all equipped with weapons and outstanding in warfare, willing to lay down their lives for my sake.

Sloka 10

aparyāptaṃ tad asmākaṃ balaṃ bhīṣmābhirakṣitam
paryāptaṃ tvidam eteṣāṃ balaṃ bhīmābhirakṣitam

aparyaptam = unlimited, vast, extensive; tat = that; asmakam = of ours; balam = strength; bhisma = by Bhisma; abhiraksitam = well protected; paryaptam = limited; tu = but; idam = all these; etesam = of the Pandavas; balam = strength; bhima = by Bhima; abhiraksitam = well protected.

"Unlimited is our strength, well protected by Bhishma, while the strength of the Pandavas' army is limited, well protected by Bhima.

Sloka 11

ayaneṣu ca sarveṣu yathābhāgam avasthitāḥ
bhīṣmam evābhirakṣantu bhavantaḥ sarva eva hi

ayanesu = in the strategic places; ca = also; sarvesu = all; yatha-bhagam = as planned; avasthitah = standing, placed; bhismam = to Bhisma; eva = certainly; abhiraksantu = provide cover; bhavantah = till the end; sarve = all; evahi = firmly.

"Placing yourselves in the strategic places, all of you should provide cover to Bhisma firmly till the end as planned."

Sloka 12

tasya sañjanayan harṣaṃ kuruvṛddhaḥ pitāmahaḥ
siṃhanādaṃ vinadyocchaiḥ śaṅkhaṃ dadhmau pratāpavān

tasya = his; sanjanayan = increasing; harsam = joy, happiness; kuru-vrddhah = grand old man of kurus (Bhisma); pitamahah = the grandfather; simha-nadam = lion's roar; vinadya = sound, noise;

uccaih = very loudly; sankham = conchshell; dadhmau = blew; pratapa-van = the valiant.

"Then valiant Bhishma, the grand old man of Kurus and the great grandfather, blew his conch that sounded like the roar of a lion, increasing the joy (of Duryodhana).

Sloka 13

tataḥ śaṅkhāś ca bheryaś ca paṇavānakagomukhāḥ
sahasaivābhyahanyanta sa śabdas tumulobhavat

tatah = thereafter; sankhah = conches; ca = also; bheryah = kettle drums; ca = and; panava-anaka = trumpets and drums; go-mukhah = horns; sahasa = suddenly; eva = certainly; abhyahanyanta = all at once; sah = that; sabdah = sound; tumulah = tumultuous; abhavat = resulted.

"Then many conches, large drums, small drums, kettle drums, and horns were all blown suddenly at once and the resulting sound was tumultuous.

Sloka 14

tataḥ śvetair hayair yukte mahati syandane sthitau
mādhavaḥ pāṇḍavaś caiva divyau śaṅkhau pradaghmatuḥ

tatah = thereafter; svetaih = by white; hayaih = horses; yukte = yoked; mahati = in a great; syandane = chariot; sthitau = seated, ensconced; madhavah = Krishna; pandavah = Arjuna; ca = also; eva = certainly; divyau = divine, heavenly, celestial; sankhau = conchshells; pradadhmatuh = sounded.

"Then seated in a great chariot, drawn by white horses, Krishna and Arjuna, also blew their divine conches.

Sloka 15

pāñcajanyaṃ hṛṣīkeśo devadattaṃ dhanañjayaḥ
pauṇḍraṃ dadhmau mahāśaṅkhaṃ bhīmakarmā vṛkodaraḥ

pancajanyam = Pancajanyam; hrsika-isah = Krishna; devadattam = Devadattam; dhanam-jayah = Arjuna; paundram = Paundra;

dadhmau = blew; maha-sankham = big conchshell; bhima-karma = mighty deeds; vrka-udarah = perrson with great hunger.

"Then Krishna, Arjuna and Bhima of mighty deeds and voracious stomach blew their conches named Panchajanyam, Devadatta and the big Paundra.

Sloka 16

anañtavijayaṃ rājā kuntīputro yudhiṣṭhiraḥ
nakulaḥ sahadevaś ca sughoṣamaṇipuṣpakau

ananta-vijayam = Anantavijayam; raja = the king; kunti-putrah = the son of Kunti; yudhisthirah = Yudhisthira; nakulah = Nakula; sahadevah = Sahadeva; ca = and; sughosa-manipuspakau = Sughosa and Manipuspaka.

"Yudhishtira, the son of Kunti, and Nakula and Sahadeva (blew) Anantavijayam, Manipushpaka and Sughosha

Sloka 17

kāśyaś ca parameṣvāsaḥ śikhaṇḍī ca mahārathaḥ
dhṛṣṭadyumno virāṭaś ca sātyakiś cāparājitaḥ

kasyah = an epithet for the king of Kasi; ca = and; parama-isu-asah = the great archer; sikhandi = Sikhandi; ca = also; maha-rathah = great charioteer; dhrstadyumnah = Dhrstadyumna; viratah = Virata; ca = also; satyakih = Satyaki; ca = and; aparajitah = undefeated or invincible.

"The King of Kasi, the great archer Sikhandi, the great charioteer Dhristadyumna, Virata and the invincible Satyaki.

Sloka 18

drupado draupadeyāś ca sarvaśaḥ pṛthivīpate
saubhadraś ca mahābāhuḥ śaṅkhān dadhmuḥ pṛthakpṛthak

drupadah = Drupada; draupadeyah = the sons of Draupadi; ca = and; sarvasah = all; prthivi-pate = O lord of the earth; saubhadrah = the son of Subhadra; ca = also; maha-bahuh = very strong; sankhan = conchshells; dadhmuh = blew; prthak prthak = each separately.

"O Lord of the earth, Drupada, the sons of Draupadi, and the mighty son of Subhadra also blew their conches separately.

Soka 19

sa ghoṣo dhārtarāṣṭrāṇāṃ hṛdayāni vyadārayat
nabhaś ca pṛthivīṃ caiva tumulobhyanunādayan

sah = that; ghosah = din, noise; dhartarastranam = of the sons of Dhrtarastra; hrdayani = hearts; vyadarayat = shook, startled, disturbed; nabhah = the sky; ca = also; prthivim = the earth; ca = also; eva = certainly; tumulah = tumultous; abhyanunadayan = reverberating.

"That tumultuous din reverberating through the sky and the earth certainly shook the hearts of the sons of Dhritarashtra.

Sloka 20

atha vyavasthitān dṛṣṭvā dhārtarāṣṭrān.h kapidhvajaḥ
pravṛtte śastrasaṃpāte dhanur udyamya pāṇḍavaḥ

atha = thereupon; vyavasthitan = situated; drstva = watching; dhartarastran = the sons of Dhrtarastra; kapi-dhvajah = with the flag of Hanuman mounted on his chariot; pravrtte = disposed; sastra = arrows; sampate = ready to come down; dhanuh = bow; udyamya = taking up, getting ready; pandavah = the son of Pandu (Arjuna).

"Thereupon, watching the arrows waiting to come down from the sons of Dhritarashtra and taking up his bow, the son of Pandu whose flag atop the chariot bore the image of Hanuman...

Sloka 21

hṛṣīkeśaṃ tadā vākyam idam āha mahīpate
senayor ubhayor madhye rathaṃ sthāpaya mecyuta

Hrisikesam = to Krishna; tada = that; vakyam = speech, words, sentence; aha = said; mahipate = O lord of the earth; senayoh = armies; idam = this; ubhayoh = two, both; madhye = between; ratham = chariot; sthapaya = stop; me = my; acyuta = Achyuta.

O Lord of the earth, (Arjuna) said these words to Krishna, "O Achyuta, stop the chariot between the two armies.'"

Sloka 22

yāvad etān nirikṣehaṃ yoddhukāmān avasthitān
kair mayā saha yoddhavyam asmin raṇasamudyame

yavatas = all or as as many as ; etan = all these; nirikse = see, take a look; aham = I; yoddhu-kaman = raring to fight; avasthitan = present; kaih = with whom; maya = by me; saha = with; yoddhavyam = fight; asmin = in this; rana = war; samudyame = exertion, work hard.

"That I (may) look at all these, who are present here, raring to fight and with whom I may have to strive in this war.

Sloka 23

yotsyamānān avekṣehaṃ ya etetra samāgatāḥ
dhārtarāṣṭrasya durbuddher yuddhe priyacikīrṣavaḥ

yotsyamanan = those who will be fighting; avekse = let me see; aham = I; ye = who; ete = those; atra = here; samagatah = assembled; dhartarastrasya = son of Dhrtarastra; durbuddheh = evil minded; yuddhe = in the battle priya = pleasing; cikirsavah = wishing.

"Let me also see those who have assembled here to fight, wishing to please the evil minded son of Dhritarashtra (Duryodhana)."

Sloka 24

evam ukto hṛṣīkeśo guḍākeśena bhārata
senayor ubhayor madhye sthāpayitvā rathottamam

sanjayah = Sanjaya; uvaca = said; evam = thus; uktah = told, spoken, addressed; hrsikesah = Hrisikesa; gudakesena = by Gudakesa; bharata = O Bharata; senayoh = of the armies; ubhayoh = of both; madhye = in between; sthapayitva = station; ratha-uttamam = the finest chariot.

Sanjaya said, "O, Bharata, thus spoken by Arjuna, Krishna stationed their excellent chariot in between the two armies.

Sloka 25

bhīṣmadroṇapramukhataḥ sarveṣāṃ ca mahīkṣitām
uvāca pārtha paśyaitān samavetān kurūn iti

bhisma = Bhisma; drona = Drona; pramukhatah = facing, in front of; sarvesam = all; ca = also; mahi-ksitam = rulers of the earth; uvaca = said; partha = O Partha); pasya = behold; etan = all of them; samavetan = assembled; kurun = kurus; iti = thus.

"In front of Bhishma, Drona and all the rulers of the earth, said Krishna, 'Partha, see all the Kurus.'"

Sloka 26

tatrāpaśyat sthitān pārthaḥ pitṛn atha pitāmahān
ācāryān mātulān bhrātṛn putrān pautrān sakhīṃs tathā

tatra = there; apasyat = saw; sthitan = standing; parthah = Arjuna; pitrn = fathers; atha = also; pitamahan = grandfathers; acaryan = teachers; matulan = maternal uncles; bhratrn = brothers; putran = sons; pautran = grandsons; sakhin = friends; tatha = too.

"There Arjuna saw standing fathers, also grandfathers, teachers, maternal uncles, brothers, sons, grandsons, friends...

Sloka 27

śvaśurān suhṛdaś caiva senayor ubhayor api
tān samīkṣya sa kaunteyaḥ sarvān bandhūn avasthitān

svasuran = fathers-in-law; suhrdah = amiable, good hearted; ca = also; eva = certainly; senayoh = of the armies; ubhayoh = of both api = including; tan = all of them; samiksya = saw; sah = he; kaunteyah = Arjuna; sarvan = all kinds of; bandhun = relatives; avasthitan = standing in position.

"Fathers-in-law and also amiable people in both the armies. After Arjuna saw all kinds of relatives standing in their respective positions.

Sloka 28

kṛpayā parayāviṣṭo viṣīdann idamabravīt
dṛṣṭvemaṃ svajanaṃ kṛṣṇa yuyutsuṃ samupasthitam

krpaya = by compassion; paraya = great; avistah = overcome, filled with; visidan = with sadness; idam = thus; abravit = spoke; dṛṣṭva = see; mama = my; svajanaṃ = own people; kṛṣṇa = O Krish na; yuyutsuṃ = ready to fight; samupasthitam = gathered.

"Overcome with great compassion and filled with sadness, Arjuna spoke thus,'O Krishna, seeing my own people gathered here ready to fight'.

Sloka 29

sīdanti mama gātrāṇi mukhañ ca pariśuṣyati
vepathuś ca śarīre me romaharṣaś ca jāyate

sidanti = shaking; mama = my; gatrani = limbs; mukham = mouth; ca = also; parisusyati = parched.; vepathuh = trembling of the body; ca = also; sarire = on the body; me = my; roma-harsah = hairs standing on end; ca = also; jayate = is taking place;

"My limbs are shaking, mouth is parched, body is trembling and the hair on my body is standing on end.

Sloka 30

gāṇḍīvaṃ straṃsate hastāt tvak caiva paridahyate
na ca śaknomy avasthātuṃ bhramatīva ca me manaḥ

gandivam = Gandivam, Arjuna's bow; sramsate = slipping; hastat = from the hands; tvak = skin; ca = and; eva = certainly; paridahyate = burning; na = nor; ca = and; saknomi = am I able; avasthatum = stand; bhramati = reeling; iva = as; ca = and; me = my; manah = mind;

"Gandivam is slipping from my hands, my skin is burning all over; I am not able to stand , and my mind is reeling.

Sloka 31

nimittāni ca paśyāmi viparītāni keśava
na ca śreyonupaśyāmi hatvā svajanam āhave

nimittani = bad omens; ca = and; pasyami = I foresee; viparitani = inauspicious, the opposite; kesava = O Kesava; na = not; ca = and; sreyah = good; anupasyami = foresee; hatva = by killing; sva-janam = own people; ahave = in the battle, fight;

"And I see inauspicious omens, O Kesava. Nor do I foresee any good from killing my own people in the battle.

Sloka 32

na kāṅkṣe vijayaṃ kṛṣṇa na ca rājyaṃ sukhāni ca
kiṃ no rājyena govinda kiṃ bhogair jīvitena vā

na = notr; kankse = desire; vijayam = victory; krsna = O Krsna; na = not; ca = and; rajyam = kingdom; sukhani = happiness thereof; ca = and; kim = what; nah = to us; rajyena = kingdom; govinda = O Govinda; kim = what; bhogaih = enjoyment; jivitena = living.

"I do not desire victory O Krishna, nor kingdom, nor the joy of having it. Of what use, O Govinda, kingdom or enjoyment or even living?

Sloka 33

yeṣām arthe kāṅkṣitaṃ no rājyaṃ bhogāḥ sukhāni ca
ta imevasthitā yuddhe prāṇāṃs tyaktvā dhanāni ca

yesam = for whom; arthe = sake kanksitam = desired; nah = our; rajyam = kingdom; bhogah = enjoyment; sukhani = happiness; ca = and; te = they; ime = these; avasthitah = stand, arrayed; yuddhe = in the battle; pranan = lives; tyaktva = renouncing; dhanani = riches; ca = and;

"Those for whose sake (we) desire kingdom, enjoyment and happiness, they are stand (here) in the battle, renouncing their lives and riches.

Sloka 34

ācāryāḥ pitaraḥ putrās tathaiva ca pitāmahāḥ
mātulāḥ śvaśurāḥ pautrāḥ śyālāḥ sambandhinas tathā

acaryah = teachers; pitarah = fathers; putrah = sons; tatha = thus; eva = even; ca = and; pitamahah = grandfathers; matulah = maternal uncles; svasurah = fathers-in-law; pautrah = grandsons; syalah = brothers-in-law; sambandhinah = relatives; tatha = as well as.

"Teachers, fathers, sons, and thus even grandfathers, maternal uncles, fathers-in-law, grandsons, brothers-in-law and other kinsmen.

Sloka 35

etān na hantum icchhāmi ghnatopi madhusūdana
api trailokyarājyasya hetoḥ kiṃ nu mahīkṛte

etan = all these; na = never; hantum = for killing; icchami = do I wish; ghnatah = being killed; api = even; madhusudana = O Madhusudana; api = even if; trai-lokya = of the three worlds; rajyasya = of the kingdoms; hetoh = for the sake; kim = what to speak of; nu = only; mahi-krte = for the sake of the earth.

"I do not wish to kill them, even though they may, O Madhusudana, not even for the lordship of the three worlds. Then what to speak of the earth?

Sloka 36

nihatya dhārtarāṣṭrān naḥ kā prītiḥ syājanārdana
pāpam evāśrayed asmān hatvaitān ātatāyinaḥ

nihatya = by slaying; dhartarastran = the sons of Dhrtarastra; nah = our; ka = what; pritih = pleasure; syat = will there be; janardana = O Janardana; papam = sin; eva = certainly; asrayet = take shelter; asman = us; hatva = by killing; etan = all these; atatayinah = aggressors.

"By slaying the sons of Dhritarashtra, what pleasure will be ours, O Janardhana? Sin will certainly abide in us if we kill these aggressors.

Sloka 37

tasmān nārhā vayaṃ hantuṃ dhārtarāṣṭrān svabāndhavān
svajanaṃ hi kathaṃ hatvā sukhinaḥ syāma mādhava

tasmat = therefore; na = not; arhah = right, authority, deserving; vayam = we; hantum = to kill; dhartarastran = the sons of Dhrtarastra; sa-bandhavan = relations; sva-janam = own people; hi = certainly; katham = how; hatva = by killing; sukhinah = happy; syama = become; madhava = Madhava.

"Therefore we do not have the right to kill the sons of Dhritarashtra, our relations and our own people. Certainly O Madhava, how can we be happy by killing (them)?

Sloka 38

yadyapyete na paśyanti lobhopahatacetasaḥ
kulakṣayakṛtaṃ doṣaṃ mitradrohe ca pātakam

yadi = if; api = certainly; ete = they; na = do not; pasyanti = see; lobha = greed; upahata = destroyed; cetasah = mind, heart, soul; kula-ksaya = destruction or decline of the family; krtam = done; dosam = impurityl, defect; mitra-drohe = betraying one's friends; ca = also; patakam = great sin;

"Even though they, with their hearts and minds destroyed by greed, do not perceive the greatsin of destroying their own family and betrayal of their own friends.

Sloka 39

kathaṃ na jñeyam asmābhiḥ pāpād asmān nivartitum
kulakṣayakṛtaṃ doṣaṃ prapaśyadbhir janārdana

katham = why; na = not; jneyam = known; asmabhih = by us; papat = from sins; asmat = from these; nivartitum = to cease; kula-ksaya = the destruction of the family; krtam = by doing so; dosam = impurity, blemish; prapasyadbhih = by those who can see; janardana = Janardana.

"But why should we not, who know the sin arising from the destruction of the family, cease doing it to avoid the blemish, O Janardhana?

Sloka 40

kulakṣaye pranaśyanti kuladharmāḥ sanātanāḥ
dharme naṣṭe kulaṃ kṛtsnam adharmobhibhavaty uta

kula-ksaye = with the destruction of the family; pranasyanti = perish, come to an end, disintegrate; kula-dharmah = caste duties; sanatanah = eternal; dharme = law, lawful; naste = is destroyed; kulam = family; krtsnam = entire, whole; adharmah = lawlessness, adharma; abhibhavati = overwhelms; uta = it is said.

"It is said that with the destruction of the family, the caste duties perish and the eternal law gets destroyed, (wherby) lawlessness overwhelms the whole family.

Sloka 41

adharmābhibhavāt kṛṣṇa praduṣyanti kulastriyaḥ
strīṣu duṣṭāsu vārṣṇeya jāyate varṇasaṅkaraḥ

adharma = irreligiousness; abhibhavat = predominance, prevalence; krsna = O Krishna; pradusyanti = defiled, become impure; kula-striyah = family women; strisu = women; dustasu = fall into evil ways; varsneya = O descendant of Vrsni; jayate = arise, takes place; varna-sankarah = intermixture of castes.

"With the prevalence of irreligiousness, O Krishna, women become impure and when them falls into evil ways, o descendent of Vrisni, intermixture of castes arise.

Sloka 42

saṅkaro narakāyaiva kulaghnānāṃ kulasya ca
patanti pitaro hy eṣāṃ luptapiṇḍodakakriyāḥ

sankarah = inter mixture; narakaya = hell; eva = certainly; kula-ghnanam = destroyers of family; kulasya = of the family; ca = also; patanti = descend to hell, decline, ruined; pitarah = ancestors; hi =

certainly; esam = of them; lupta = become violated, neglected; pinda = sacrificial offerings to departed souls; udaka = water; kriyah = sacrificial acts.

"With the intermixture of duties, the destroyers of family and (members of) the family descend to hell. Neglected, their ancestors fall (down to earth), as they do not receive the sacrificial offering of food, water and (the merit of) sacrificial acts.

Sloka 43

doṣair etaiḥ kulaghnānāṃ varṇasaṅkarakārakaiḥ
utsādyante jātidharmāḥ kuladharmāś ca śāśvatāḥ 1.43

dosaih = because of such misdeeds; etaih = these; kula-ghnanam = destroyers of the family; varna-sankara = admixture of castes; karakaih = perpetrators of; utsadyante = causes devastation; jati-dharmah = social order; kula-dharmah = family traditions; ca = and; sasvatah = eternal.

"Because of the misdeeds of these destroyers of family and perpetrators of the admixture of the castes, the eternal social order and the family traditions are destroyed.

Sloka 44

utsannakuladharmāṇāṃ manuṣyāṇāṃ janārdana
narake niyataṃ vāso bhavatīty anuśuśruma

utsanna = destroyed, ruined, uprooted; kula-dharmanam = of the family traditions; manusyanam = of such people; janardana = O Janardana; narake = in hell; niyatam = certainly, inevitably; vasah = abode; bhavati = it so happens; iti = thus; anususruma = heard from the masters.

"O Janardana, I happened to hear from the masters that the abode of those who destroy their family traditions(dharma), is invetably in the hell.

Sloka 45

**aho bata mahat pāpaṃ kartuṃ vyavasitā vayam
yad rājyasukhalobhena hantuṃ svajanam udyatāḥ**

aho = alas; bata = how unfortunate it is; mahat = great; papam = sins; kartum = committing; vyavasitah = decided; vayam = we; yat = so that; rajya = kingdom; sukha = pleasure; lobhena = out of greed; hantum = to kill; sva-janam = own people; udyatah = preparing, getting ready.

"Alas, how unfortunate it is that we are preparing to commit the great sin of killing our own people out of greed for the pleasure of kingdom.

Sloka 46

**yadi mām apratīkāram aśastraṃ śastrapāṇayaḥ
dhārtarāṣṭrā raṇe hanyus tan me kṣemataraṃ bhavet**

yadi = even if; mam = unto me; apratikaram = merciful, without being vengeful; asastram = unarmed; sastra-panayah = armed with weapons; dhartarastrah = the sons of Dhrtarastra; rane = in the battle; hanyuh = may kill; tat = that; me = mine; ksema-taram = better; bhavet = become.

"It is much better if the sons of Dhritarashtra, armed with weapons, kill me when I am unarmed and not in a vengeful mood to fight."

Sloka 47

**evam uktvārjunaḥ saṅkhye rathopastha upāviśat
visṛjya saśaraṃ cāpaṃ śokasaṃvignamānasaḥ**

sanjayah = Sanjaya; uvaca = said; evam = thus; uktva = saying; arjunah = Arjuna; sankhye = in the the battle; ratha = chariot; upasthe = situated on; upavisat = sat down again; visrjya = setting aside; sa-saram = along with arrows; capam = the bow; soka = by sorrow; samvigna = distressed, disturbed; manasah = within the mind.

Said Sanjaya," Saying thus, Arjuna sat down in his chariot, setting aside his bow and arrows, with his mind distressed by sorrow."

End of Chapter 1

iti srīmadbhāgavadgītāsupanisatsu brahmavidyāyām yogasāstre
srikrisnārjunasamvāde arjunavisādayogo nāma prathamo 'dhyayah

iti = thus; srīmadbhāgavadgītā = in the sacred Bhagavadgita; upanisatsu = in the Upanishad; brahmavidyāyām = the knowledge of the absolute Brahman; yogasāstre = the scripture of yoga; srikrisnārjunasamvāde = the dialogue between Sri Krishna and Arjuna; arjunavisādayogo nāma = by name Arjuna's sorrow; prathamo 'dhyayah = first chapter;

Thus ends the first chapter named the Yoga of Arjuna's Sorrow, in the Upanishad of the sacred Bhagavadgita, the knowledge of the Absolute Brahman, the scripture on yoga, and the debate between Lord Krishna and Arjuna.

2 – The Yoga of Knowledge

Sloka 1

sañjaya uvāca
taṃ tathā kṛpayāviṣṭam aśrupūrṇākulekṣaṇam
viṣīdantam idaṃ vākyam uvāca madhusūdanaḥ

sanjayah uvaca = Sanjaya said; tam = to him; tatha = thus; krpaya = with compassion; avistam = entered, possessed, overwhelmed, overpowered; asru-purna = full of tears; akula = distressed; iksanam = eyes; visidantam = unhappy, sad, ; idam = this; vakyam = words; uvaca = spoke,said; madhu-sudanah = Madhusudana.

Sanjaya said, "Thus overwhelmed with compassion, Madhusudana spoke these words to him (Arjuna who was) with tearful eyes, distressed and unhappy."

Sloka 2

śrībhagavān uvāca
kutas tvā kaśmalam idaṃ viṣame samupasthitam
anāryajuṣṭam asvargyam akīrtikaram arjuna

sri-bhagavan uvaca = said the Supreme Lord; kutah = from where; tva = to you; kasmalam = dejection, disgraceful; idam = this; visame = critical situation; samupasthitam = entered, settled; anarya = ignoble, ignominious, dishonorable; justam = practiced by; asvargyam = disqualify for heavenly life; akirti = infamy; karam = causing; arjuna = O Arjuna.

The Supreme Lord said, "From where did these disgraceful thoughts practiced by dishonorable people settled (in your mind) in this critical situation, O Arjuna, which disqualify you for heavenly life and cause infamy?

Sloka 3

klaibyaṃ mā sma gamaḥ pārtha naitat tvayyupapadyate
kṣudraṃ hṛdayadaurbalyaṃ tyaktvottiṣṭha paraṃtapa

klaibyam = cowardliness, mental weakness, timidity; masmagamah = do not succumb; partha = Partha; na = not; etat = this; tvayi = to you; upadyate = suit, appropriate; ksudram = lowly, mean, base, vile; hrdaya = heart; daurbalyam = weakness; tyaktva = leave aside; uttistha = get up; param-tapa = O chastiser of the enemies

"O Partha, do not succumb to cowardliness. It does not suit you. Leave aside the lowly weakness of your heart, O chastiser of the enemies, and get ready."

Sloka 4

arjuna uvāca
kathaṃ bhīṣmam ahaṃ sāṅkhye droṇaṃ ca madhusūdana
iṣubhiḥ pratiyotsyāmi pūjārhāv arisūdana

arjunah uvaca = Arjuna said; katham = how; bhismam = to Bhisma; aham = I; sankhye = in the battle; dronam = to Drona; ca = and; madhu-sudana = Madhusudana; isubhih = with arrows; pratiyotsyami = repulse, counter attack; puja-arhau = venerable, qualified for woship; ari-sudana = slayer of enemies.

Arjuna said, "O Madhusudana, how am I going to attack venerable Bhishma and Drona in the battle with my arrows, O slayer of enemies?

Sloka 5

gurūn ahatvā hi mahānubhāvān śreyo bhoktuṃ bhaikṣyam apīha loke
hatvārthakāmāṃstu gurunihaiva bhuñjjīya bhogān rudhirapradigdhān

gurun = teachers; ahatva = not killing; hi = certainly; maha-anubhavan = elderly people; sreyah = highest good, appropriate; bhoktum = eating; bhaiksyam = begging; api = even; ihaloke = in this world; hatva = killing; artha = wealth; kaman = pleasure; tu = but; gurun = teachers; iha =here, this; eva = certainly; bhunjiya = enjoying, eating; bhogan = food, enjoyments; rudhira = blood; pradigdhan = stained.

"In this world not killing the teachers and the elders is the highest good. Eating the food from begging is certainly preferable here to enjoying the bloodstained food (earned) by killing teachers for wealth and pleasure.

Sloka 6

na caitadvidmaḥ kataran no garīyo yad vā jayema yadi vā no jayeyuḥ
yān eva hatvā na jijīviṣāmas tevasthitāḥ pramukhe dhārtarāṣṭrāḥ

na = not; ca = and; etat = this; vidmah = do know; katarat = which one; nah = for us; gariyah = more improtant; yat = that; va = either; jayeyu = be conquered; yadi = if; va = or; (yadiva = otherwise); nah = us; jayema = conquer; yan = those; eva = certainly; hatva = by killing; na = not; jijivisamah = desire to live; te = all of them; avasthitah = standing; pramukhe = in front, arrayed, facing; dhartarastrah = the sons of Dhrtarastra.

" Not do I know which one is more important for us, to conquer them or to be conquered by them, by killing whom we do not certainly wish to live, even all these sons of Dhritarashtra, (who are now) standing in front of us.

Sloka 7

kārpaṇyadoṣopahatasvabhāvaḥ pṛcchāmi tvāṃ dharmasaṃmūḍhacetāḥ
yac chreyaḥ syān niścitaṃ brūhi tan me śiṣyastehaṃ śādhi māṃ tvāṃ prapannam

karpanya = meekness, wretchedness, miserliness; dosa = impurity; upahata = afflicted with, struck by; sva-bhavah = own state, inherent nature, natural disposition; prcchami = I am asking; tvam = you; dharma = duty; sammudha = deluded, confused; cetah = in citta, mind; yat = what; sreyah = better; syat = may be; niscitam = decidedly, clearly; bruhi = tell; tat = that; me = to me; sisyah = disciple; te = yours; aham = I am; sadhi = instruct; mam = me; tvam = to You; prapannam = surrendered.

"With my own state afflicted by the impurity of meekness and my mind confused about the duty I am asking you to tell me clearly which is better. I am your disciple. Instruct me. I have surrendered to you.

Sloka 8

na hi prapaśyāmi mamāpanudyād yac chokam ucchoṣaṇam indriyāṇām
avāpya bhūmāv asapatnam ṛddhaṃ rājyaṃ surāṇām api cādhipatyam

na = not; hi = certainly; prapasyami = I see; mama = my; apanudyat = may dispel; yat = that; sokam = sorrow, grief; ucchosanam = heat; indriyanam = in the senses; avapya = obtaining; bhumau = on the earth; asapatnam = unrivalled; rddham = rich, prosperous; rajyam = kingdom; suranam = over the divinities; api = even; ca = and; adhipatyam = suzerainty, sovereignty, dominion, rule.

"I do not see that obtaining a prosperous kingdom upon earth and even suzerainty over the divinities would dispel my sorrow or the heat in my senses."

Sloka 9

sañjaya uvāca
evam uktvā hṛṣīkeśaṃ guḍākeśaḥ paraṃtapaḥ
na yotsya iti govindam uktvā tūṣṇīṃ babhūva ha

sanjayah uvaca = Sanjaya said; evam = tin this manner; uktva = having said; hrsikesam = unto Hrisikesa; gudakesah = Gudakesa; parantapah = terror of the enemies; na=not; yotsye = shall fight; iti = thus; govindam = to Govinda; uktva = having said; tusnim = silent; babhuva = became; ha = certainly.

Sanjaya said, "Having spoken in this manner to Hrisikesa, (and) having said to Govinda,'I will not fight,' Gudakesa became silent.

Sloka 10

tam uvaca hṛṣīkeśah prahasann iva bharata
senayor ubhayor madhye visidantam, idam vacah

tam = to him; uvaca = said; hrsikesah = Hrisikesa; prahasan = laughingly; iva = in this manner; bharata = Bharata; senayoh = of the armies; ubhayoh = of both ; madhye = in the middle; visidantam = grief stricken; idam = these; vacah = words.

"To him (who was) grief stricken, Hrisikesa said these words laughingly in this manner in between the two armies, O Bharata.

Sloka 11

śrībhagavān uvāca
aśocyān anvaśocas tvaṃ prajñāvādāṃś ca bhāṣase
gatāsūn agatāsūṃś ca nānuśocanti paṇḍitāḥ

sri-bhagavan uvaca = Sri Bhagavan said; asocyan = not to be grieved for; anvasocah = you are grieving; tvam = you; prajna-vadan = wise arguments; ca = and; bhasase = speak; gata = gone, past; asun = life; agata = not past; asun = life; ca = also; na = not; anusocanti = grieve; panditah = knowledgeable people.

The Supreme Lord said, "You are grieving for (those) who should not be grieved for. You have put forth wise arguments. But (truly) knowledgeable people do not grieve for life that is gone or yet to be gone.

Sloka 12

natv evāhaṃ jātu nāsaṃ na tvaṃ neme janādhipāḥ
na caiva na bhaviṣyāmaḥ sarve vayam ataḥ param

na = not; tu = indeed; eva = and; aham = I; jatu = a time; na = not; asam = existed; na = not; tvam = you; na = not; ime = these; jana-adhipah = rulers of the people; na = not; ca = and; eva = certainly; na = not; bhavisyamah = exist in future; sarve = all; vayam = we; atah param = here after.

"There was not a time when I did not exist, nor you, nor all these kings. Also, we will not cease to exist in future after we depart from here.

Sloka 13

dehinosmin yathā dehe kaumāraṃ yauvanaṃ jarā
tathā dehāntaraprāptir dhīras tatra na muhyati

dehinah = indweller of the body; asmin = in this; yatha = as; dehe = in the body; kaumaram = childhood; yauvanam = youth; jara = old age; tatha = In the same way; deha-antara = another body; praptih = attain; dhirah = the sober; tatra = in such matters; na = not; muhyati = deluded.

"Just as the dweller of the body passes from childhood to youth to old age, in the same manner he attains another body. Therefore, in such matters the wise do not get deluded.

Sloka 14

mātrāsparśās tu kaunteya śītoṣṇasukhaduḥkhadāḥ
āgamāpāyinonityās tāṃs titikṣasva bhārata

matra =matter, material world, material objects; sparsah = contact, touching; tu = indeed; kaunteya = Kaunteya; sita = cold; usna = heat; sukha = pleasure; duhkha = pain; -dah=giving, producing; agama = coming; apayinah = going; anityah = impermanent; tan = these; titiksasva = bear with, tolerate; bharata = Bharata.

"Indeed contact with matter, O Kaunteya, (is) giving cold, heat, pleasure and pain. (They are) impermanent, coming and going. Bear with them, O Bharata.

Sloka 15

yaṃ hi na vyathayanty ete puruṣaṃ puruṣarṣabha
samaduḥkhasukhaṃ dhīraṃ somṛtatvāya kalpate

yam = whom; hi = certainly; na = not; vyathayanti = trouble; ete = these; purusam = person; purusa-rsabha = best among men; sama =

equal; duhkha = pain, sorrow; sukham = pleasure, happiness; dhiram = firm, stable; sah = he; amrtatvaya = for liberation, eternal life; kalpate = fit, qualified.

"O best among men, whom these do not trouble, (who is) equal to pleasure and pain (and) stable, he is fit for liberation.

Sloka 16

nāsato vidyate bhāvo nābhāvo vidyate sataḥ
ubhayor api dṛṣṭo.antas tv anayos tattvadarśibhiḥ

na = not, never; asatah = of the non existient; vidyate = is; bhavah = existence, state, being; na = not; abhavah = does not exist; avidyate = is not; satah = of the existent; ubhayoh = of the two; api = also; drstah = seen; antah = concluded, determined; tu = indeed; anayoh = of them; tattva = the essence of That; darsibhih = by the seers.

"The non-existent has no existence; the existent does not not-exist. (Thus) the seers who have seen the essence of That reached the conclusion about the two.

Sloka 17

avināśi tu tad viddhi yena sarvam idaṃ tatam
vināśam avyayasyāsya na kaścit kartum arhati

avinasi = indestructible; tu = but; tat = that; viddhi = know; yena = by whihc; sarvam = the whole universe; idam = this; tatam = pervaded; vinasam = destruction; avyayasya = of the unchangeable; asya = of this; na=not; kascit = anyone; kartum = to do; arhati = is able.

"Know that to be indestructible by which all this is pervaded. None can do the destruction of that unchangeable One.

Sloka 18

antavanta ime dehā nityasyoktāḥ śarīriṇaḥ
anāśinoprameyasya tasmād yudhyasva bhārata

anta-vantah = have an end; ime = these; dehah = bodies; nityasya = eternal; uktah = said; saririnah = the embodied anasinah = indestructible; aprameyasya = immeasurable; tasmat = therefore; yudhyasva = fight; bharata = Bharata.

"These bodies of the embodied Self, (which is) said to be eternal, indestructible (and) immeasurable, have an end. Therefore, O Bharata, fight.

Sloka 19

ya enaṃ vetti hantāraṃ yaś cainaṃ manyate hatam
ubhau tau na vijānīto nāyaṃ hanti na hanyate

yah = the one; enam = this; vetti = knows; hantaram = the killer, slayer, destroyer; yah = the one; ca = and; enam = this; manyate = thinks; hatam = killed; ubhau = both; tau = they; na = not; vijanitah = know; na = not; ayam = this; hanti = kills; na = not; hanyate = is killed.

"One who knows this as the killer and the one who thinks this as the killed both of them do not know that this neither kills nor gets killed.

Sloka 20

na jāyate mriyate vā kadācin nāyaṃ abhūtvā bhavitā vā na bhūyaḥ
ajo nityaḥ śāśvatoyaṃ purāṇo na hanyate hanyamāne śarīre

na = not; jayate = born; mriyate = dies; va = either; kadacit = at any time; na = not; ayam = this; abhutva = not existed in the past; abhavita = not exist in future; va = or; na = not; bhuyah = the state of becoming; ajah = unborn; nityah = eternal; sasvatah = permanent; ayam = this; puranah = the most ancient; na = never; hanyate = is killed; hanyamane = being killed; sarire = body.

"(This Self is) neither born nor dies. At no time it did not non-exist in the past; will not non-exist in future; or will not become existence again. Unborn, eternal, permanent, and the most ancient, this is not killed when the body is killed.

Sloka 21

vedāvināśinaṃ nityaṃ ya enam ajam avyayam
kathaṃ sa puruṣaḥ pārtha kaṃ ghātayati hanti kam

veda = knows; avinasinam = indestructible; nityam = eternal; yah = who; enam = this; ajam = unborn; avyayam = inexhaustible; katham = how; sah = he; purusah = person; partha = O Partha; kam = whom; ghatayati = prompt to kill; hanti = kill; kam = whom.

"(He) who knows that this (Self) is indestructible, eternal, unborn and inexhaustible, how can such person kill or instigate (others) to kill?

Sloka 22

vāsāṃsi jīrṇāni yathā vihāya navāni gṛhṇāti naroparāṇi
tathā śarīrāṇi vihāya jīrṇāni anyāni saṃyāti navāni dehī

vasamsi = clothes; jirnani = torn, worn out; yatha = just as; vihaya = discards; navani = new; grhnati = accepts; narah = a person; aparani = various, several different; tatha = in that way; sarirani = bodies; vihaya = discards; jirnani = worn out, aged; anyani = another; samyati = obtains, gets, receives, accepts; navani = new; dehi = the embodied.

"Just as a person discards worn out clothes and wears several different (ones), in the same manner the embodied (Self) discards aged and worn out bodies and obtains new (ones).

Sloka 23

nainaṃ chindanti śastrāṇi nainaṃ dahati pāvakaḥ
na cainaṃ kledayanty āpo na śoṣayati mārutaḥ

na = not; enam = this; chindanti = cut, divide, pierce; sastrani = weapons; na = not; enam = this; dahati = burn; pavakah = fire; na = never; ca = and; enam = this; kledayanti = soak, moisten; apah = water; na = not; sosayati = dries; marutah = wind.

"Weapons cannot cut or pierce this (Self); fire cannot burn this (Self); water cannot soak it; and wind cannot cannot dry (It).

Sloka 24

acchedyoyam adāhyoyam akledyośoṣya eva ca
nityaḥ sarvagataḥ sthāṇur acaloyaṃ sanātanaḥ

acchedyah = impervious, impenetrable; ayam = this; adahyah = incombustible; ayam = this; akledyah = insoluble; asosyah = unparchable; eva = certainly; ca = and; nityah = eternal; sarva-gatah = all-pervading; sthanuh = constant, fixed; acalah = immovable; ayam = this; sanatanah = perpetual, everlasting.

"This (Self) is impenetrable, incombustible, insoluble, cannot be dried, eternal and certainly this (Self is) eternal, all-pervading, constant, immovable, and everlasting.

Sloka 25

avyaktoyam acintyoyam avikaryoyam ucyate
tasmād evaṃ viditvainaṃ nānuśocitum arhasi 2.25

avyaktah = invisible; ayam = this; acintyah = not reachable by thought, incomprehensible; ayam = this; avikaryah = unchangeable; ayam = this; ucyate = said to be; tasmat = therefore; evam = thus, like this; viditva = knowing well; enam = this; na = not; anusocitum = grieve, repent; arhasi = deserve.

"Invisible is this; unreachable by thought is this; unchangeable is this. Therefore knowing well thus, this is not to be repented for.

Sloka 26

atha cainaṃ nityajātaṃ nityaṃ vā manyase mṛtam
tathāpi tvaṃ mahābāho naivaṃ śocitum arhasi 2.26

atha = if, otherwise; ca = and; enam = this; nitya-jatam = born continuously; nityam = eternally; va = or; manyase = think; mrtam = dies; tatha api = even; tvam = you; maha-baho = O mighty-armed one; na =not; evam = thus; socitum = grieve, lament; arhasi = deserve.

"Otherwise if you think (that) this is born continuously or dies constantly, even then, O mighty armed one, this is not to be repented for.

Sloka 27

jātasya hi dhruvo mṛtyur dhruvaṃ janma mṛtasya ca
tasmād aparihāryerthe na tvaṃ śocitum arhasi

jatasya = For those who are born; hi = indeed; dhruvah = certain; mrtyuh = death; dhruvam = certain; janma = birth; mrtasya = for the dead; ca = and; tasmat = therefore; apariharye = that which is unavoidable; arthe = regarding; na = not; tvam = you; socitum = lament; arhasi = deserve.

"For those who are born, indeed, death is certain and for those who die, birth is certain. Therefore, regarding that which is unavoidable, you should not grieve.

Sloka 28

avyaktādīni bhūtāni vyaktamadhyāni bhārata
avyaktanidhanāny eva tatra kā paridevanā

avyakta = unmanifested; adinin= in the beginning; bhutani =beings, elemental selves; vyakta = manifested; madhyani = in the middle; bharata = Bharata; avyakta = unmanifested; nidhanani = upon destruction; eva = also; tatra = for that; ka = what; paridevana = lamentation, complaint, wailing.

"O Bharata, the beings are unmanifested in the beginning, manifested in the middle and unmanifested again in the end upon death or destruction. For that, what (is the need) to grieve?

Sloka 29

āścaryavat paśyati kaścid enam āścaryavad vadati tathaiva cānyaḥ
āścaryavac cainam anyaḥ śṛṇoti śrutvāpy enaṃ veda na caiva kaścit

ascarya-vat = as amazing, wonderful; pasyati = see; kascit = one; enam = this; ascarya-vat = amazing; vadati = speak; tatha =similarly; eva = indeed; ca = and; anyah = another; ascarya-vat = as wonderful or amazing; ca = and; enam = this; anyah = others; srnoti = hear; srutva = having heard; api = even; enam = this; veda = do know; na = never; ca = and; eva = certainly; kascit = anyone.

"One beholds this as wonderful; similarly indeed another speaks of this as a wonder; and another hears of this as wonderful. Yet having heard, none knows this certainly.

Sloka 30

dehī nityam avadhyoyaṃ dehe sarvasya bhārata
tasmāt sarvāṇi bhūtāni na tvaṃ śocitum arhasi

dehi = the indweller of the body; nityamavadhyah = can never be slaughtered; ayam = this; dehe = in the body; sarvasya = in all; bharata = Bharata; tasmat = therefore; sarvani = all; bhutani = living beings; na = not; tvam = you; socitum = worry, grieve; arhasi = deserve.

"The indweller of the body is eternal. This (who is) in the bodies of all can never be slaughtered, O Bharata. Therefore, you should not grieve for living beings (when they die).

Sloka 31

svadharmam api cāvekṣya na vikampitum arhasi
dharmyād dhi yuddhāc chreyonyat kṣatriyasya na vidyate

sva-dharmam = one own duty; api = also; ca = indeed; aveksya = considering; na = not; vikampitum = to waver, hesitate; arhasi = deserve; dharmyat = with regard to duty; hi = in fact, indeed; yuddhat = than fighting; sreyah = better; anyat = no other; ksatriyasya = of a ksatriya, warrior; na = not; vidyate = exist.

"Indeed, considering your own duty also, you should not waver. In fact, with regard to duty none other is better for a warrior than fighting

Sloka 32

yadṛcchayā copapannaṃ svargadvāram apāvṛtam
sukhinaḥ kṣatriyāḥ pārtha labhante yuddham īdṛśam

yadrcchaya = happening by coincidence, by chance or by fate; ca = and; upapannam = happened; svarga = heaven; dvaram = door; apavrtam = open; sukhinah = happy; ksatriyah = warrior; partha = Partha; labhante = get, obtain, attain; yuddham = war; idrsam = like this.

"Happy are the warriors, O Partha, who get (a chance to fight in) a war like this, which presents itself coincidentally and opens the doors of heaven (to them).

Sloka 33

atha cet tvam imaṃ dhārmyaṃ saṅgrāmaṃ na kariṣyasi
tataḥ svadharmaṃ kīrtiṃ ca hitvā pāpam avāpsyasi

atha = now, here, so also; cet = if; tvam = you; imam = this; dharmyam = dutiful; sangramam = battle, fighting, war; na = not; karisyasi = fight, do; tatah = then; sva-dharmam = own duty; kirtim = fame, reputation; ca = and; hitva = thrown away; papam = sin; avapsyasi = gain, incur, attain.

"Now, if you do not fight this dutiful war, then you will incur sin, casting away your own duty and your fame.

Sloka 34

akīrtiṃ cāpi bhūtāni kathayiṣyanti tevyayām
saṃbhāvitasya cākīrtir maraṇād atiricyate

akirtim = infamy; ca = and; api = besides; bhutani = beings; kathayisyanti = speak about, narrate; te = of your; avyayam = ceaselessly; sambhavitasya = for a respectable person; ca = and; akirtih = dishonor; maranat = death; atiricyate = worse than.

"Besides, beings would ceaselessly speak about your infamy; and to a respectable person dishonor is worse than death.

Sloka 35

bhayād raṇād uparataṃ maṃsyante tvāṃ mahārathāḥ
yeṣāṃ ca tvaṃ bahumato bhūtvā yāsyasi lāghavam

bhayat = because of fear; ranat = from the battle; uparatam = withdrawn; mamsyante = will think; tvam = of you; maha-rathah = great charioteers; yesam = by whom; ca = and; tvam = you; bahu-matah = thought higly; bhutva = having been; yasyasi = will go; laghavam = smallness, littleness, disrespect, dishonor.

"The great charioteers (like Karna and Bhishma) will think that you withdrew from the battlefield out of fear. By whom you have been held in high esteem, you will fall into dishonor and disrepute.

Sloka 36

avācyavādāṃś ca bahūn vadiṣyanti tavāhitāḥ
nindantas tava sāmarthyaṃ tato duḥkhataraṃ nu kim

avacya = improper, indecent, unspeakable; vadan = words; ca = and; bahun = many; vadisyanti = will say; tava = your; ahitah = ill-wishers, enemies; nindantah = defame, blame, denigrate; tava = your; samarthyam = power, force, ability; tatah = than; duhkha-taram = very painful; nu = of course; kim = what.

"You enemies and ill wishers will say many improper and indecent worlds, defaming your power and ability. What can be more painful than this?

Sloka 37

hato vā prāpsyasi svargaṃ jitvā vā bhokṣyase mahīm
tasmād uttiṣṭha kaunteya yuddhāya kṛtaniścayaḥ 2.37

hatah = by getting killed; va = or; prapsyasi = you will gain; svargam = heaven; jitva = by winning; va = or; bhoksyase = enjoy; mahim = the earth; tasmat = therefore; uttistha = stand up, get up; kaunteya = Kaunteya, son of Kunti; yuddhaya = for the battle; krta = to act, to fight; niscayah = determination.

"You will either attain heaven by getting killed (in the battle) or enjoy the earth by winning. Therefore, O Kaunteya, stand up to fight with determination.

Sloka 38

sukhaduḥkhe same kṛtvā lābhālābhau jayājayau
tato yuddhāya yujyasva naivaṃ pāpam avāpsyasi 2.38

sukha = happiness, pleasure; duhkhe = sorrow, pain; same = alike, same; krtva =treating; labha-alabhau = gain and loss; jaya-ajayau = victory and defeat; tatah = then; yuddhaya = for the fighting; yujyasva = get ready; na = not; evam = thus; papam = sin; avapsyasi = incur, obtain, gain.

"Treating alike (both) happiness and sorrow, gain and loss, victory and defeat you should get ready to fight

Sloka 39

eṣā tebhihitā sāṅkhye buddhir yoge tv imāṃ śṛṇu
buddhyā yukto yayā pārtha karmabandhaṃ prahāsyasi

esa = this; te = to you; abhihita = spoken, declared, imparted; sankhye = Sankhya; buddhih = intelligence; yoge = yoga; tu = but; imam = to this; srnu = listen; buddhya = concerning intelligence; yuktah = endowed, filled with, joined; yaya = by which; partha = Prtha; karma-bandham = the bondage of karma; prahasyasi = release from.

"This teaching (whch has been) imparted to you (so far) is Sankhya; but (now), endowed with intelligence, listen to the yoga of intelligence (buddhi yoga), by which you will be released from the bondage of action.

Sloka 40

nehābhikramanāśosti pratyavāyo na vidyate
svalpam apy asya dharmasya trāyate mahato bhayāt

na = not; iha = here; abhikrama = effort; nasah = loss; asti =is; pratyavayah = harm; na = not; vidyate = there is; svalpam = little; api

= even; asya = of this; dharmasya = of this dutifulness; trayate = saves, protects; mahatah = great; bhayat = fear of mortal life.

"Here there is no loss of effort, no harm. Even a little of this dutifulness saves one from the great fear.

Sloka 41

vyavasāyātmikā buddhir ekeha kurunandana
bahuśākhā hy anantāś ca buddhayovyavasāyinām

vyavasaya-atmika = resolute; buddhih = discriminating intelligence; eka = only one; iha = in this; kuru-nandana = scion of the Kurus; bahu-sakhah = various branches; hi = indeed; anantah = endless; ca = and; buddhi= mind; avyavasayinam = without determination.

"The discriminating intelligence of the resolute is one (pointed); whereas endless with many branches indeed is the discriminating intelligence of the irresolute.

Sloka 42

yām imāṃ puṣpitāṃ vācaṃ pravadanty avipaścitaḥ
vedavādaratāḥ pārtha nānyad astīti vādinaḥ

yam= all; imam = these; puspitam = flowery; vacam = words; pravadanti = speak; avipascitah = people with poor discernment; veda-vada-ratah = delight in the discussion of the Vedas; partha = Prtha; na = not; anyat = other; asti =is; iti = thus; vadinah = declare.

All these people with poor discernment speak flowery words (and) take delight in the discussion of the Vedas, O Partha, declaring that there is nothing else other than this.

Sloka 43

kāmātmānaḥ svargaparā janmakarmaphalapradām
kriyāviśeṣabahulāṃ bhogaiśvaryagatiṃ prati

kama-atmanah = mind filled with desires; svarga-parah = heaven as the highest goal; janma-karma-phala-pradam = birth as the fruit of actions.; kriya-visesa = special rites and rituals; bahulam = various; bhoga = enjoyment; aisvarya = wealth; gatim = attaining, obtaining; prati = for the sake of.

"Minds filled with desires, heaven as the highest goal, (assuming) birth as the fruit of actions, they engaged in various special rites and rituals for the sake of attaining wealth and enjoyment.

Sloka 44

bhogaiśvaryaprasaktānāṃ tayāpahṛtacetasām
vyavasāyātmikā buddhiḥ samādhau na vidhīyate

bhoga = enjoyment; aisvarya = wealth; prasaktanam = intense desire, obsession; taya = by that; apahrta= stolen, lost, carried away; cetasam = mind; vyavasaya-atmika = one pointed; buddhih = discriminating intelligence; samadhau = setting; na = not; vidhiyate =become fixed, established.

"With intense desire for enjoyment and wealth, the mind lost by that, the setting of one-pointed intelligence does not become established.

Sloka 45

traiguṇyaviṣayā vedā nistraiguṇyo bhavārjuna
nirdvandvo nityasatvastho niryogakṣema ātmavān

trai-gunya = regarding the triple gunas; visayah = topic, subject matter; vedah = Vedas; nistraigunyah = without the gunas; bhava = be; arjuna = Arjuna; nirdvandvah = without the pairs of opposites; nitya-sattva-sthah = ever established in sattva; niryoga-ksemah = without concern for wealth or acquisitions and wellbeing; atma-van = remain established in the self.

"The Vedas are about the triple gunas. (But) O Arjuna (you should) remain established in the Self, to be without duality, ever established in sattva and indifferent to wealth and wellbeing.

Sloka 46

yāvān artha udapāne sarvataḥ saṃplutodake
tāvān sarveṣu vedeṣu brāhmaṇasya vijānataḥ

yavan = as much; arthah = purpse; uda-pane = well, reservoir, pool ; sarvatah = everywhere; sampluta-udake = water in a flood or deluge; tavan = so much; sarvesu = all; vedesu = in the Vedas; brahmanasya = of Brahman; vijanatah = one who knows.

"As much purpose the water in a well serves when there is a deluge, so much do all the Vedas for a brahmana who has knowledge (of the Self).

Sloka 47

karmaṇy evādhikāras te mā phaleṣu kadācana
mā karmaphalahetur bhūr mā te saṅgostv akarmaṇi

karmani = for actions; eva = certainly; adhikarah = right; te = your; ma = never; phalesu = for the fruit; kadacana = at any time; ma = never; karma-phala = fruit of actions; hetuh = cause; bhuh = become; ma = do not; te = your; sangah = attachment; astu = have; akarmani =inaction.

"Your right is certainly for the actions alone but not for the fruit (of your actions). Do not become the cause of the fruit of your actions. Nor should you have attachment to inaction.

Sloka 48

yogasthaḥ kuru karmāṇi saṅgaṃ tyaktvā dhanañjaya
siddhyasiddhyoḥ samo bhūtvā samatvaṃ yoga ucyate

yoga-sthah = established in yoga; kuru = perform; karmani = actions; sangam = attachment; tyaktva = renouncing; dhananjaya = Dhananjaya; siddhi-asiddhyoh = gain and loss; samah = equal; bhutva = becoming; samatvam = Sameness or equanimity; yogah = yoga; ucyate = is called.

Meanuing

"Established in yoga, perform actions, renouncing attachment O Dhanajaya, becoming equal to gain and loss. Sameness or equanimity is called yoga.

Sloka 49

dūreṇa hy avaraṃ karma buddhiyogād dhanañjaya
buddhau śaraṇam anviccha kṛpaṇāḥ phalahetavaḥ

durena = in a very bad manner; hi = inferior; avaram = inferior; karma = action; buddhi-yogat = buddhiyoga, yoga of equnimity; dhananjaya = Dhananjaya; buddhau = of the discriminating intelligence; saranam =refuge; anviccha = seek; krpanah = poor, pitiable, wretched who are devoid of judgment; phala-hetavah = for the fruit of actions.

"In a very bad manner, inferior is action to the yoga of equanimity, O Dhananjaya. seek refuge in discriminating intelligence. The wretched, who are devoid of judgment, seek the fruit of action.

Sloka 50

buddhiyukto jahātīha ubhe sukṛtaduṣkṛte
tasmād yogāya yujyasva yogaḥ karmasu kauśalam

buddhi-yuktah = with buddhi or discriminating intelligence; jahati = rejects, lets go; iha = here, in this world; ubhe = in both; sukrta-duskrte = good and bad deeds; tasmat = therefore; yogaya = for the sake of yoga; yujyasva = get ready, be prepared; yogah = yoga; karmasu = in doing karma, in performing actions; kausalam = skillfulness, cleverness.

"With discriminating intelligence let go of both good and bad deeds. Therefore, get ready for the sake of yoga (to perform you duty). Yoga is skillfulness in action.

Sloka 51

karmajaṃ buddhiyuktā hi phalaṃ tyaktvā manīṣiṇaḥ
janmabandhavinirmuktāḥ padaṃ gacchhanty anāmayam

karma-jam =born out of actions; buddhi-yuktah = with equanimity and discernment; hi = indeed; phalam = fruit, result; tyaktva = renounce, give up; manisinah = great among men; janma-bandha = bondage to life or birth; vinirmuktah = liberated; padam = exalted state, position; gacchanti = go; anamayam = Siva or Vishnu, healthy, sound, beyond name and forms.

"Endowed with equanimity and discernment, the great among men renounce the results born of actions. Released from the bondage of life (they) reach the exalted state of Siva or Vishnu.

Sloka 52

yadā te mohakalilaṃ buddhir vyatitariṣyati
tadā gantāsi nirvedaṃ śrotavyasya śrutasya ca

yada = when; te = your; moha = delusion; kalilam = dense, turbidity, confusion,; buddhih = discriminating intelligence; vyatitarisyati = transcend, go beyond; tada = then; ganta asi = shall go; nirvedam = dispassion; srotavyasya = what should be heard; srutasya = has been heard; ca = and

"When the turbid mire of your delusion is transcended with discriminating intelligence, then you shall attain dispassion to what is heard and yet to be heard.

Sloka 53

śrutivipratipannā te yadā sthāsyati niścalā
samādhāv acalā buddhis tadā yogam avāpsyasi

sruti = the Vedas; vipratipanna = conflicting ideas; te = your; yada = when; sthasyati = remains; niscala = stable, firm; samadhau = self-absorption; acala = immovable, unshakeable; buddhih = sameness or samatva buddhi arising from discriminating intelligence; tada = them; yogam = the state of yoga; avapsyasi = you will attain.

"When your mind, which is troubled by the conflicting statement of the Vedas, becomes stable and self-absorbed,

then you will attain that state (yoga) of unshakeable equanimity."

Sloka 54

arjuna uvāca
sthitaprajñasya kā bhāṣā samādhisthasya keśava
sthitadhīḥ kiṃ prabhāṣeta kim āsīta vrajeta kim

arjunah uvaca = Arjuna said; sthita-prajnasya = of one who has stable intelligence; ka = what; bhasa = definition, description; samadhi-sthasya = of the state of self-absorption; kesava = Kesava; sthita-dhih = the self-absorbed; kim = what; prabhaseta = may speak; kim = how; asita = sits; vrajeta = walks; kim = how.

Arjuna asked, 'What is the description of the one who has stable intelligence and (who) is in the state of self-absorption. How does the self-absorbed (person) speak or walk?'

Sloka 55

śrībhagavān uvāca
prajahāti yadā kāmān sarvān pārtha manogatān
ātmany evātmanā tuṣṭaḥ sthitaprajñas tadocyate

sri-bhagavan uvaca = the Supreme Lord said; prajahati = renounces; yada = when; kaman = desires; sarvan = all types; partha = Partha; manah-gatan = happening or arising in the mind; atmani = in the Self; eva = alone; atmana = by the Self; tustah = satisfied; sthita-prajnah = stable person; tada = then; ucyate = is said, called.

"The Supreme Lord said, 'Renouncing all types of desires arising in the mind, O Partha, whoever remains satisfied in the Self by Self alone, he is called a person of stable intelligence.

Sloka 56

duḥkheṣv anudvignamanāḥ sukheṣu vigataspṛhaḥ
vītarāgabhayakrodhaḥ sthitadhīr munir ucyate

duhkhesu = in sorrow; anudvigna-manah = who is not disturbed; sukhesu = in happiness; vigata-sprhah = who is free from desires; vita = free from; raga = passion; bhaya = fear; krodhah = anger; sthita-dhih = stable and firmed minded; munih = a sage; ucyate = is called.

"Who is undisturbed when there is adversity, indifferent to happiness, free from attachment, fear and anger, he is called a sage of stable and firm mind.

Sloka 57

yaḥ sarvatrānabhisnehas tattatprāpya śubhāśubham
nābhinandati na dveṣṭi tasya prajñā pratiṣṭhitā

yah = who; sarvatra = everywhere; anabhisnehah = without attachment; tat = that; tat = that; prapya = achieving; subha = good; asubham = bad; na = not; abhinandati = welcomes, appreciates; na = nor; dvesti = dislikes or rerjects; tasya = of his; prajna = discriminating wisdom; pratisthita = firmly fixed.

"Who is without attachment everywhere, who neither seeks that which is good nor rejects that which is bad upon attaining it, that person's discriminating intelligence is firmly fixed.

Sloka 58

yadā saṃharate cāyaṃ kūrmoṅgānīva sarvaśaḥ
indriyāṇīndriyārthebhyas tasya prajñā pratiṣṭhitā 2.58

yada = when; samharate = draws in fully; ca =and; ayam = this one; kurmah = tortoise; angani = limbs; iva = just as; sarvasah = wholly, completely; indriyani = the senses; indriya-arthebhyah = from the sense objects; tasya = his; prajna = discriminating intelligence; pratisthita = becomes firmly established.

"When this one draws fully (his) senses from the sense objects, like a tortoise wholly (withdraws its) limbs, his discriminating intelligence becomes firmly established.

Sloka 59

viṣayā vinivartante nirāhārasya dehinaḥ
rasavarjaṃ rasopy asya paraṃ dṛṣṭvā nivartate

visayah = sense objects; vinivartante = turn away, recede; niraharasya = without food, abstaining, fasting; dehinah = of the embodied; rasa-varjam = leaving aside or excepting the taste; rasah = taste; api =even that; asya = of his; param = supreme transcendental; drstva = upon seeing; nivartate = ceases, falls away.

"The Sense objects recede from the embodied being who abstains from food, excepting the taste. Even that taste falls away from him upon seeing the supreme transcendental Self.

Sloka 60

yatato hy api kaunteya puruṣasya vipaścitaḥ
indriyāṇi pramāthīni haranti prasabhaṃ manaḥ

yatatah = while endeavoring; hi = indeed; api = even; kaunteya = Kaunteya; purusasya = of the person; vipascitah =of the discriminating wise; indriyani = the senses; pramathini = turbulent, unsteady; haranti = snatch away; prasabham = forcibly; manah = the mind.

"Indeed even while endeavoring (to withdraw the senses), O Kaunteya, the senses snatch away forcibly the mind of the discriminating wise person

Sloka 61

tāni sarvāṇi saṃyamya yukta āsīta matparaḥ
vaśe hi yasyendriyāṇi tasya prajñā pratiṣṭhitā

tani = of them; sarvani = all; samyamya = restraining; yuktah = self-absorbed; asita = sit; mat-parah = on Me as the supreme; vase = in control; hi = certainly; yasya = whose; indriyani = senses; tasya = of him; prajna = wisdom, higher intelligence; pratisthita = firmly established or stabilized.

"Restraining them all, one should sit self-absorbed, Me as the Supreme. Certainly whose senses are under control, his intelligence is firmly stabilized.

Sloka 62

dhyāyato viṣayān puṃsaḥ saṅgas teṣūpajāyate
saṅgāt sañjāyate kāmaḥ kāmāt krodhobhijāyate

dhyayatah = by dwelling; visayan = sense objects; pumsah = of the person; sangah = attachment; tesu = in them (sense objects); upajayate = is born; sangat = attachment; sanjayate = develops; kamah = desire; kamat = from desire; krodhah = anger; abhijayate = arises.

"By constantly dwelling upon the sense objects, one develops attachment with them. From attachment is born desire; and from desire arises anger.

Sloka 63

krodhād bhavati saṃmohaḥ saṃmohāt smṛtivibhramaḥ
smṛtibhraṃśād buddhināśo buddhināśāt praṇaśyati

krodhat = from anger; bhavati = develops; sammohah = delusion; sammohat = from delusion; smrti = of memory, law books; vibhramah = loss; smrti-bhramsat = from loss of memory; buddhi-nasah = loss of discriminating intelligence; buddhi-nasat = loss of discriminating intelligence; pranasyati = perishes.

"From anger develops delusion, from delusion (arises) confusion of memory, from confusion of memory (arises) loss of discriminating intelligence and when discriminating intelligence is lost, life is lost.

Sloka 64

rāgadveṣavimuktais tu viṣayān indriyaiś caran
ātmavaśyair vidheyātmā prasādam adhigacchati

raga = attraction; dvesa = aversion; vimuktaih = released; tu = but; visayan = sense objects; indriyaih = with the senses; caran = moving; atma-vasyaih = under own control; vidheya-atma = the self-disciplined; prasadam = peace and clarity; adhigacchati = attains.

"But by moving among the sense objects the senses that are free from attraction and aversion and under his own control, the self-disciplined (person) attains peace and clarity.

Sloka 65

prasāde sarvaduḥkhānāṃ hānir asyopajāyate
prasannacetaso hy āśu buddhiḥ paryavatiṣṭhate

prasade = in serenity; sarva = all; duhkhanam = sorrows; hanih = destruction, removal, eradication; asya = of his; upajayate = ensue; prasanna = serene, pleasant cetasah = mind; hi = indeed; asu = soon; buddhih = discriminating intelligence; pari = sufficiently, firmly; avatisthate = established.

"In (the state of) serenity follows the destruction of all his sorrows. Indeed, with serene mind soon his discriminating intelligence is firmly established.

Sloka 66

nāsti buddhir ayuktasya na cāyuktasya bhāvanā
na cābhāvayataḥ śāntir aśāntasya kutaḥ sukham.

na= not; asti = there is; buddhih = discriminating intelligence; ayuktasya = the unsteady or uncontrolled; na = not; ca = and; ayuktasya = unsteady, uncontrolled; bhavana = concentration; na = not; ca = and; abhavayatah = one without concentration; santih = peace; asantasya = for the one without peace; kutah = where is; sukham = happiness.

"For the unsteady, there is no discriminating intelligence and for the unsteady no concentration (either). For him without concentration there is no peace and for the one without peace how can there be happiness?

Sloka 67

indriyāṇāṃ hi caratāṃ yan manonuvidhīyate
tad asya harati prajñāṃ vāyur nāvam ivāmbhas

indriyanam = of the senses; hi = for; caratam = wandering, moving; yat = that; manah = mind; anuvidhiyate = in obedience or according to; tat = that; asya = of him; harati = carries away, takes away; prajnam = wisdom or understanding arising from discriminating intelligence; vayuh = the wind; navam = a boat; iva = like; ambhasi = on the water.

For the mind that is in obedience to the wandering senses, that (mind) of him carries away the wisdom like the wind (carries away) the boat on the waters.

Sloka 68

tasmād yasya mahābāho nigṛhītāni sarvaśaḥ
indriyāṇīndriyārthebhyas tasya prajñā pratiṣṭhitā

tasmat = therefore; yasya = whose; maha-baho = O mighty-armed one; nigrhitani = withdrawn, restrained; sarvasah = in all respects; indriyani = the senses; indriya-arthebhyah = from the sense objects; tasya = of him; prajna = discriminating intelligence; pratisthita = firmly established.

"Therefore, O mighty armed (Arjuna), whose senses are withdrawn in all respects from the sense objects, the discriminating intelligence of him is firmly established.

Sloka 69

yā niśā sarvabhūtānāṃ tasyāṃ jāgarti saṃyamī
yasyāṃ jāgrati bhūtāni sā niśā paśyato muneḥ

ya = that which; nisa = night; sarva = all; bhutanam = for the beings; tasyam = in that; jagarti = wakeful; samyami = th e self-restrained; yasyam = in which; jagrati = awake; bhutani = beings; sa = that is; nisa = night; pasyatah = sees; muneh = the silent sage.

"That which is night for all beings in that the self-restrained remains awake; in which the beings are awake, that is night for the silent sage.

Sloka 70

āpūryamāṇam acalapratiṣṭhaṃ samudram āpaḥ praviśanti yadvat
tadvat kāmā yaṃ praviśanti sarve sa śāntim āpnoti na kāmakāmī

apuryamanam = Ever full to the brim; acala-pratistham = unmoving and unchanged; samudram = the ocean; apah = waters; pravisanti = enter; yadvat = as; tadvat = so; kamah = desires; yam = to whom; pravisanti = enter; sarve = all; sah = that person; santim = peace; apnoti = attained; na = not; kama-kami = pursuer of desires.

Just as the waters that enter from all sides the ocean that is always full, unmoving and unchanged so are all the desires that enter a person who has attained peace. Not so, who is the pursuer of desires.

Sloka 71

vihāya kāmān yaḥ sarvān pumāṃś carati niḥspṛhaḥ
nirmamo nirahaṃkāraḥ sa śāntim adhigacchhati

vihaya = having renounced; kaman = all desires; yah = who; sarvan = all; puman = the person; carati = moves about; nihsprhah = without longing; nirmamah = without the sense of ownership; nirahankarah = without egoism; sah = he; santim = peace; adhigacchati = attains.

"That man attains peace, who having renounced all desires, moves about without longing, without the sense of ownership, (and) without egoism.

Sloka 72

eṣā brāhmī sthitiḥ pārtha naināṃ prāpya vimuhyati
sthitvāsyām antakālepi brahmanirvāṇam ṛcchati

esa = this; brahmi = highest, Brahman; sthitih = state; partha = Partha; na = not; enam = this; prapya = having attained; vimuhyati = is deluded; sthitva = thus established; asyam = in this; anta-kale = end time, last stages of life; api = also; brahma-nirvanam = union, dissolution or absorption into Brahman; rcchati = attains.

"This is the highest state, O Partha; having attained this, one does not become deluded. Thus established in this (state), at the end of life, one attains absorption into Brahman, the Supreme Self."

Sloka 73

iti srīmadbhāgavadgītāsupanisatsu brahmavidyāyām
yogasāstre
srikrisnārjunasamvāde sāmkhyayogo nāma dvitiyo 'dhyayah

iti = thus; srīmadbhāgavadgītā = in the sacred Bhagavadgita; upanisatsu = in the Upanishad; brahmavidyāyām = the knowledge of the absolute Brahman; yogasāstre = the scripture of yoga; srikrisnārjunasamvāde = the dialogue between Sri Krishna and Arjuna; sāmkhyayogo nāma = by name samkhya yoga; dvitiya = second; adhyayah = chapter;

Thus ends the second chapter named the Yoga of Knowledge in the Upanishad of the sacred Bhagavadgita, the knowledge of the Absolute Brahman, the scripture on yoga, and the debate between Lord Krishna and Arjuna.

3 – The Yoga of Action

Sloka 1

arjuna uvāca
jyāyasī cet karmaṇas te matā buddhir janārdana
tat kiṃ karmaṇi ghore māṃ niyojayasi keśava

arjunah = Arjuna; uvaca = said; jyayasi = superior; cet = if; karmanah = to action; te = your; mata = thought, opinion; buddhih = discriminating intelligence; janardana = Janardana; tat = then; kim = why; karmani = in action; ghore = horrible, awful, hideous, terrible; mam = me; niyojayasi = engaging me; kesava = O Kesava.

Arjuna said, "O Janardana, if in your opinion discriminating intelligence is superior to actions then why are you engaging me in hideous actions, O Kesava?

Sloka 2

vyāmiśreṇeva vākyena buddhiṃ mohayasīva me
tad ekaṃ vada niścitya yena śreyoham āpnuyām

vyamisrena = mixed, ambiguous, conflicting; iva = as it is ; vakyena = statements; buddhim = understanding arising from discriminating intelligence; mohayasi = confused, bewildered; iva = as; me = my; tat = therefore; ekam = one; vada = please tell; niscitya = with clarity or certainty; yena = by which; sreyah = highest good; aham = I; apnuyam = may attain.

"With conflicting and ambiguous statements, as it is, you have confused my understanding. Therefore, tell me clearly that by which I may attain the highest good."

Sloka 3

śrībhagavān uvāca
lokesmin dvividhā niṣṭhā purā proktā mayānagha
jñānayogena sāṅkhyānāṃ karmayogena yogināṃ

sri-bhagavan uvaca = said the Supreme Lord; loke = in the world; asmin = this; dvi-vidha = two kinds of; nistha = discipline, steadfastness, faith; pura = in the past; prokta = declared; maya = by Me; anagha = sinless one; jnana-yogena = by the yoga of knowledge; sankhyanam = for the wise men of knowledge; karma-yogena = yoga of action; yoginam = for the practitioners of yoga.

The Supreme Lord said, "O sinless one, two types of disciplines were declared by Me in this world in the past: the yoga of knowledge for the men of knowledge and the yoga of action for the practitioners of yoga

Sloka 4

na karmaṇām anārambhān naiṣkarmyaṃ puruṣośnute
na ca saṃnyasanād eva siddhiṃ samadhigacchati

na = without; karmanam = from actions; anarambhat = by not doing; naiskarmyam = idleness, inactivity, exemption from the consequences of actions; purusah = person; asnute = attain; na = nor; ca = also; sannyasanat = by renunciation; eva = only; siddhim = fulfillment; samadhigacchati = attain

"A person does not attain freedom from the consequences of his actions by abstaining from actions; nor does he attain fulfillment by renunciation alone.

Sloka 5

na hi kaścit kṣaṇam api jātu tiṣṭhaty akarmakṛt
kāryate hy avaśaḥ karma sarvaḥ prakṛtijair guṇaiḥ

na = not; hi = because,for; kascit = anyone; ksanam = moment; api = even; jatu = even; tisthati = exist, remain; akarma-krt = without performing action; karyate = made to do; hi = indeed; avasah = without their own accord or active involvement; karma = actions; sarvah = all; prakrti-jaih = born of Prakriti or Nature; gunaih = qualities.

"Because no one can remain even for a moment without performing actions. Indeed, all are made to perform actions helplessly by the qualities born of Nature.

Sloka 6

karmendriyāṇi saṃyamya ya āste manasā smaran
indriyārthān vimūḍhātmā mithyācāraḥ sa ucyate

karma-indriyani = organs of action; samyamya = controlling; yah = who; aste = remains; manasa = by the mind; smaran = recollecting, remembering; indriya-arthan = sense objects; vimudha = deluded; atma = soul; mithya-acarah = practitioner of improper or deceitful conduct; sah = he; ucyate = is called.

"Controlling the organs of action, he who remains thinking of the sense objects, that deluded soul is called a practitioner of delusion.

Sloka 7

yas tv indriyāṇi manasā niyamyārabhaterjuna
karmaindriyaiḥ karmayogam asaktaḥ sa viśiṣyate

yah = he who; tu = but, however; indriyani = the senses; manasa = the mind; niyamya = restraining; arabhate = begins, practices; arjuna = Arjuna; karma-indriyaih = organs of actions; karma-yogam = yoga of action; asaktah = without attachment; sah = that one, he; visisyate = special, better, stands apart, distinguished.

"However, he who practices the yoga of action with the organs of action, O Arjuna, restraining the senses with the mind, without attachment, that one is special.

Sloka 8

niyataṃ kuru karma tvaṃ karma jyāyo hy akarmaṇaḥ
śarīrayātrāpi ca te na prasidhyed akarmaṇaḥ

niyatam = ordained, obligatory; kuru = perform; karma = duties; tvam = you; karma = action; jyayah = superior; hi = cetainly; akarmanah = to inaction; sarira = bodily; yatra = journey, survival, maintenance; api = even; ca = and; te = your; na = not; prasiddhyet = will not be possible; akarmanah = without action.

"You (shall) perform ordained actions. Certainly action is superior to inaction; and with inaction, even the journey of the body will not be possible.

Sloka 9

yajñārthāt karmaṇonyatra lokoyaṃ karmabandhanaḥ
tadarthaṃ karma kaunteya muktasaṅgaḥ samācara

yajna-arthat = for the sake of sacrifice; karmanah = action; anyatra = otherwise; lokah = the world; ayam = this ; karma-bandhanah = bound by actions; tadartham = for That; karma = actions; kaunteya = O son of Kunti; mukta-sangah = free from attachment; samacara = do, perform.

"For the sake of sacrifice only are actions. Otherwise, this world is bound by action. O son of Kunti , for That sake only, free from attachment, perform your actions.

Sloka 10

sahayajñāḥ prajāḥ sṛṣṭvā purovāca prajāpatiḥ
anena prasaviṣyadhvam eṣa vostv iṣṭakāmadhuk

saha = along with; yajnah = sacrificial rituals; prajah = living beings; srstva = having created; pura = in the remote antiquity; uvaca = said; praja-patih = Brahma, the creator of beings; anena = by this; prasavisyadhvam = grow and mulitiply; esah = certainly; vah = your; astu = let it be; ista = what is desired; kama-dhuk = the giver or fulfiller.

"In the remote antiquity, having created sacrificial rituals along with living beings, Brahma Prajapati declared, "By this only you shall grow and multiply. Let it be your fulfiller of desires and wishes."

Sloka 11

devān bhāvayatānena te devā bhāvayantu vaḥ
parasparaṃ bhāvayantaḥ śreyaḥ param avāpsyatha

devan = gods, devas; bhavayata = you nourish; anena = with this; te = those; devah = gods, devas; bhavayantu = nourish; vah = you;

parasparam = mutually, each other; bhavayantah = nourishing; sreyah = good; param = the highest, supreme; avapsyatha = you should obtain.

"Nourish the gods with this (sacrifice) and those gods will nourish you. Thus nourishing each other, you will obtain the highest good.

Sloka 12

iṣṭān bhogān hi vo devā dāsyante yajñabhāvitāḥ
tair dattān apradāyaibhyo yo bhuṅkte stena eva saḥ

istan = desired; bhogan = enjoyments; hi = indeed; vah = to you; devah = gods, devas; dasyante = confer; yajna-bhavitah = nourished by the sacrifices; taih = by them; dattan = what has been given; apradaya = without giving; ebhyah = to them; yah = who; bhunkte = enjoys; stenah = thief; eva = certainly; sah = is he.

"Indeed, nourished by the sacrifices (you perform), the gods confer upon you the desired enjoyments. He who enjoys what has been given by them without giving them in return is certainly a thief

Sloka 13

yajñaśiṣṭāśinaḥ santo mucyante sarvakilbiṣaiḥ
bhuñjate te tv aghaṃ pāpā ye pacanty ātmakāraṇāt

yajna-sista = what is left of the sacrifice; asinah = those who eat; santah = the pious; mucyante = are freed; sarva = all kinds of; kilbisaih = from sins; bhunjate = incur; te = those; tu = but; agham = sin; papah = sinners, unholy people; ye = those who; pacanti = cook; atma-karanat = for themselves

"The pious who eat what is left of a sacrifice are freed from all kinds of sins, but those evil (persons) verily eat sin, who cook food for themselves.

Sloka 14

annād bhavanti bhūtāni parjanyād annasaṃbhavaḥ
yajñād bhavati parjanyo yajñaḥ karmasamudbhavaḥ

annat = from food; bhavanti = come into existence; bhutani = beings; parjanyat = from rains; anna = food; sambhavah = is created; yajnat = from the sacrifice; bhavati = arise; parjanyah = rains; yajnah = sacrifice; karma = obligatory duties; samudbhavah = origin.

"From food beings come into existence; from rains is created food; from sacrifice arise rains; and sacrifice has obligatory work as its origin.

Sloka 15

karma brahmodbhavaṃ viddhi brahmākṣarasamudbhavam
tasmāt sarvagataṃ brahma nityaṃ yajñe pratiṣṭhitam

karma = work; brahma = Brahma; udbhavam = originated; viddhi = know; brahma = Brahman; aksara = the Imperishable; samudbhavam = manifested; tasmat = therefore; sarva-gatam = all-pervading; brahma = Brahman; nityam = eternally; yajne = in sacrifice; pratisthitam = situated.

"Know that action originated from Brahma and Brahma originated directly from the Supreme Brahman. Therefore the all pervading Brahman is eternally situated in all acts of sacrifice.

Sloka 16

evaṃ pravartitaṃ cakraṃ nānuvartayatīha yaḥ
aghāyur indriyārāmo moghaṃ pārtha sa jīvati

evam = thus; pravartitam = moving; cakram = wheel; na = not; anuvartayati = follows; iha = here, in this; yah = who; agha-ayuh = sinful life; indriya-aramah = indulging or resting in the senses; mogham = in vain; partha = Partha; sah = he; jivati = lives.

"He who does not follow here the wheel thus moving, whose life is sinful, indulging in the senses, in vain O Partha, he lives.

Sloka 17

yas tv ātmaratir eva syād ātmatṛptaś ca mānavaḥ
ātmany eva ca saṃtuṣṭas tasya kāryaṃ na vidyate

yah = who; tu = but; atma-ratih = delights in self; eva = only; syat = remains; atma-trptah = satisfied by self; ca = and; manavah = human being; atmani = in the self; eva = only; ca = and; santustah = happy, contended; tasya = for him; karyam = duty; na = no; vidyate = arising from the Vedas.

"But the person who delights in the Self, is satisfied by the Self and happy within the Self, for such a person duty does not arise from the Vedas.

Sloka 18

naiva tasya kṛtenārtho nākṛteneha kaścana
na cāsya sarvabhūteṣu kaścid arthavyapāśrayaḥ

na = not; eva = at all; tasya = for him; krtena = by performing duty; arthah = interest; na = not; akrtena = without performing duty; iha = in this world; kascana = whatever; na = no; ca = and; asya = for him; sarva-bhutesu = in all living beings; kascit = any; artha = object; vyapasrayah = dependence

"For him there is no interest at all in performing duty or not performing it. For him there is no dependence, whatsoever, on any object and on any living being.

Sloka 19

tasmād asaktaḥ satataṃ kāryaṃ karma samācara
asakto hy ācaran karma param āpnoti pūruṣaḥ

tasmat = therefore; asaktah = not attached, not feeling interested, disinterest; satatam = always; karyam = obligatory; karma = work; samacara = perform; asaktah = disinterest; hi = certainly; acaran = performing; karma = work; param = the Supremet; apnoti = attains; purusah = a person.

"Therefore, always perform your obligatory work without attachment. Certainly, by performing work without attachment a person attains the Supreme Self.

Sloka 20

karmaṇaiva hi saṃsiddhim āsthitā janakādayaḥ
lokasaṃgraham evāpi saṃpaśyan kartum arhasi

karmana = through work; eva = only; hi = for; samsiddhim = equanimity, sameness; asthitah = attained; janaka-adayah = Janaka and others; loka-sangraham = welfare of the world; eva = and; api = also; sampasyan = for the sake of; kartum = do your duty; arhasi = you should.

"Through work only sameness attained by (king) Janaka and others. Also, for the welfare of the world do your duty you should.

Sloka 21

yadyad ācarati śreṣṭhas tattad evetaro janaḥ
sa yat pramāṇaṃ kurute lokas tad anuvartate

yadyad = whatever; acarati = does; sresthah = a great person or a superior person; tattat = that that; eva = only; itarah = other; janah = people; sah = he; yat = whatever; pramanam = example, standard; kurute = sets; lokah = the world; tat = that; anuvartate = follows.

"Whatever a superior person does, that only other people (do). Whatever example or standard he sets, the world follows that.

Sloka 22

na me pārthāsti kartavyaṃ triṣu lokeṣu kiṃcana
nānavāptam avāptavyaṃ varta eva ca karmaṇi

na = no; me = for me; partha = Partha; asti = there is; kartavyam = duty to do; trisu = in the three; lokesu = worlds; kincana = whatsoever; na = not; anavaptam = not gained; avaptavyam = to be gained; varte = engage; eva = also; ca = and; karmani = in obligatory duty.

"For me, O Partha, there is no duty to do in the three worlds whatsoever; and nothing not gained that should be gained. Yet, I also engage in obligatory duty.

Sloka 23

yadi hy ahaṃ na varteyaṃ jātu karmaṇy atandritaḥ
mama vartmānuvartante manuṣyāḥ pārtha sarvaśaḥ

yadi = if; hi = indeed; aham = I; na = not; varteyam = continue doing; jatu = always; karmani = in duty; atandritah = unwaveringly or undistracted; mama = My; vartma = path; anuvartante = follow; manusyah = people; partha = O Partha; sarvasah = in every way, everywhere.

"If indeed I do not always continue doing my duty unwaveringly, people will follow my path in every way, O Partha.

Sloka 24

utsīdeyur ime lokā na kuryāṃ karma ced aham
saṃkarasya ca kartā syām upahanyām imāḥ prajāḥ

utsideyuh = would be destroyed; ime = these; lokah = worlds; na = do not; kuryam = perform; karma = duty, actions; cet = if; aham = I; sankarasya = intermingling of castes; ca = and; karta = the perpetrator; syam = would become; upahanyam = cause harm; imah = these; prajah = people.

"These worlds would be destroyed if I do not perform actions; I would be the perpetrator of the confusion of castes and cause considerable harm to these people.

Sloka 25

saktāḥ karmaṇy avidvāṃso yathā kurvanti bhārata
kuryād vidvāṃs tathāsaktaś cikīrṣur lokasaṃgraham

saktah = with attachment; karmani = actions; avidvamsah = the ignorant; yatha = as; kurvanti = perform; bharata = Bharata; kuryat = act; vidvan = the knowledgeable; tatha = thus; asaktah = without attachment; cikirsuh = desiring to; loka-sangraham = welfare of the world

"O Bharata, just as the ignorant people perform their actions with attachment the knowledgeable must act without attachment, desiring the welfare of the world.

Sloka 26

na buddhibhedaṃ janayed ajñānāṃ karmasaṃginām
joṣayet sarvakarmāṇi vidvān yuktaḥ samācaran

na = not; buddhi-bhedam = mental conflict; janayet = cause; ajnanam = among the ignorant; karma-sanginam = attachment to action; josayet = make them do; sarva = all; karmani = duties; vidvan = learned; yuktah = in an appropriate manner; samacaran = performing, practicing.

"Without causing confusion or mental conflicts among the ignorant (who are) attached to their actions, the knowledgeable person should encourage them to perform all their duties, performing his own duties in an appropriate manner.

Sloka 27

prakṛteḥ kriyamāṇāni guṇaiḥ karmāṇi sarvaśaḥ
ahaṃkāravimūḍhātmā kartāham iti manyate

prakrteh = of nature; kriyamanani = actions are performed; gunaih = by the qualities; karmani = actions; sarvasah = all types of; ahankara-vimudha = deluded by ego; atma = the being; karta = doer; aham = I; iti = thus; manyate = thinks.

"All types of action are performed by the gunas arising from Nature. Deluded by the ego, the being, thus thinks, "I am the doer."

Sloka 28

tattvavit tu mahābāho guṇakarmavibhāgayoḥ
guṇā guṇeṣu vartanta iti matvā na sajjate

tattva-vit = the knower of the nature of things, a person of knowledge; tu = but; maha-baho = mighty-armed one; guna-karma = gunas and actions; vibhagayoh = divisions; gunah = qualities; gunesu = in the qualities; vartante = reside; iti = thus; matva = having thought; na = not; sajjate = becomes attached.

"But O mighty armed one, he who knows the nature of things and the division of the gunas and actions does not become attached, thinking thus, 'the gunas resided among the gunas.'

Sloka 29

prakṛter guṇasaṃmūḍhāḥ sajjante guṇakarmasu
tān akṛtsnavido mandān kṛtsnavin na vicālayet

prakrteh = of Nature; guna-sammudhah = deluded by the gunas; sajjante = become attached; guna-karmasu = in guna related activities; tan = those; akrtsna-vidah = the ignorant; mandan = poor intellect; krtsna-vit = the knowers of all; na = not; vicalayet = disturb.

"Deluded by the gunas of Nature, the ignorant become attached to the actions arising from the gunas. The knowers of all should not disturb men of poor intellect.

Sloka 30

mayi sarvāṇi karmāṇi saṃnyasyādhyātmacetasā
nirāśīr nirmamo bhūtvā yudhyasva vigatajvaraḥ

mayi = to Me; sarvani = all ; karmani = actions; sannyasya = renouncing; adhyatma = in the Self; cetasa = fixing the mind; nirasih = without expectations; nirmamah = without the sense of ownership; bhutva = by remaining; yudhyasva = fight; vigata-jvarah = without feverish agitation.

"Renouncing all actions to Me, fixing your mind upon the Self, free from expectations and sense of ownership, fight without feverish agitation.

Sloka 31

ye me matam idaṃ nityam anutiṣṭhanti mānavāḥ
śraddhāvantonasūyanto mucyante tepi karmabhiḥ

ye = those; me = My; matam = teachings, doctrines; idam = this; nityam = always, constantly; anutisthanti = follow; manavah = human beings, people; sraddha-vantah = with great faith; anasuyantah = without envy, indignation or intolerance; mucyante = are freed; te = they; api = also; karmabhih = from actions.

"Those people who constantly follow my teachings with great faith and without envy or intolerance are also freed from actions.

Sloka 32

ye tv etad abhyasūyanto nānutiṣṭhanti me matam
sarvajñānavimūḍhāṃs tān viddhi naṣṭān acetasaḥ

ye = those who; tu = but; etat = this; abhyasuyantah = out of envy; na = do not; anutisthanti = follow; me = My; matam = teaching, doctrine; sarva-jnana = knowledge of the all pervading Self; vimudhan = deluded; tan = they; viddhi = know; nastan = ruined; acetasah = without discriminating intelligence, without mindfulness.

"But those who, out of envy, do not follow my teaching know them to be deluded about the knowledge of the all pervading Self, ruined and lacking in discriminating intelligence.

Sloka 33

sadṛśaṃ ceṣṭate svasyāḥ prakṛter jñānavān api
prakṛtiṃ yānti bhūtāni nigrahaḥ kiṃ kariṣyati

sadrsam = accordingly; cestate = acts; svasyah = his own; prakrteh = Nature; jnana-van = a wise person; api = even; prakrtim = nature; yanti = follow; bhutani = living beings; nigrahah = restraint or suppression; kim = what; karisyati = can do.

"Even a wise person acts according to his own nature. All living beings follow their own nature. What restraint or suppression can do?

Sloka 34

indriyasyendriyasyārthe rāgadveṣau vyavasthitau
tayor na vaśam āgacchhet tau hy asya paripanthinau

indriyasya = of the senses; indriyasya arthe = in the sense objects; raga = attraction; dvesau = aversion; vyavasthitau = situated, rest, located; tayoh = their; na = not; vasam = influence, control; agacchet = should (one) come; tau = they; hi = certainly; asya = his; paripanthinau = obstacles, stumbling blocks.

"Attraction and aversion for the sense objects are established in the senses. One should not come under their influence. They are the major obstacles (to liberation).

Sloka 35

śreyān svadharmo viguṇaḥ paradharmāt svanuṣṭhitāt
svadharme nidhanaṃ śreyaḥ paradharmo bhayāvahaḥ

sreyan = superior; sva-dharmah = own duty; vigunah = defective, devoid of merit; para-dharmat = duty of another; svanusthitat = perfectly done, well performed; sva-dharme = one's own duty; nidhanam = death; sreyah = better; para-dharmah = duty of another;; bhaya-avahah = fraught with fear, fear producing.

"Even if defective, one's own duty is superior to the duty of another that is well performed. Better is death while doing one's own duty. The duty of another is fraught with fear and danger."

Sloka 36

arjuna uvāca
atha kena prayuktoyaṃ pāpaṃ carati pūruṣaḥ
anicchann api vārṣṇeya balād iva niyojitaḥ

arjunah uvaca = Arjuna said; atha = now then; kena = by what; prayuktah = induced; ayam = one; papam = sin; carati = commit; purusah = a person; anicchan = against will; api = even; varsneya = O Varsneya; balat = by force; iva = as if; niyojitah = compelled.

Said Arjuna, "Now then, O Varsneya, induced by what does one commit sin against one's will as if one were compelled by force?"

Sloka 37

śrībhagavān uvāca
kāma eṣa krodha eṣa rajoguṇasamudbhavaḥ
mahāśano mahāpāpmā viddhy enam iha vairiṇam

sri-bhagavan uvaca = said God Supreme; kamah = desire; esah = this; krodhah = anger; esah = this; rajah-guna = the quality of rajas; samudbhavah = is born, arises; maha-asanah = greatly devourer; maha-papma = greatly sinner; viddhi = know; enam = this; iha = here in this world; vairinam = the enemy.

"The Supreme Lord said, "This desire, the anger, born of the quality of rajas, is the great devourer, the great sinner. Know that here in the world this is the enemy.

Sloka 38

dhūmenāvriyate vanhir yathādarśo malena ca
yatholbenāvṛto garbhas tathā tenedam āvṛtam

dhumena = by smoke; avriyate = enveloped; vahnih = fire; yatha = as; adarsah = mirror; malena = by impurities; ca = and; yatha = as; ulbena = by womb; avrtah = is covered; garbhah = fetus; tatha = so; tena = by that; idam = this; avrtam = is enveloped.

"As by smoke fire is enveloped, as a mirror by impurities and as by womb is covered the fetus so is by that (desire) this is enveloped.

Sloka 39

āvṛtaṃ jñānam etena jñānino nityavairiṇā
kāmarupeṇa kaunteya duṣpūreṇānalena ca

avrtam = enveloped; jnanam = wisdom, knowledge; etena = by this; jnaninah = of the wise; nitya-vairina = eternal enemy; kama-rupena = in the form of desire; kaunteya = Kaunteya, son of Kunti; duspurena = insatiable; analena = by the fire; ca = and.

"O Kaunteya, wisdom is enveloped by this eternal enemy of the wise in the form of desire which is an insatiable fire.

Sloka 40

indriyāṇi mano buddhir asyādhiṣṭhānam ucyate
etair vimohayaty eṣa jñānam āvṛtya dehinam

indriyani = the senses; manah = the mind; buddhih = the discriminating intelligence; asya = of this; adhisthanam = the seat; ucyate = said to be; etaih = by these; vimohayati = deludes; esah = of this; jnanam = wisdom; avrtya = enveloped; dehinam = the embodied.

"The senses, the mind, and the discriminating intelligence are said to be its seat; with them it deludes the embodied Self by veiling the wisdom."

Sloka 41

tasmāt tvam indriyāṇy ādau niyamya bharatarṣabha
pāpmānaṃ prajahi hy enaṃ jñānavijñānanāśanam

tasmat = therefore; tvam = you; indriyani = senses; adau = in the beginning; niyamya = by restraining; bharata-rsabha = the best among the Bharatas; papmanam = sin; prajahi = slay, control; hi = indeed; enam = this; jnana = knowledge; vijnana = higher knowledge; nasanam = destroyer.

"Therefore, O best of the Bharatas, restraining the senses in the very beginning slay the sin, which is indeed the destroyer of knowledge and wisdom.

Sloka 42

indriyāṇi parāṇy āhur indriyebhyaḥ paraṃ manaḥ
manasas tu parā buddhir yo buddheḥ paratas tu saḥ

indriyani = senses; parani = superior; ahuh = say; indriyebhyah = to the senses; param = superior; manah = the mind; manasah = to the mind; tu = also; para = superior; buddhih = discriminating intelligence; yah = one who; buddheh = to the intelligence; paratah = superior; tu = but; sah = He.

"(They) say that the senses are superior; superior to the senses is the mind; superior to the mind is the discriminating intelligence; the one superior to the discriminating intelligence is He.

Sloka 43

evaṃ buddheḥ paraṃ buddhvā saṃstabhyātmānam ātmanā
jahi śatruṃ mahābāho kāmarūpaṃ durāsadam

evam = thus; buddheh = to discriminating intelligence; param = superior; buddhva = by knowing; samstabhya = by establishing; atmanam = the ego self; atmana = by the Self; jahi = slayt; satrum = the enemy; maha-baho = O mighty-armed one; kama-rupam = the form of desire; durasadam = formidable.

"Thus knowing the Self as superior to the discriminating intelligence, establishing the ego-self within the Self, O mighty armed one, slay the enemy in the form of desire, which is formidable

Conclusion

iti srīmadbhāgavadgītāsupanisatsu brahmavidyāyām
yogasāstre
srikrisnārjunasamvāde karmayogo nāma tritiyo 'dhyayah

iti = thus; srīmadbhāgavadgītā = in the sacred Bhagavadgita; upanisatsu = in the Upanishad; brahmavidyāyām = the knowledge of the absolute Brahman; yogasāstre = the scripture of yoga; srikrisnārjunasamvāde = the dialogue between Sri Krishna and

Arjuna; karmayogo nāma = by name karma yoga; tritiya = thirdd; adhyayah = chapter;

Thus ends the third chapter named Yoga of Action in the Upanishad of the divine Bhagavadgita, the knowledge of the Absolute, the yogic scripture, and the debate between Arjuna and Lord Krishna.

4 – The Yoga of Knowledge with Renunciation of Action

Sloka 1

imaṃ vivasvate yogaṃ proktavān aham avyayam
vivasvān manave prāha manur ikṣvākavebravīt

sri-bhagavan uvaca = the Supreme Lord said; imam = this; vivasvate = to Vaivasvata; yogam = yoga; proktavan = taught; aham = I; avyayam = imperishable; vivasvan = Vivasvan; manave = to the first born Manu; praha = taught; manuh = Manu; iksvakave = to King Iksvaku; abravit = taught.

The Supreme Lord said, "I taught this imperishable yoga to Vaivasvata; Vaivasvan taught it to Manu; Manu taught this to king Iksvaku.

Sloka 2

evaṃ paramparāprāptam imaṃ rājarṣayo viduḥ
sa kāleneha mahatā yogo naṣṭaḥ paraṃtapa 4.2

evam = thus; parampara = regular succession; praptam = having received, gained, obtained; imam = this; raja-rsayah = the saintly kings; viduh = knew; sah = this; kalena = in the course of time; iha = here; mahata = great; yogah = yoga; nastah = lost; parantapa = Parantapa.

"Thus having received the knowledge through regular succession, the saintly kings knew this (yoga); but, O destroyer of the foes, in course of time this great yoga was lost in this world.

Sloka 3

sa evāyaṃ mayā tedya yogaḥ proktaḥ purātanaḥ
bhaktosi me sakhā ceti rahasyaṃ hy etad uttamam

sah = that; eva =indeed; ayam = this; maya = by Me; te = to you; adya = today; yogah = yoga; proktah = taught; puratanah = greatly ancient;

bhaktah = devotee; asi = you are; me = My; sakha = friend; ca = and; iti = because; rahasyam = secret; hi = for; etat = this; uttamam = great, utmost.

"That yoga of great antiquity, (which is) indeed this, has been taught to you by Me today because you are my devotee and friend, for it is an utmost secret.

Sloka 4

arjuna uvāca
aparaṃ bhavato janma paraṃ janma vivasvataḥ
katham etad vijānīyāṃ tvam ādau proktavān iti

arjunah uvaca = Arjuna said; aparam = later; bhavatah = Your; janma = birth; param = earlier; janma = birth; vivasvatah = of Vivasvan; katham = how; etat = this; vijaniyam = may I to understand; tvam = You; adau = in the beginning; proktavan = taught; iti = thus.

Said Arjuna," Later was your birth. The birth of Vaivsvan was earlier. How may I understand this that in the beginning You taught (him)?"

Sloka 5

śrībhagavānuvāca
bahūni me vyatītāni janmāni tava cārjuna
tāny ahaṃ veda sarvāṇi na tvaṃ vettha paraṃtapa

sri-bhagavan uvaca = the glorious Bhagavan said; bahuni = many; me = my; vyatitani = have gone by; janmani = births; tava = of yours; ca = and; arjuna = O Arjuna; tani = those; aham = I; veda = know; sarvani = all; na = not; tvam = you; vettha = know; parantapa = O destroyer of the foes.

The Supreme Lord said,"Many births of mine have gone by and those of yours, O Arjuna. I know them all, but you do not know, O destroyer of the foes.

Sloka 6

ajopi sann avyayātmā bhūtānām īśvaropi san
prakṛtiṃ svām adhiṣṭhāya saṃbhavāmy ātmamāyayā

ajah = unborn; api = although; san = I am; avyaya = imperishable; atma = self; bhutanam = living being; isvarah = the Lord; api = although; san = I am; prakrtim = Nature; svam = My own; adhisthaya = presiding over ; sambhavami = I take birth; atma-mayaya = by My own Power of Maya.

"Although I am unborn and imperishable, although I am the Lord of all beings, presiding over My own Nature, I manifest by my own power of Maya

Sloka 7

yadā yadā hi dharmasya glānir bhavati bhārata
abhyutthānam adharmasya tadātmānaṃ sṛjāmy aham

yada yada = whenever; hi = surely; dharmasya = duty and virtue; glanih = decline; bhavati = there is; bharata = Bharata; abhyutthanam = increase, ascendence; adharmasya = vice and evil; tada = then; atmanam = Myself; srjami = manifest; aham = I.

"O Bharata, whenever there is a decline of virute and ascendance of evil, then I surely manifest Myself .

Sloka 8

paritrāṇāya sādhūnāṃ vināśāya ca duṣkṛtām
dharmasaṃsthāpanārthāya saṃbhavāmi yuge yuge 4.8

paritranaya = for the protection; sadhunam = of the good, righteous, virtuous; vinasaya = for the destruction of; ca = and; duskrtam = the wicked; dharma = moral laws and religious duties; samsthapana-arthaya = for the sake of establishing; sambhavami = I incarnate Myself; yuge yuge = from time to time.

"For the protection of the good and for the destruction of the wicked, and for the sake of establishing the moral laws and religious duties, I incarnate (upon earth) from time to time.

Sloka 9

janma karma ca me divyam evaṃ yo vetti tattvataḥ
tyaktvā dehaṃ punarjanma naiti mām eti sorjuna

janma = birth; karma = actions; ca = and; me = My; divyam = divine; evam = thus; yah = who; vetti = knows; tattvatah = correctly, truly, really; tyaktva = leaving; deham = the body; punarjanma = rebirth; na = never; eti = come; mam = to Me; eti = come; sah = he; arjuna = O Arjuna.

"He who thus knows correctly My divine birth and My actions, would never have rebirth upon leaving his body. He comes to Me, O Arjuna.

Sloka 10

vītarāgabhayakrodhā manmayā mām upāśritāḥ
bahavo jñānatapasā pūtā madbhāvam āgatāḥ

vita = free from; raga = passion; bhaya = fear; krodhah = anger; mat-maya = fully absorbed in Me; mam = to Me; upasritah = taking refuge; bahavah = many; jnana = knowledge; tapasa = by penance or austerity; putah = purified; mat-bhavam = My state; agatah = attained.

"Free from passion, fear, anger, fully absorbed in Me, taking refuge in Me, purified by the austerity of knowledge, many attained My State.

Sloka 11

ye yathā māṃ prapadyante tāṃs tathaiva bhajāmy aham
mama vartmānuvartante manuṣyāḥ pārtha sarvaśaḥ

ye = who; yatha = in whatever; mam = to Me; prapadyante = they approach; tan = them; tatha = in the same manner; eva = even; bhajami = reward; aham = I; mama = My; vartma = path; anuvartante = do follow; manusyah = human beings; partha = Partha; sarvasah = in every way, in all respects.

"In whatever (manner) they approach Me, in the same manner I reward them, O Partha, human beings follow My path in every way.

Sloka 12

kāṃkṣantaḥ karmaṇāṃ siddhiṃ yajanta iha devatāḥ
kṣipraṃ hi mānuṣe loke siddhir bhavati karmajā

kanksantah = desiring; karmanam = of actions; siddhim = success; yajante = perform sacrifices; iha = here, in this world; devatah = the divinities; ksipram = quickly; hi = indeed; manuse loke = in the world of human beings; siddhih bhavati = success achieved; karma-ja = born of actions.

"Desiring success in actions they perform sacrifices here for the divinities. Indeed, in this world of humans, success is achieved quickly from actions.

Sloka 13

cāturvarṇyaṃ mayā sṛṣṭaṃ guṇakarmavibhāgaśaḥ
tasya kartāram api māṃ viddhy akartāram avyayam

catuh-varnyam = the four castes; maya = by Me; srstam = created; guna = quality; karma = action; vibhagasah = division of; tasya = of that; kartaram = the creator; api = although; mam = Me; viddhi = know; akartaram = non-doer; avyayam = inexhaustible

"The four castes are created by Me based on the division of actions arising from the gunas. Although I am the creator of that (division of castes), Know Me as the inexhaustible non-doer.

Sloka 14

na māṃ karmāṇi limpanti na me karmaphale spṛhā
iti māṃ yobhijānāti karmabhir na sa badhyate

na = not; mam = Me; karmani = actions; limpanti = taint; na = not; me = My; karma-phale = fruit of actions; sprha = desire; iti = thus; mam =

Me; yah = who; abhijanati = know; karmabhih = by action; na = not; sah = he; badhyate = bound.

"Actions do not taint Me, nor the fruit of action is sought by Me. He who knows Me thus, is not bound by actions.

Sloka 15

evaṃ jñātvā kṛtaṃ karma pūrvair api mumukṣubhiḥ
kuru karmaiva tasmāt tvaṃ pūrvaiḥ pūrvataraṃ kṛtam

evam = thus; jnatva = knowing; krtam = performed; karma = actions; purvaih = ancient; api =even; mumuksubhih = seekers of liberation; kuru = perform; karma = actions; eva = even; tasmat = therefore; tvam = you; purvaih = by the ancient; purva-taram = in the past ages; krtam = performed.

"Knowing thus, actions were performed even by the ancient seekers of liberation. Therefore even you (should) perform actions as were performed by the ancient ones in the past ages.

Sloka 16

kiṃ karma kimakarmeti kavayopy atra mohitāḥ
tat te karma pravakṣyāmi yaj jñātvā mokṣyaseśubhāt

kim = what is; karma = action; kim = what is; akarma = inaction; iti = thus; kavayah = the intelligent; api = even; atra = about; mohitah = confused, bewildered; tat = that; te = you; karma = action; pravaksyami = I shall explain; yat = which; jnatva = knowing; moksyase = will be liberated; asubhat = from the misfortune.

"Even the intelligent are confused about what action is and what inaction is. I shall explain to you that action, by knowing which you will be liberated from this great misfortune.

Sloka 17

karmaṇo hy api boddhavyaṃ boddhavyaṃ ca vikarmaṇaḥ
akarmaṇaś ca boddhavyaṃ gahanā karmaṇo gatiḥ

karmanah = of actions; hi = indeed; api = even; boddhavyam = should be known; boddhavyam = should be known; ca = also; vikarmanah = wrong action; akarmanah = inaction; ca = and; boddhavyam = should be known; gahana = mysterious; karmanah = of actions; gatih = the way or path.

"Indeed actions even should be known; also wrong actions should be known; and inaction should be known. Mysterious is the path of action.

Sloka 18

karmaṇyakarma yaḥ paśyed akarmaṇi ca karma yaḥ
sa buddhimān manuṣyeṣu sa yuktaḥ kṛtsnakarmakṛt

karmani = in action; akarma = inaction; yah = he who; pasyet = perceives; akarmani = in inaction; ca = and; karma = action; yah = who; sah = he; buddhi-man = wise; manusyesu = among people; sah = he; yuktah = engaged in yoga; krtsna-karma-krt = although performs actions.

"He who perceives inaction in action and action in inaction, he is wise among people. He is engaged in yoga although performs actions.

Sloka 19

yasya sarve samārambhāḥ kāmasaṃkalpavarjitāḥ
jñānāgnidagdhakarmāṇaṃ tam āhuḥ paṇḍitaṃ budhāḥ

yasya = whose; sarve = all; samarambhah = undertakings; kama = desire; sankalpa = decisions; varjitah = are devoid of; jnana = knowledge; agni = fire; dagdha = burnt away; karmanam = actions; tam = him; ahuh = call; panditam = learned; budhah = the wise.

"He whose all undertakings are free from desire induced decisions, whose actions are burnt away in the fire of knowledge, the wise call him learned.

Sloka 20

tyaktvā karmaphalāsaṅgaṃ nityatṛpto nirāśrayaḥ
karmaṇy abhipravṛttopi naiva kiṃcit karoti saḥ

tyaktva = having given up; karma-phala-asangam = attachment tothe fruit of actions; nitya = always; trptah = contended; nirasrayah = depending on nothing; karmani = in actions; abhipravrttah = engaged; api =also; na = not; eva = even though; kincit = anything; karoti = does; sah = he.

"Having given up attachment to the fruit of actions, always contended, also depending on nothing, he does not do anything even though (he is engaged in actions).

Sloka 21

nirāśīr yatacittātmā tyaktasarvaparigrahaḥ
śārīraṃ kevalaṃ karma kurvan nāpnoti kilbiṣam

nirasih = without desire or expectation; yata = controlled; citta-atma = mind; tyakta = giving up; sarva = all; parigrahah = possessions; sariram = body; kevalam = only; karma = actions, functions; kurvan = doing so; na = not; apnoti = acquires, incurs; kilbisam = sin.

"Without desire or expectation, with the mind under control, giving up all possessions, performing only body related functions, even acting, he incurs no sin.

Sloka 22

yadṛcchālābhasaṃtuṣṭo dvandvātīto vimatsaraḥ
samaḥ siddhāv asiddhau ca kṛtvāpi na nibadhyate

yadrccha = unintentionally, by chance or coincidence; labha = gain; santustah = contended; dvandva = pairs of opposites, duality; atitah = transcending; vimatsarah = free from envy; samah = equal; siddhau = in success; asiddhau = failure; ca = and; krtva = while performing actions; api = even, although; na = not; nibadhyate = is bound.

"Contended with what comes by chance, transcending the pairs of opposites or duality, free from envy, equal to success and failure, he is not bound even while performing actions.

Sloka 23

gatasaṅgasya muktasya jñānāvasthitacetasaḥ
yajñāyācarataḥ karma samagraṃ pravilīyate

gata-sangasya = past attachments; muktasya =of the liberated; jnana-avasthita = established in knowledge; cetasah = mind; yajnaya = for the sake of sacrifice; acaratah = performs; karma = actions; samagram = completely; praviliyate = dissolved or destroyed.

"For the liberated person, who is free from past attachments, whose mind is established in knowledge, actions performed for the sake of a sacrifice are completely dissolved.

Sloka 24

brahmārpaṇaṃ brahma havir brahmāgnau brahmaṇā hutam
brahmaiva tena gantavyaṃ brahmakarmasamādhinā

brahma = Brahman; arpanam = the act of offering; brahma = the Supreme Brahman; havih = oblation, the offering,; brahma = Brahman; agnau = sacrificial fire; brahmana = by brahman; hutam = the pouring; brahma = Brahman; eva = surely; tena = by him; gantavyam = attained, reached; brahma = Brahman; karma = actions; samadhina = by complete absorption

"The act of offering is Brahman; the oblation is Brahman; the burnt offering is poured into the fire of Brahman by Brahman. Brahman is surely attained by him who performs actions fully absorbed in Brahman.

Sloka 25

daivam evāpare yajñaṃ yoginaḥ paryupāsate
brahmāgnāv apare yajñaṃ yajñenaivopajuvhati

daivam = divinities; eva = only; apare = other, some; yajnam = sacrifices; yoginah = yogis; paryupasate = perform; brahma = Brahman; agnau = in the fire of; apare = some others; yajnam = sacrifice; yajnena = by the sacrifice; eva = even; upajuhvati = pouring.

"Some yogis perform sacrifices for the divinities. Others perform sacrifice by pouring the sacrifice in the fire of Brahman.

Sloka 26

śrotrādīnīndriyāṇy anye saṃyamāgniṣu juvhati
śabdādīn viṣayān anya indriyāgniṣu juvhati

srotra-adini = ears etc.; indriyani = senses; anye = others; samyama = of self-restraint; agnisu = in the fire; juhvati = pour; sabda-adin = sound etc.; visayan = sense objects; anye = others; indriya = of the senses; agnisu = in the fire; juhvati = pour.

"Some pour sense organs such as ears etc., in the fire of self-restraint; others pour sense-objects (such as) sounds etc., into the fire of the sense organs.

Sloka 27

sarvāṇīndriyakarmāṇi prāṇakarmāṇi cāpare
ātmasaṃyamayogāgnau juvhati jñānadīpite

sarvani = all; indriya = senses; karmani = activities; prana-karmani = activities of the vital breath; ca =and; apare = others; atma-samyama = self-stabilization; yoga = yoga; agnau = in the fire of; juhvati = offer; jnana-dipite = ignited by knowledge.

"Others offer all the activities of the senses and the activities of the vital breath into the fire of self-stabilization, ignited by knowledge.

Sloka 28

dravyayajñās tapoyajñā yogayajñās tathāpare
svādhyāyajñānayajñāś ca yatayaḥ saṃśitavratāḥ

dravya-yajnah = sacrifice with matieral wealth; tapah-yajnah = sacrifice with austerities; yoga-yajnah = sacrifice with yoga; tatha = in the same manner; apare = others; svadhyaya = sacrifice with self-study; jnana-yajnah = sacrifice with knowledge; ca = and on the other; yatayah = self-restrained ascetics; samsita = taken to strict; vratah = vows.

"In the same manner, others do sacrifice with material wealth, with austerities, with yoga, with self-study, and with knowledge. Self-restrained ascetics do it with strict vows

Sloka 29

apāne juvhati prāṇaṃ prāṇepānaṃ tathāpare
prāṇāpānagatī ruddhvā prāṇāyāmaparāyaṇāḥ

apane = in apana; juhvati = offer, pour; pranam = in prana prane = prana; apanam = in apana; tatha = in the same manner; apare = others; prana = prana; apana = apana; gati = movement; ruddhva = restraining; prana-ayama = pranayama; parayanah = devoted to, absorbed in, adhering to.

"Similarly, others offer prana in apana, apana in prana, restraining the movements of prana and apana and devoted to the practice of pranayama.

Sloka 30

apare niyatāhārāḥ prāṇān prāṇeṣu juvhati
sarvepy ete yajñavido yajñakṣapitakalmaṣāḥ

apare = others; niyata = restrained; aharah = food; pranan = vital breath; pranesu = in the vital breath; juhvati = offer; sarve = all; api = also; ete = these; yajna-vidah = knowers of sacrifice; yajna = sacrifices; ksapita = cleansed; kalmasah = impurities.

"Others restraining food, offer their vital breath into the vital breath. All these are knowers of the sacrifice, with their impurities cleansed by sacrifices.

Sloka 31

yajñaśiṣṭāmṛtabhujo yānti brahma sanātanam
nāyaṃ lokosty ayajñasya kutonyaḥ kurusattama

yajna-sista = remains of the sacrifice; amrta-bhujah = eat the sweet food; yanti = go, reach; brahma = Brahman; sanatanam = eternal; na = not; ayam = this; lokah = world; asti = there is; ayajnasya = those who do not perform sacrifices; kutah = where; anyah = the other; kuru-sattama = O best amongst the Kurus.

"Those who eat the sweet remains of the sacrificial food go to the eternal Brahman. This world is not for those who do not perform sacrifices. Then, where is the question of the other worlds, O best among theKurus?

Sloka 32

evaṃ bahuvidhā yajñā vitatā brahmaṇo mukhe
karmajān viddhi tān sarvān evaṃ jñātvā vimokṣyase

evam = thus; bahu-vidhah = various types; yajnah = sacrifices; vitatah = spread out, extended; brahmanah = Brahman; mukhe = face; karma-jan = to be born of actions; viddhi = know; tan = then; sarvan = all; evam = thus; jnatva = knowing; vimoksyase = be liberated.

"Thus various kinds of sacrifices spread out from the face of Brahman. Know them all to be born of action. Knowing thus you will be liberated.

Sloka 33

śreyān dravyamayād yajñāj jñānayajñaḥ paraṃtapa
sarvaṃ karmākhilaṃ pārtha jñāne parisamāpyate

sreyan = better; dravya-mayat = using materials; yajnat = sacrifice; jnana= knowledge; yajnah = sacrifice; parantapa = O destroyer of enemies; sarvam = all; karma = actions; akhilam = totally; partha = Partha; jnane = in knowledge; parisamapyate = culminate.

"O destroyer of the enemies, better than the material sacrifice is the sacrifice done with knowledge. O Partha, all actions culminate totally in knowledge.

Sloka 34

tad viddhi praṇipātena paripraśnena sevayā
upadekṣyanti te jñānaṃ jñāninas tattvadarśinaḥ

tat = that; viddhi = know, realize; pranipatena = prostrating, falling at one's feet, obeissance; pariprasnena = by asking questions; sevaya = by rendering service; upadeksyanti = give initiation; te = to you; jnanam = knowledge; jnaninah = the knowledgeable; tattva = truth; darsinah = the seers.

"Know that by falling at the feet, asking questions and doing service. The enlightened ones, the seers of truth, initiate you into knowledge.

Sloka 35

yaj jñātvā na punar moham evaṃ yāsyasi pāṇḍava
yena bhūtāny aśeṣeṇa drakṣyasy ātmany atho mayi

yat = that; jnatva = by knowing; na = not; punah = again; moham = delusion; evam = in this manner; yasyasi = fall into; pandava = O Pandava; yena = by which; bhutani = all living beings; asesani = without exception; draksyasi = you will see; atmani = in the Self; atho = and so also; mayi = in Me.

"Knowing that you should not fall into delusion again in this manner, O Pandava, by which you will see all beings in the Self and so also in Me.

Sloka 36

ced asi pāpebhyaḥ sarvebhyaḥ pāpakṛttamaḥ
sarvaṃ jñānaplavenaiva vṛjinaṃ saṃtariṣyasi

api = even; cet = if; asi = are; papebhyah = of the sinners; sarvebhyah = of all; papa-krttamah = sinner; sarvam = all; jnana-plavena = by the raft of knowledge; eva = alone, only; vrjinam = the ocean of sin, misery or wickedness; santarisyasi = cross over.

"Even if you are the worst sinner of all sinners, you will cross the ocean of sin, misery and wickedness by the raft of knowledge alone.

Sloka 37

yathaidhāṃsi samiddhognir bhasmasāt kuruterjuna
jñānāgniḥ sarvakarmāṇi bhasmasāt kurute tathā

yatha = just as; edhamsi = wood; samiddhah = blazing; agnih = fire; bhasmasat = to ashes; kurute = reduces; arjuna = O Arjuna; jnana-agnih = the fire of knowledge; sarva-karmani = all actons; bhasmasat = to ashes; kurute = reduces; tatha = similarly.

"As the blazing fire reduces the wood to ashes, O Arjuna, the fire of knowledge reduces to ashes all actions

Sloka 38

na hi jñānena sadṛśaṃ pavitram iha vidyate
tat svayaṃ yogasaṃsiddhaḥ kālenātmani vindati

na = not; hi = indeed; jnanena =to knowledge; sadrsam = comparable; pavitram = sacred, pure; iha = here, in this world; vidyate = is; tat = that; svayam = by itself; yoga = yoga; samsiddhah = perfected, ready, prepared; kalena = in course of time; atmani = in himself; vindati = knows, realizes.

"There is nothing as sacred as knowledge in this world. That person who has perfected himself skillfully in yoga will realize the Self in due time.

Sloka 39

śraddhāvāṃl labhate jñānaṃ tatparaḥ saṃyatendriyaḥ
jñānaṃ labdhvā parāṃ śāntim acireṇādhigacchati

sraddha-van = a faithful aspirant; labhate = gains; jnanam = knowledge; tat-parah = intent on, exclusively devoted to; samyata = controlled; indriyah = organs of action and perception; jnanam =

knowledge; labdhva = attained; param = supreme; santim = peace; acirena = soon, quickly; adhigacchati = attains.

"A faithful aspirant, who is intent and has control over the organs of action and perception, gains knowledge. Having gained knowledge, he quickly attains supreme peace.

Sloka 40

ajñaś cāśraddadhānaś ca saṃśayātmā vinaśyati
nāyaṃ lokosti na paro na sukhaṃ saṃśayātmanaḥ

ajnah = the one devoid of knowledge, the ignorant; ca = and; asraddadhanah = one without the wealth of faith; ca = and; samsayatma = doubting mind; vinasyati = perishes; na = not; ayam = this; lokah = world; asti = there is; na = not; parah = next world; na = not; sukham = happiness; samsayatmanah = skeptic.

"The one without knowledge, without the wealth of faith and with doubting mind perishes. For the skeptic there is neither this world nor the next world nor happiness.

Sloka 41

yogasaṃnyastakarmāṇaṃ jñānasaṃchinnasaṃśayam
ātmavantaṃ na karmāṇi nibadhnanti dhanaṃjaya

yoga = yoga; sannyasta = renounced; karmanam = actions; jnana = knowledge; sanchinna = dispelled or destroyed; samsayam = doubts; atma-vantam = conquered the Self; na = not; karmani = work; nibadhnanti = do not bind; dhananjaya = O Dhananjaya.

"Actions do not bind him O Dhananjaya, who has renounced actions through yoga, whose doubts have dispelled by knowledge, and who has conquered the Self.

Sloka 42

tasmād ajñānasañbhūtaṃ hṛtsthaṃ jñānāsinātmanaḥ
chittvainaṃ saṃśayaṃ yogam ātiṣṭhottiṣṭha bhārata

tasmat = therefore; ajnana-sambhutam = born out of ignorance; hrt-stham = in the heart; jnana = knowledge; asina = by the sword;

atmanah = of your own; chittva = cutting asunder; enam = this; samsayam = doubt; yogam = yoga; atistha = becoming firmly established; uttistha = stand up to fight; bharata = O descendant of Bharata.

"Therefore cut asunder this doubt of yours, which is born out of ignorance and ensconced in your heart, with the sword of the knowledge, becoming firmly established in yoga, O Bharata.

Conclusion

iti srīmadbhāgavadgītāsupanisatsu brahmavidyāyām yogasāstre
srikrisnārjunasamvāde jnānakarmasanyāsayogo nāma caturdho 'dhyayah

iti = thus; srīmadbhāgavadgītā = in the sacred Bhagavadgita; upanisatsu = in the Upanishad; brahmavidyāyām = the knowledge of the absolute Brahman; yogasāstre = the scripture of yoga; srikrisnārjunasamvāde = the dialogue between Sri Krishna and Arjuna; jnānakarmasanyāsayogo nāma = by name yoga of knowledge with renunciation of action; tritiya = thirdd; adhyayah = chapter;

Thus ends the fourth chapter named The Yoga of Knowledge with Renunciation of Action in the Upanishad of the divine Bhagavadgita, the knowledge of the Absolute, the yogic scripture, and the debate between Arjuna and Lord Krishna.

5 – The Yoga of Renunciation of Action

Sloka 1

arjuna uvāca
saṃnyāsaṃ karmaṇāṃ kṛṣṇa punar yogaṃ ca śaṃsasi
yac chreya etayor ekaṃ tan me brūhi suniścitam

arjunah uvaca = Arjuna said; sannyasam = renunciation; karmanam = of actions; Krishna = O Krsna; punah = again; yogam = yoga; ca = and; samsasi = you praise; yat = which; sreyah = is betterl; etayoh = of these two; ekam = one; tat = that; me = to me; bruhi = please tell; suniscitam = decisively, clearly.

Arjuna said, "You praise both renunciation of actions, O Krishna, and again yoga of action. Which is better of these two that you tell me clearly?"

Sloka 2

śrībhagavān uvāca
saṃnyāsaḥ karmayogaś ca niḥśreyasakarāv ubhau
tayos tu karmasaṃnyāsāt karmayogo viśiṣyate

sri-bhagavan uvaca = the Supreme Lord said; sannyasah = renunciation; karma-yogah = yoga of action; ca = and; nihsreyasa-karau = lead to liberation; ubhau = both; tayoh = of the two; tu = however; karma-sannyasat = of renunciation of action; karma-yogah = yoga of action; visisyate = excels.

"The Supreme Lord said, "Renunciation and yoga of action both lead to liberation; of the two, however, the yoga of action excels over the renunciation of action.

Sloka 3

jñeyaḥ sa nityasaṃnyāsī yo na dveṣṭi na kāṅkṣati
nirdvandvo hi mahābāho sukhaṃ bandhāt pramucyate

jneyah = should be known; sah = he; nitya = always; sannyasi = engaged in renunciation; yah = who; na = never; dvesti = hates; na = not; kanksati = desires; nirdvandvah = free from dualities and pairs of opposities; hi = in fact; maha-baho = O mighty-armed; sukham = is easily, comfortably; bandhat = from bonds; pramucyate = is liberated.

"He who neither hates nor desires should be known as the one who is ever engaged in renunciation. Indeed, free from dualities and pairs of opposites, O mighty-armed, he is liberated easily from all bonds.

Sloka 4

sāṃkhyayogau pṛthag bālāḥ pravadanti na paṇḍitāḥ
ekam apy āsthitaḥ samyag ubhayor vindate phalam

sankhya = yoga of knowledge; yogau = yoga of action; prthak = distinct, different; balah = the young, immature, the under developed, the ignorant; pravadanti = say; na = but not; panditah = the learned ones; ekam = one; api = even; asthitah = being established; gaining mastery; samyak = properly, completely; ubhayoh = of both; vindate = gets; phalam = the fruits.

"Ignorant people say the yoga of knowledge and the yoga of renunciation are distinct, but not the wise ones. By becoming properly established even in one, one obtains the fruits of both.

Sloka 5

yat sāṃkhyaiḥ prāpyate sthānaṃ tad yogair api gamyate
ekaṃ sāṃkhyaṃ ca yogaṃ ca yaḥ paśyati sa paśyati

yat = whatever; sankhyaih = by yoga of knowledge; prapyate = obtained; sthanam = place; tat = that; yogaih = yoga of action; api = also; gamyate = reached; ekam = one; sankhyam = knowledge; ca = and; yogam = action; ca = and; yah = one who; pasyati = sees; sah = he; pasyati = sees.

"whatever place obtained by the yoga of knowledge that is also reached by the yoga of action. He who sees both knowledge and action as one (really) sees.

Sloka 6

as tu mahābāho duḥkham āptum ayogataḥ
yogayukto munir brahma nacireṇādhigacchati

sannyasah = renunciation; tu = in fact; maha-baho = O mighty-armed; duhkham = hard, difficult; aptum = attin; ayogatah = without yoga of action; yoga-yuktah = engaged in yoga of action; munih = the silent one, an ascetic; brahma = Brahman ; na cirena = quickly, sooner; adhigacchati = attains.

"Renunciation is hard to attain, , O mighty armed, without yoga of action. Engaged in yoga of action the silent one attains Brahman quickly.

Sloka 7

yogayukto viśuddhātmā vijitātmā jitendriyaḥ
sarvabhūtātmabhūtātmā kurvann api na lipyate

yoga-yuktah = skilful in the yoga of action; visuddha-atma = a pure soul; vijita-atma = self-controlled; jita-indriyah = conqueror of the sense orgas; sarva-bhuta-atma = all embodied souls; bhuta-atma = the embodied Self; kurvan api = even when engaged in work; na = not; lipyate = is not tainted.

"He who is skilful in the yoga of action, the pure soul, self-controlled, conqueror of the sense organs, the embodied Self of all the embodied souls, even when engaged in actions is not tainted.

Sloka 8

naiva kiṃcit karomīti yukto manyeta tattvavit
paśyañ śṛṇvan spṛśañ jighrann aśnan gacchan svapañ śvasan

na = not; eva = indeed; kincit = anything; karomi = I do; iti = thus; yuktah = established in yoga; manyeta = thinks; tattva-vit = knower of truth; pasyan = seeing; srnvan = hearing; sprsan = touching; jighran = smelling; asnan = eating; gacchan = walking; svapan = dreaming; svasan = breathing.

"Established in yoga, the knower of truth should think, 'I do nothing," while seeing, hearing, touching, smelling, tasting, walking, dreaming and breathing.

Sloka 9

pralapan visṛjan gṛhṇann unmiṣan nimiṣann api
indriyāṇīndriyārtheṣu vartanta iti dhārayan

pralapan = speaking; visrjan = releasing; grhnan = grasping; unmisan = opening; nimisan = closing; api = even; indriyani = the senses; indriya-arthesu = engaged with the sense objecs; vartante = exisit; iti = thus; dharayan = holding.

"While speaking, releasing, grasping, opening, closing, he thinks, 'The senses are engaged with the sense objects.'

Sloka 10

brahmaṇy ādhāya karmāṇi saṅgaṃ tyaktvā karoti yaḥ
lipyate na sa pāpena padmapatram ivāmbhasā

brahmani = Brahman; adhaya = by dedicating, placing, offering; karmani = actions; sangam = attachment; tyaktva = giving up; karoti = performs actions; yah = who; lipyate = is tainted; na = not; sah = he; papena = by sin; padma-patram = lotus leaf; iva = like; ambhasa = in the water.

"By offering all actions to Brahman, giving up attachment, whoever performs actions is not tainted by sins, just like the lotus leaf in the water.

Sloka 11

kāyena manasā buddhyā kevalair indriyair api
yoginaḥ karma kurvanti saṅgaṃ tyaktvātmaśuddhaye

kayena = with the body; manasa = with the mind; buddhya = with the intelligence; kevalaih = only, merely, exclusively; indriyaih = with the senses; api = even; yoginah = yogis; karma = actions; kurvanti = perform; sangam = attachment; tyaktva = giving up; atma = self; suddhaye = for the purification.

"Giving up attachment, the yogis perform actions only with the body, the mind, intelligence and even sense organs for their self-purification.

Sloka 12

yuktaḥ karmaphalaṃ tyaktvā śāntim āpnoti naiṣṭhikīm
ayuktaḥ kāmakāreṇa phale sakto nibadhyate

yuktah = the one engaged in yoga; karma-phalam = fruit of actions; tyaktva = giving up; santim = peace; apnoti = attains; naisthikim = decisiveness, firmness, resoluteness; ayuktah = the one not established in yoga; kama-karena = due to desire, impelled by desire; phale = in fruit; saktah = interested, drawn; nibadhyate = is bound, becomes responsible.

"The one established in yoga, giving up the fruit of actions, attains peace arising from resoluteness. The one not established in yoga, drawn to the fruit of action, impelled by desire, becomes bound.

Sloka 13

sarvakarmāṇi manasā saṃnyasyāste sukhaṃ vaśī
navadvāre pure dehī naiva kurvan na kārayan

sarva = all; karmani = actions; manasa = mentally; sannyasya = renouncing, giving up; aste = remains; sukham = in happiness; vasi = the self-controlled; nava-dvare = nine gates; pure = in the city; dehi = the embodied; na = not; eva = indeed; kurvan = performing actions; na = not; karayan = causing action.

"Renouncing all actions mentally, the self-controlled embodied one remains happily in the city of nine gates, neither performing actions nor causing them.

Sloka 14

na kartṛtvaṃ na karmāṇi lokasya sṛjati prabhuḥ
na karmaphalasaṃyogaṃ svabhāvas tu pravartate

na = not; kartrtvam = doership; na = not; karmani = actions; lokasya = of the world; srjati = creates; prabhuh = the Lord; na = not; karma-phala = fruit of actions; samyogam = union, attachment; svabhavah = by inherent nature; tu = indeed; pravartate = behave, act.

"The Lord creates neither doership nor actions of the world; nor has He attachment to the fruit of His actions. By Nature indeed, actions arise.

Sloka 15

nādatte kasyacit pāpaṃ na caiva sukṛtaṃ vibhuḥ
ajñānenāvṛtaṃ jñānaṃ tena muhyanti jantavaḥ

na = not; adatte = accepts; kasyacit = anyone's; papam = sin; na = not; ca = and; eva = even; su-krtam = good deeds; vibhuh = the Mighty, Supreme, Omniscient Being; ajnanena = by ignorance; avrtam = enveloped; jnanam = knowledge; tena = by that; muhyanti = deluded; jantavah = the living beings

"The Supreme Lord accepts neither sins nor good deeds of anyone. Knowledge is enveloped by ignorance. By that, the living beings are deluded.

Sloka 16

jñānena tu tad ajñānaṃ yeṣāṃ nāśitam ātmanaḥ
teṣām ādityavaj jñānaṃ prakāśayati tat param

jnanena = by knowledge; tu = but; tat = that; ajnanam = ignorance; yesam = of whom; nasitam = destroyed; atmanah = of the Self; tesam = their; aditya-vat = like the sun; jnanam = knowledge; prakasayati = illuminates, shines forth; tat param = that Supreme Reality.

"But in whom that ignorance becomes destroyed by knowledge, their knowledge, like the sun, illuminates that Supreme Reality.

Sloka 17

tadbuddhayas tadātmānas tanniṣṭhās tatparāyaṇāḥ
gacchanty apunarāvṛttiṃ jñānanirdhūtakalmaṣāḥ

tat-buddhayah = those whose intelligence is fixed in that; tat-atmanah = those who have That as their Self; tat-nisthah = those whose thoughts are firmly fixed in That; tat-parayanah = those who are intensely devoted to That as their goal; gacchanti = attain; apunah-avrttim = state of non-return; jnana = knowledge; nirdhuta = cleansed; kalmasah = impurities.

"Those whose intelligence is fixed in That, those who have That as their Self, those whose thoughts are firmly fixed in That, those who are intensely devoted to That, attain the state of non-return, with their knowledge cleansed of all impurities.

Sloka 18

vidyāvinayasaṃpanne brāhmaṇe gavi hastini
śuni caiva śvapāke ca paṇḍitāḥ samadarśinaḥ

vidya = knowledge; vinaya = gentle behavior, good conduct; sampanne = endowed with; brahmane = on a brahmana; gavi = on the cow; hastini = on the elephant; suni = on the dog; ca = and; eva = even sva-pake = lowly person, an unclean person who cooks dog meat and eats it; ca = and; panditah = the learned ones; sama-darsinah = look equally.

"The learned ones look equally upon a brahmana who is endowed with right knowledge and gentle conduct, a cow, an elephant, a dog and even a lowly and unclean person.

Sloka 19

ihaiva tair jitaḥ sargo yeṣāṃ sāmye sthitaṃ manaḥ
nirdoṣaṃ hi samaṃ brahma tasmād brahmaṇi te sthitāḥ

iha = here in this world; eva = itself; taih = by them; jitah = conquered; sargah = rebirth, creation, succession of life; yesam = whose; samye = in sameness; sthitam = established; manah = mind; nirdosam = without defects, impurities; hi = alone; samam = equal to all; brahma = Brahman; tasmat = therefore; brahmani = in Brahman; te = they; sthitah = are established.

"In this world itself rebirth is conquered by them whose minds are established in sameness. Brahman alone is without defects and equal to all. Therefore, they are established in Brahman.

Sloka 20

na prahṛṣyet priyaṃ prāpya nodvijet prāpya cāpriyam
sthirabuddhir asaṃmūḍho brahmavid brahmaṇi sthitaḥ

na = not; prahrsyet = rejoice; priyam = what is pleasant; prapya = gaining; na = not; udvijet = feeling unhappy, disturbed, agitated; prapya = gaining; ca = and; apriyam = what is unpleasant; sthira-buddhih = stable mind; asammudhah = without being deluded; brahma-vit = the knower of Brahman; brahmani = in Brahman; sthitah = established.

"Neither rejoicing upon gaining what is pleasant nor feeling unhappy upon gaining what is unpleasant, stable minded, without being deluded, the knower of Brahman remains established in Brahman

Sloka 21

bāhyasparśeṣv asaktātmā vindaty ātmani yat sukham
sa brahmayogayuktātmā sukham akṣayam aśnute

bahya-sparsesu = in external contacts; asakta-atma = disinterested; vindati = finds; atmani = in the self; yat = that which; sukham = bliss;

sah = he; brahma-yoga = union with Brahman; yukta-atma = engaged by Self; sukham = bliss; aksayam = inexhaustible; asnute = enjoys.

"Disinterested in external contact with sense objects, he finds bliss which is within his own Self. With his Self fully absorbed in Brahman and in union with Him, he enjoys inexhaustible bliss

Sloka 22

ye hi saṃsparśajā bhogā duḥkhayonaya eva te
ādyantavantaḥ kaunteya na teṣu ramate budhaḥ

ye = those; hi = indeed; samsparsa-jah = born from contact with sense objects; bhogah = enjoyments; duhkha = suffering and sorrow; yonayah = source, womb; eva = indeed; te = they are; adi = beginning; anta = end; vantah = they have; kaunteya = O son of Kunti; na = not; tesu = in them; ramate = take pleasure, indugle; budhah = wise person, discriminating person.

"Indeed, those enjoyments which are born from contact with sense objects are the source of suffering and sorrow. They have a beginning and an end. O son of Kunti, a wise person does not take pleasure **in them.**

Sloka 23

śaknotīhaiva yaḥ soḍhuṃ prāk śarīravimokṣaṇāt
kāmakrodhodbhavaṃ vegaṃ sa yuktaḥ sa sukhī naraḥ

saknoti = able to do, can; iha = here; eva = itself; yah = he who; sodhum = withstand, tolerate; prak = before; sarira = body; vimoksanat = death, departing; kama = lust; krodha = anger; udbhavam = source, produced from; vegam = intensity, force, impulse; sah = he; yuktah = established in yogi; sah = he; sukhi = happy; narah = human being.

"He who is able to withstand here itself, before departing from the body, the intensity of anger and lust, he is established in yoga and he is a happy human being.

Sloka 24

yontaḥsukhontarārāmas tathāntarjyotir eva yaḥ
sa yogī brahmanirvāṇaṃ brahmabhūtodhigacchati

yah = who; antah-sukhah = internally happy; antah-aramah = internally restful and blissful; tatha = so also; antah-jyotih = ligh within; eva = has; yah = anyone; sah = that; yogi = practitioner of yoga; brahma-nirvanam = absorption in Brahman; brahma-bhutah = Supreme Being; adhigacchati = attains.

"He who is internally happy, internally restful and blissful and who has light within, that practitioner of yoga attains Brahman and becomes absorbed in Him.

Sloka 25

labhante brahmanirvāṇam ṛṣayaḥ kṣīṇakalmaṣāḥ
chinnadvaidhā yatātmānaḥ sarvabhūtahite ratāḥ

labhante = gain, attani; brahma-nirvanam = absorption in Brahman; rsayah = the seers; ksina-kalmasah = with their impurities greatly reduced; chinna dvaidhah = duality destryoed; yata-atmanah = in control of themselves; sarva-bhuta = in all living being; hite = welfare; ratah = engaged.

"The seers attain absorption in Brahman, with their impurities greatly reduced, their duality destroyed, their organs under their self-control and who are engaged in the welfare of all living beings.

Sloka 26

kāmakrodhaviyuktānāṃ yatīnāṃ yatacetasām
abhito brahmanirvāṇaṃ vartate viditātmanām

kama = lust; krodha = anger; vimuktanam = freed; yatinam = the ascetics who practice self-restraings; yata-cetasam = minds under control; abhitah = from both sides, near; brahma-nirvanam = absorption in Brahman; vartate = there is; vidita-atmanam = having known the Self.

"For the ascetics who are freed from lust and anger, who practice self-restraint, who have their minds under control, who have known the Self, there is absorption in Brahman either way.

Sloka 27

sparśān kṛtvā bahir bāhyāṃś cakṣuś caivāntare bhruvoḥ
prāṇāpānau samau kṛtvā nāsābhyantaracāriṇau

sparsan = the sense objects; krtva = Keeping; bahih = outgoing; bahyan = external; caksuh = eyes; ca = and; eva = certainly; antare = within; bhruvoh = between the eye brows; prana-apanau = prana and apana breaths; samau = equal; krtva = doing so; nasa-abhyantara = within in the nostrins; carinau = moving.

"Keeping the sense objects outgoing and external, with the eyes fixed between the eye brows, making the prana and apana breaths equal while moving within the nostrils.

Sloka 28

yatendriyamanobuddhirmunir mokṣaparāyaṇaḥ
vigatecchābhayakrodho yaḥ sadā mukta eva saḥ

yata = restraining, controlling; indriya = senses; manah = mind; buddhih = intelligence; munih = the silent one; moksa = liberation; parayanah = devotedly or intently pursuing; vigata = free; iccha = desire; bhaya = fear; krodhah = anger; yah = one who; sada = forever; muktah = liberated; eva = even; sah = he.

"Restraining his senses, mind, and intelligence, the silent ascetic, intently pursuing liberation, freed from desires, fear, and anger, is he who is forever liberated.

Sloka 29

bhoktāraṃ yajñatapasāṃ sarvalokamaheśvaram
suhṛdaṃ sarvabhūtānāṃ jñātvā māṃ śāntim ṛcchati

bhoktaram = the enjoyer; yajna = sacrifices; tapasam = penances and austerities; sarva-loka = all worlds; maha-isvaram = the Supreme Lord;

su-hrdam = the friend; sarva = all; bhutanam = of the living beings; jnatva = thus knowing; mam = Me; santim = peace; rcchati = one attains.

"He attains peace by knowing me thus as the enjoyer of sacrifices and austerities, the Supreme Lord of all the worlds, (and) the friend of all living beings."

Conclusion

iti srīmadbhāgavadgītāsupanisatsu brahmavidyāyām yogasāstre
srikrisnārjunasamvāde sanyāsayogo nāma pancamo 'dhyayah

iti = thus; srīmadbhāgavadgītā = in the sacred Bhagavadgita; upanisatsu = in the Upanishad; brahmavidyāyām = the knowledge of the absolute Brahman; yogasāstre = the scripture of yoga; srikrisnārjunasamvāde = the dialogue between Sri Krishna and Arjuna; sanyāsayogo nāma = by name yoga of renunciation of action; pancama = fifth adhyayah = chapter;

Thus ends the fifth chapter named Sanyasa Yoga or the Yoga of Renunciation of action in the Upanishad of the divine Bhagavadgita, the knowledge of the Absolute, the yogic scripture, and the debate between Arjuna and Lord Krishna.

6 – The Yoga of Self-absorption

Sloka 1

śrībhagavān uvāca
anāśritaḥ karmaphalaṃ kāryaṃ karma karoti yaḥ
sa saṃnyāsī ca yogī ca na niragnir na cākriyaḥ

sri-bhagavan uvacajay = the Supreme Lord said; anasritah = without depending; karma-phalam = fruit of action; karyam = duty related; karma = actions; karoti = performs; yah = he who; sah = he; sannyasi = sanyashi; ca = and; yogi = yogi; ca = and; na = not; nih = without; agnih = fire; na = nor; ca = and; akriyah = without obligatory duties.

"Said the Lord Supreme, "He who performs duty related action, without depending upon the fruit of his action, he is a sanyasi and a yogi; not he, who does not keep the fires and who does not perform obligatory actions.

Sloka 2

yaṃ saṃnyāsam iti prāhur yogaṃ taṃ viddhi pāṇḍava
na hy asaṃnyastasaṃkalpo yogī bhavati kaścana

yam = what; sannyasam = renunciation; iti = thus; prahuh = they call; yogam = yoga; tam = that; viddhi = know; pandava = O son of Pandu; na = not; hi = indeed; asannyasta = without giving up; sankalpah = decision, intentions; yogi = yogi; bhavati = becomes; kascana = anyone.

"What they speak of as renunciation know that as yoga, O Pandava. Indeed, without renouncing intentions none can become a yogi.

Sloka 3

āruruksor muner yogaṃ karma kāraṇam ucyate
yogārūḍhasya tasyaiva śamaḥ kāraṇam ucyate

aruruksoh = of the one who is wishing to ascend; muneh = muni, ascetic, sage; yogam = the state of yoga; karma = actions; karanam = the cause, means; ucyate = is said to be; yoga = state of yoga; arudhasya = one who has ascended; tasya = his; eva = certainly; samah

= even mindedness; karanam = the means, causae; ucyate = is said to be.

"For the sage who is trying to ascend to the state of yoga, action is said to be the means. For the one who has ascended to the state of yoga, even mindedness is said to be the means

Sloka 4

yadā hi nendriyārtheṣu na karmasv anuṣajjate
sarvasaṃkalpasaṃnyāsī yogārūḍhas tadocyate

yada = when; hi = only, truly; na = not; indriya-arthesu = for sense gratification, or sense objects; na = not; karmasu = in actions; anusajjate = is attached; sarva-sankalpa = all desires or intentions; sannyasi = he who has renounced; yoga-arudhah = established in yoga; tada = then; ucyate = is said to be.

"Truly when a sanyasi who has renounced all desires and intentions is attached neither to sense objects nor to actions, then is he said to be established in yoga.

Sloka 5

uddhared ātmanātmānaṃ nātmānam avasādayet
ātmaiva hy ātmano bandhur ātmaiva ripur ātmanaḥ

uddharet = one should deliver, help, uplift; atmana = by oneself; atmanam = oneself; na = not; atmanam = the Self; avasadayet = debase, degrade; atma = oneself; eva = surely; hi = for; atmanah = one's own; bandhuh = relation, friend; atma = the Self; eva = surely; ripuh = enemy; atmanah = one's own.

"One should uplift oneself by oneself; one should not debase oneself. Surely, the Self is one's own friend and surely one's own enemy.

Sloka 6

bandhur ātmātmanas tasya yenātmaivātmanā jitaḥ
anātmanas tu śatrutve vartetātmaiva śatruvat

bandhuh = friend; atma = the self; atmanah = by self; tasya = of him; yena = by whom; atma = the self; eva = very; atmana = of self; jitah = conquered; anatmanah = for one who has not conquered oneself; tu = but; satrutve = in enmity, with hostility; varteta = acts, behaves; atma eva = very self; satru-vat = as an enemy.

"Of him, who has conquered his very self by the self, his self is the friend of his self; but for him who has not conquered himself, his very self acts with hostility like an enemy.

Sloka 7

jitātmanaḥ praśāntasya paramātmā samāhitaḥ
śītoṣṇasukhaduḥkheṣu tathā mānāpamānayoḥ

jita-atmanah = who has conquered his mind and body; prasantasya = who is peaceful, tranquail; parama-atma = Supreme Self; samahitah = absorbed, intent on, concentrated on; sita = cold; usna = heat; sukha = in happiness; duhkhesu = in distress; tatha = also; mana = honor; apamanayoh = and dishonor.

"The conqueror of the mind and body, the one peaceful and absorbed in the Supreme Self, remains the same in cold and heat, pain and pleasure and honor and dishonor.

Commentary

This verse describes not only the self-conquered and self-realized yogi but also the progressive states of inner perfection and equanimity by which he reaches such a supreme state on the path of renunciation and desireless actions. The first stage in this yoga is developing control over the mind, the senses and the body through purification, withdrawal of the senses and the mind. When it is accomplished, one is able to experience peace and tranquility. When the mind is subdued, peaceful, and stable, for a yogi the practice of concentration (dharana) and contemplation (dhyana) becomes easier, which leads to absorption in the transcendental Self (Isvara) or the Supreme Self (paramatma). When a person is fully established in the Self, he becomes equal to all the dualities of life and pairs of opposites.

Sloka 8

jñānavijñānatṛptātmā kūṭastho vijitendriyaḥ
yukta ity ucyate yogī samaloṣṭāśmakāñcanaḥ

jnana = knowledge; vijnana = wisdom arising from knowledge; trpta = contented, satisfied; atma = person, soul, being; kuta-sthah = stable, firm; vijita-indriyah = master of the senses; yuktah = one who is united with God; iti = thus; ucyate = said to be; yogi = yogi; sama = equal, same; lostra = dirt, lump of clay; asma = stone; kancanah = gold.

"The contended soul with knowledge and wisdom, firmly stable, master of the senses, united with the Self, is said to be the yogi who regards as same a lump of clay, stone and gold.

Sloka 9

suhṛnmitrāryudāsīnamadhyasthadveṣyabandhuṣu
sādhuṣv api ca pāpeṣu samabuddhir viśiṣyate

su-hrt = well wisher, kind-hearted; mitra = friend; ari = enemy; udasina = indifferent, unconcerned; madhya-stha = mediator; dvesya = haters; bandhusu = relations; sadhusu = saints; api = also; ca = and; papesu = to the sinners; sama-buddhih = being equal; visisyate = he excels.

"He excels who has equanimity towards well wishers, friends, enemies, indifferent people, mediators, haters, relations, saints and also sinners.

Sloka 10

yogī yuñjīta satatam ātmānaṃ rahasi sthitaḥ
ekākī yatacittātmā nirāśīr aparigrahaḥ

yogi = a yogi; yunjita = concentrate; satatam = always, constantly; atmanam = upon Self; rahasi = in a secret or a solitary place; sthitah = staying, sitting; ekaki = alone; yata-citta-atma = with mind and the body under control; nirasih = without desires; aparigrahah = without grasping.

"A yogi should concentrate upon the Self constantly, staying alone in a secret or solitary place, with his mind and body under control, without desires and without grasping (the sense objects).

Sloka 11

śucau deśe pratiṣṭhāpya sthiram āsanam ātmanaḥ
nātyucchritaṃ nātinīcaṃ cailājinakuśottaram

sucau = in a clean; dese = place, location or area; pratisthapya = having established, stationed, sett up; sthiram = firm; asanam = seat, base, support; atmanah = of his own; na = not; ati = very; ucchritam = high; na = not; ati = very; nicam = low; caila-ajina = cloth and deerskin; kusottaram = kusa grass;

"In a clean place, having established a firm seat of his own, neither very high nor very low, covered with cloth, deer skin and kusa grass.

Sloka 12

tatraikāgraṃ manaḥ kṛtvā yatacittendriyakriyaḥ
upaviśyāsane yuñjyād yogam ātmaviśuddhaye

tatra = thereupon; eka-agram = one pointed, single minded; manah = mind; krtva = doing so; yata-citta = controlling the mind; indriya = senses; kriyah = activities; upavisya = sitting on; asane = on the seat; yunjyat = execute; yogam = yoga practice; atma = heart; visuddhaye = for clarifying.

"There upon, sitting on that seat, with single minded concentration, keeping his mind, senses and activities under firm control, he should practice yoga for self-purification.

Sloka 13

samaṃ kāyaśirogrīvaṃ dhārayann acalaṃ sthiraḥ
saṃprekṣya nāsikāgraṃ svaṃ diśaś cānavalokayan

samam = straight; kaya-sirah = body and head; grivam = neck; dharayan = holding; acalam = stable, without moving; sthirah = still;

sampreksya = looking intensely at; nasikagram = tip of the nose; svam = own; disah = directions; ca = and; anavalokayan = not looking around

"Holding his body, head and neck straight, stable and still, looking intensely at the tip of his own nose, and not looking around in other directions.

Sloka 14

praśāntātmā vigatabhīr brahmacārivrate sthitaḥ
manaḥ saṃyamya maccitto yukta āsīta matparaḥ

prasanta = tranquil, peaceful, placid; atma = mind, self; vigata-bhih = without fear; brahmacari-vrate = practicing celibacy, brahmacharya; sthitah = abiding, established; manah = mind; samyamya = engaged in samyama; mat = absorbed in Me; cittah = citta, consciousness; yuktah = the adept who is united with God or the Self; asita = remain seated; mat = Me; parah = as the supreme goal.

"The adept, who is united with God, should remain seated, Me as his supreme goal, with tranquil mind, without fear, abiding in the practice of celibacy, mind engaged in samyama, and his consciousness absorbed in Me.

Sloka 15

yuñjann evaṃ sadātmānaṃ yogī niyatamānasaḥ
śāntiṃ nirvāṇaparamāṃ matsaṃsthām adhigacchati

yunjan = concentrating, united with God; evam = thus; sada = ever, constantly; atmanam = mind established in the Self; yogi = yogi; niyata-manasah = disciplined mind; santim = peace; nirvana-paramam = supreme state of liberation; mat-samstham = My peaceful abode; adhigacchati = attain.

"United with Me thus, his mind ever established in the Self, the yogi of disciplined mind attains peace, that supreme state of liberation which abides in Me.

Sloka 16

nātyaśnatas tu yogosti na caikāntam anaśnataḥ
na cātisvapnaśīlasya jāgrato naiva cārjuna

na = not; ati = excessively, voraciously; asnatah = one who eats; tu = but; yogah = yoga; asti = is; na = not; ca = and; ekantam = at all; anasnatah = who does not eat; na = not; ca = and; ati = excessively, for too long; svapna-silasya = who sleeps; jagratah = who remains awake; na = not; eva = ever; ca = and; arjuna = O Arjuna.

"O Arjuna, yoga is not for the one who eats voraciously, nor for the one who does not eat at all; not for the one who sleeps for too long, nor for the one who remains awake

Sloka 17

yuktāhāravihārasya yuktaceṣṭasya karmasu
yuktasvapnāvabodhasya yogo bhavati duḥkhahā 6.17

yukta-ahara-viharasya = one who controls his eating and enjoyment; yukta-cestasya = who controls his citta; karmasu = in actions; yukta-svapna-avabodhasya = who regulates or blanaces his sleeping and waking times; yogah = yoga; bhavati = becomes; duhkha-ha = destroyer of sorrow.

"Yoga becomes a destroyer of sorrow for him who controls his eating and enjoyment, who controls his citta, (and) who balances his sleeping and waking times.

Sloka 18

yadā viniyataṃ cittam ātmany evāvatiṣṭhate
niḥspṛhaḥ sarvakāmebhyo yukta ity ucyate tadā

yada = when; viniyatam = controlled; cittam = the citta; atmani = in the Self; eva = only; avatisthate = established; nisprhah = without desire; sarva = all; kamebhyah = craving for objects; yuktah = united and self-absorbed yogi; iti = thus; ucyate = is said to be; tada = then.

"When the mind is controlled and established in the Self only, without desires and craving for objects, then he is said to be the self-absorbed yogi.

Sloka 19

yathā dīpo nivātastho neṅgate sopamā smṛtā
yogino yatacittasya yuñjato yogam ātmanaḥ

yatha = as; dipah = a lamp; nivata-sthah = windless place; na = not; ingate = flickers; sa upama = that metaphor, example; smrta = comes to mind, remembered; yoginah = about the yogi; yata-cittasya = whose citta is under control; yunjatah = practising; yogam = union or absorption; atmanah = with the Self.

"As a lamp in a windless place does not flicker - that is the metaphor remembered about the yogi whose mind is under control and who is practicing union or absorption with the Self.

Sloka 20

yatroparamate cittaṃ niruddhaṃ yogasevayā
yatra caivātmanātmānaṃ paśyann ātmani tuṣyati

yatra = in that state of stillness; uparamate = withdrawing, ceasing, abstaining; cittam = the citta; niruddham = restrained; yoga-sevaya = by the practice of yoga; yatra = in that; ca = and; eva = only; atmana = in the Self; atmanam = the self; pasyan = by seeing; atmani = in the self; tusyati = remains satisfied.

"In that state when the mind is withdrawn, restrained by the practice of yoga, in that only seeing the self abiding in the Self, one remains satisfied within the Self only.

Sloka 21

sukham ātyantikaṃ yat tad buddhigrāhyam atīndriyam
vetti yatra na caivāyaṃ sthitaś calati tattvataḥ

sukham = happiness, bliss; atyantikam = endless, infinite; yat = which; tat = that; buddhi = discriminating intelligence; grahyam = realized, grasped; atindriyam = beyond the senses, transcendental; vetti = knows; yatra = wherein; na = not; ca = and; eva = surely; ayam = this; sthitah = situated; calati = moves, deviates; tattvatah = from the Truth or Reality.

"He does not deviate from Truth or Reality when he is established in That Infinite bliss, which is grasped by the discriminating intelligence, but which is beyond the senses.

Sloka 22

yaṃ labdhvā cāparaṃ lābhaṃ manyate nādhikaṃ tataḥ
yasmin sthito na duḥkhena guruṇāpi vicālyate

yam = which; labdhva = gaining, obtaining; ca = and; aparam = another; labham = gain; manyate = things; na = not; adhikam = greater, superior; tatah = further; yasmin = in which; sthitah = being established; na = not; duhkhena = sorrow, suffering; guruna api = more; vicalyate = vexing, troublemsom.

"Obtaining which there is no thought of another greater gain, and further, being established in which no sorrow is more vexing or troublesome.

Sloka 23

taṃ vidyād.h duḥkhasaṃyogaviyogaṃ yogasaṃjñitam
sa niścayena yoktavyo yogonirviṇṇacetasā

Tam = that; vidyat = one should know; duhkha = pain and suffering; samyoga = union, contact, assocaiton; viyogam = disassociation, separation; yoga-samjnitam = known as yoga; sah = that yoga; niscayena = with resolve; yoktavyah = should be practiced; yogah = yoga; anirvinna-cetasa = without despair and disheartedness.

"One should know that disassociation from union with pain and suffering by the name of yoga. That yoga should be practiced with resolve and without despair and disheartedness.

Sloka 24

saṅkalpaprabhavān kāmāṃs tyaktvā sarvān aśeṣataḥ
manasaivendriyagrāmaṃ viniyamya samantataḥ

sankalpa-prabhavan = induced by thoughts; kamam = desires; tyaktva = giving up; sarvan = all; asesatah = completely without exception, completely; manasa = in the mind; eva = only, itself; indriya-gramam = the entire group of sense organs; viniyamya = controlling, restraining; samantatah = equally from all sides.

"Giving up all thought induced desires, completely without exception, restraining the entire group of sense organs within the mind only from all sides equally.

Sloka 25

śanaiḥ śanair uparamed buddhyā dhṛtigṛhītayā
ātmasaṃsthaṃ manaḥ kṛtvā na kiṃcid api cintayet

sanaih-sanaih = gradually, step by step; uparamet = should withdraw; buddhya = with the help of discriminating intelligence; dhrti-grhitaya = with firm resolve; atma-samstham = in the Self; manah = mind; krtva = fixing or placing; na-kincit = nothing; api = whatsoever; cintayet = thinking of.

"(Let him) withdraw gradually step by step, with the help of discriminating intelligence, with firm resolve, fixing the mind in the Self, thinking of nothing whatsoever.

Sloka 26

yato yato niścarati manaś cañcalam asthiram
tatas tato niyamyaitad ātmany eva vaśaṃ nayet

yatah yatah = due to whatever reasons; niscarati = keeps wandering; manah = the mind; cancalam = shaking, restless; asthiram = unstable; tatah tatah = from all those causes whatever; niyamya = restrain; etat = it; atmani = own; eva = only; vasam = control; nayet = should bring

"Due to whatever reasons the restless and unstable mind keeps wandering, (he should) restrain it from all those causes whatever and bring it under his control only.

Sloka 27

praśāntamanasaṃ hy enaṃ yoginaṃ sukham uttamam
upaiti śāntarajasaṃ brahmabhūtam akalmaṣam

prasanta = placid, tranquail; manasam = mind; hi = alone, only; enam = this; yoginam = to the yogi; sukham = happiness; uttamam = supreme, the highest; upaiti = comes; santa-rajasam = subdued passions; brahma-bhutam = the Supreme Being; akalmasam = without impurities.

"Supreme happiness comes to the yogi, whose mind is placid, whose rajasic quality has been subdued, who has become one with Brahman and who is without impurities.

Sloka 28

yuñjann evaṃ sadātmānaṃ yogī vigatakalmaṣaḥ
sukhena brahmasaṃsparśam atyantaṃ sukham aśnute

yunjan =fixing his mind; evam = thus; sada = always; atmanam = within himself; yogi = yogi; vigata = freed from; kalmasah = impurities; sukhena = easily; brahma-samsparsam = direct contact with Brahman; atyantam = highest; sukham = happiness; asnute = attains.

"Thus fixing his mind always upon his Self, the yogi who is freed from all impurities easily attains direct contact with Brahman and supreme happiness.

Sloka 29

sarvabhūtastham ātmānaṃ sarvabhūtāni cātmani
īkṣate yogayuktātmā sarvatra samadarśanaḥ

sarva-bhuta-stham = in all beings; atmanam = the Self; sarva = all; bhutani = beings; ca = and; atmani = in the Self; iksate = he sees; yoga-

yukta-atma = he who is absorbed in the Self through yoga; sarvatra = everywhere; sama-darsanah = the vision of sameness.

"Absorbed in the Self through yoga and with the vision of sameness everywhere, he (the yogi) sees the Self in all beings and all beings in the Self.

Sloka 30

yo māṃ paśyati sarvatra sarvaṃ ca mayi paśyati
tasyāhaṃ na praṇaśyāmi sa ca me na praṇaśyati

yah = he who; mam = Me; pasyati = sees; sarvatra = everywhere; sarvam = all things; ca = and; mayi = in Me; pasyati = he sees; tasya = for him; aham = I; na = not; pranasyami = cease to exist; sah = he; ca = also; me = to Me; na = nor; pranasyati = ceases to exist.

"He who sees Me everywhere and sees all things in Me, I do not cease to exist for him and he does not cease to exist for Me.

Sloka 31

sarvabhūtasthitaṃ yo māṃ bhajaty ekatvam āsthitaḥ
sarvathā vartamānopi sa yogī mayi vartate

sarva-bhuta-sthitam = dweller of things; yah = he who; mam = to Me; bhajati = worships; ekatvam = oneness; asthitah = established, situated; sarvatha = always; varta-manah = present condition; api = whatever; sah = he; yogi = yogi; mayi = in Me; vartate = exists.

"He who, established in unity or oneness, worships Me as the dweller of all things, that yogi exists in Me always whatever may be his present condition

Sloka 32

ātmaupamyena sarvatra samaṃ paśyati yorjuna
sukhaṃ vā yadi vā duḥkhaṃ sa yogī paramo mataḥ

atmaaupamyena = with the Self as the standard; sarvatra = all things; samam = equally; pasyati = sees; yah = he who; arjuna = O Arjuna; sukham = happiness; va = or; yadi =whether; va = or; duhkham =

distress; sah = that; yogi = yogi; paramah = supreme; matah = considered.

"With his Self as the standard, he who sees all things equally, whether in happiness or sorrow, O Arjuna, that yogi should be considered supreme."

Sloka 33

arjuna uvāca
yoyaṃ yogas tvayā proktaḥ sāmyena madhusūdana
etasyāhaṃ na paśyāmi cañcalatvāt sthitiṃ sthirām

arjunah uvaca = Arjuna said; yah = which ayam = this; yogah = yoga; tvaya = by You; proktah = described, spoken, spoken,; samyena = by sameness; madhu-sudana = O Madhusudana, slayer of Madhu; etasya = of its; aham = I; na = do not; pasyami = see; cancalatvat = due to restlessness of the mind; sthitim = condition, state, situation; sthiram = stable.

Said Arjuna, "This yoga, which was declared by you as sameness, O Madhusudana, I am not seeing the stable condition of it, due to the restlessness of my mind.

Sloka 34

cañcalaṃ hi manaḥ kṛṣṇa pramāthi balavad dṛḍham
tasyāhaṃ nigrahaṃ manye vāyor iva suduṣkaram

cancalam = fickle, unsteady, restless; hi = surely; manah = mind; krsna = O Krsna; pramathi = turbulent; bala-vat = strong; drdham = obstinate, stong,; tasya = its; aham = I; nigraham = control; manye = think; vayoh = of the wind; iva = like; su-duskaram = difficult.

"Surely, O Krishna, the mind is fickle, turbulent, strong and obstinate. I think its control is as difficult as of the wind."

Sloka 35

śrībhagavān uvāca
asañśayaṃ mahābāho mano durnigrahaṃ calam
abhyāsena tu kaunteya vairāgyeṇa ca gṛhyate

sri-bhagavan uvaca = the Supreme Lord said; asamsayam = undoubtedly; maha-baho = O mighty-armed one; manah = mind; durnigraham = difficult to control; calam = restless; abhyasena = by repeated practice; tu = however; kaunteya = O son of Kunti; vairagyena = by dispassion and detachment; ca = and; grhyate = tamed, held in control.

The Supreme Lord said, "O mighty-armed, undoubtedly the mind is difficult to control and restless. However, O son of Kunti, through regular practice and detachment it can be tamed.

Sloka 36

asaṃyatātmanā yogo duṣprāpa iti me matiḥ
vaśyātmanā tu yatatā śakyovāptum upāyataḥ

asamyata-atmana = by a person who has an uncontrolled mind; yogah = the state of yoga; dusprapah = difficult to obtain; iti = thus; me = My; matih = opinion; vasya-atmana = with regard to a person who has control over his mind; tu = but; yatata = strives hard; sakyah = possible; avaptum = to achieve; upayatah = through the means.

"The state of yoga is difficult to obtain by a person who has an uncontrolled mind, thus is My opinion; but it is possible to achieve through the means by a person who has control over his mind and who strives hard."

Sloka 37

arjuna uvāca
ayatiḥ śraddhayopeto yogāc calitamānasaḥ
aprāpya yogasaṃsiddhiṃ kāṃ gatiṃ kṛṣṇa gacchati

Translatin

arjunah uvaca = Arjuna said; ayatih = an unrestrained yogi; sraddhaya = with faith; upetah = endowed with, possessed of; yogat = from yoga; calita = wandering, agitated, shaken; manasah = mind; aprapya = without gaining; yoga-samsiddhim = proper preparation or perfection in yoga; kam = what; gatim = goal, destination; krsna = O Krsna; gacchati = goes.

Arjuna said, "The unrestrained yogi endowed with faith, with wandering mind, not gaining perfection or readiness in yoga, in which direction, O Krishna, he goes?

Sloka 38

kacchin nobhayavibhraṣṭaś chinnābhram iva naśyati
apratiṣṭho mahābāho vimūḍho brahmaṇaḥ pathi

kaccit = does he; na = not; ubhaya-vibhrastah = fallen from both; chinna = torn, broken,; abhram = cloud; iva = like; nasyati = perishes; apratisthah = without stability or position; maha-baho = O mighty-armed; vimudhah = deluded; brahmanah = Brahman; pathi = on the path.

"O mighty-armed, would he not perish like a broken cloud, fallen from both, without stability, deluded on the path to Brahman?

Sloka 39

etan me saṃśayaṃ kṛṣṇa chettum arhasy aśeṣataḥ
tvadanyaḥ saṃśayasyāsya chettā na hy upapadyate

etat = this is; me = my; samsayam = doubt; krsna = O Krsna; chettum = dispel; arhasi = you have to; asesatah = completely; tvat = than You; anyah = other; samsayasya = of the doubt; asya = of this; chetta = dispeller, remover; na = never; hi = surely; upapadyate = is to be found.

"O Krishna, you should dispel this doubt completely; other than You, no other dispeller of this doubt can be surely found.

Sloka 40

śrībhagavān uvāca
pārtha naiveha nāmutra vināśas tasya vidyate
na hi kalyāṇakṛt kaścid durgatiṃ tāta gacchati

sri-bhagavan uvaca = the Supreme Lord said; partha = O Partha; na = not; eva = surely; iha = here in this world; na = not; amutra = in the next world; vinasah = downfall, destruction; tasya = for him; vidyate = there is; na = not; hi = surely; kalyana-krt = perfoms auspicious actins; kascit = anyone; durgatim = in the direction of the hell, adversity, difficulty; tata = thereafter; gacchati = goes.

"The Supreme Lord said, "O Partha, certainly world there is no downfall for him in this world and in the next. My son, surely, no one who performs auspicious deeds goes in the direction of the hell.

Sloka 41

prāpya puṇyakṛtāṃ lokān uṣitvā śāśvatīḥ samāḥ
śucīnāṃ śrīmatāṃ gehe yogabhraṣṭobhijāyate

prapya = having attained; punya-krtam = righteous, meritorius; lokan = worlds; usitva = having dwelt; sasvatih = countless, eternal; samah = years; sucinam = of the pious; sri-matam = of the prosperous; gehe = in the house of; yoga-bhrastah = the yogi who has stumbled on the faith; abhijayate = is born.

"Having attained the worlds of the righteous people and having dwelt there for countless years, the yogi who stumbles on the path of yoga is born in the house of the pious and the prosperous

Sloka 42

athavā yoginām eva kule bhavati dhīmatām
etad dhi durlabhataraṃ loke janma yad īdṛśam

athava- = or; yoginam = of yogis; eva = even; kule = in the family of; bhavati = is born; dhi-matam = of great wisdom and intelligence; etat = such; hi = indeed; durlabha-taram = very difficult to attain; loke = in this world; janma = birth; yat idrsam = the one like this.

"Or he is born in the family of yogis of great wisdom and intelligence. Indeed a birth such as this one is very difficult to attain in this world.

Sloka 43

tatra taṃ buddhisaṃyogaṃ labhate paurvadehikam
yatate ca tato bhūyaḥ saṃsiddhau kurunandana

tatra = there; tam = that; buddhi-samyogam = united with buddhi; labhate = becomes, gains; paurva = of previous; dehikam = bodily existence; yatate = he strives; ca = and; tatah = than before; bhuyah = seriously; samsiddhau = readiness or preparedness in yoga; kuru-nandana = O son of Kuru.

"O son of Kuru, there he becomes united with the intelligence of his previous bodily existence and strives more seriously than before for readiness in yoga.

Sloka 44

pūrvābhyāsena tenaiva hriyate hy avaśopi saḥ
jijñāsur api yogasya śabdabrahmātivartate

purva = past; abhyasena = practice; tena = by that; eva = for surely; hriyate = is attracted; hi = surely; avasah = uncontrollably; api = besides, moreover; sah = he; jijnasuh = the inquisitive seeker; api = also; yogasya = of yoga; sabda-brahma = the sounds of vedic hymns; ativartate = surpasses, goes beyond.

"Surely, by that past practice he is attracted very uncontrollably; besides, the inquisitive seeker of yoga goes beyond the sounds of the Vedic hymns.

Sloka 45

prayatnād yatamānas tu yogī saṃśuddhakilbiṣaḥ
anekajanmasaṃsiddhas tato yāti parāṃ gatim

prayatnat = striving, effort, exertion, endeavor; yatamanah = subdued mind; tu = indeed; yogi = yogi; samsuddha = cleansed; kilbisah = of all sins; aneka = several, many; janma = births; samsiddhah = equanimity gained; tatah = thereby; yati = goes; param-gatim = highest world of Brahman.

"By striving with subdued mind, cleansed of all sins, indeed the yogi, with equanimity gained through several births, thereby goes to the highest world of Brahman

Sloka 46

tapasvibhyodhiko yogī jñānibhyopi matodhikaḥ
karmibhyaś cādhiko yogī tasmād yogī bhavārjuna

tapasvibhyah = those who practice austerities; adhikah = higher, greater, superior; yogi = the yogi; jnanibhyah = those who pursue knowledge; api = also, even, in addition; matah = regarded, considered; adhikah = higher, greater, superior; karmibhyah = those who perform their obligatory duties; ca = and; adhikah = higher, greater, superior; yogi = the yogi; tasmat = therefore; yogi = yogi; bhava = just become; arjuna = O Arjuna.

"A yogi is higher than those who practice austerities; regarded as higher than those who purse knowledge on the path of wisdom and superior to those who perform their obligatory duties on the path of action. Therefore, O Arjuna, become a yogi.

Sloka 47

yoginām api sarveṣāṃ madgatenāntarātmanā
śraddhāvān bhajate yo māṃ sa me yuktatamo mataḥ

yoginam = among the yogis; api = moreover; sarvesam = all; mat-gatena = turned towards Me; antah-atmana = with his mind; sraddha-van = with faith; bhajate = worships; yah = who; mam = Me ; sah = he; me = by Me; yukta-tamah = most skilful yogi; matah = regarded.

"Moreover, among all the yogis, he who worships Me with his mind turned towards Me, with faith, he is regarded by Me as the most skillful yogi.

Conclusion

iti srīmadbhāgavadgītāsupanisatsu brahmavidyāyām yogasāstre

srikrisnārjunasamvāde ātmasamyamayogo nāma shasto 'dhyayah

iti = thus; srīmadbhāgavadgītā = in the sacred Bhagavadgita; upanisatsu = in the Upanishad; brahmavidyāyām = the knowledge of the absolute Brahman; yogasāstre = the scripture of yoga; srikrisnārjunasamvāde = the dialogue between Sri Krishna and Arjuna; ātmasamyamayogo nāma = by name yoga of self-control; shatah = sixth; adhyayah = chapter;

Thus ends the sixth chapter named the Yoga of Self-absorption in the Upanishad of the divine Bhagavadgita, the knowledge of the Absolute, the yogic scripture, and the debate between Arjuna and Lord Krishna.

7 – The Yoga of Knowledge and Wisdom

Sloka 1

śrībhagavān uvāca
mayy āsaktamanāḥ pārtha yogaṃ yuñjan madāśrayaḥ
asaṃśayaṃ samagraṃ māṃ yathā jñāsyasi tac chṛṇu

sri-bhagavan uvaca = the Supreme Lord said; mayi = to Me; asakta = devoted, interest, aspiration; manah = mind; partha = O Partha; yogam = yoga; yunjan = practicing; mat-asrayah = take refuge in Me; asamsayam = without any doubt, undoubtedly; samagram = completely in all aspects; mam = to Me; yatha = as much as; jnasyasi = you will know; tat = that; srnu = listen.

"Said the Lord Supreme, "With mind devoted to Me, practicing yoga, taking refuge in Me, listen O Partha, how you will know Me in all respects without any doubt.

Sloka 2

jñānaṃ tehaṃ savijñānam idaṃ vakṣyāmy aśeṣataḥ
yaj jñātvā neha bhūyo.anyaj jñātavyam avaśiṣyate

jnanam = higher knowledge; te = to you; aham = I; sa = along with; vijnanam = worldly knowledge; idam = this; vaksyami = will explain; asesatah = in full, without any remains; yat = which; jnatva = knowing; na = not; iha = in this world; bhuyah = again; anyat = nothing else; jnatavyam = knowable; avasisyate = remains to be known.

"I will explain to you in detail the higher knowledge along with this worldly knowledge, knowing which nothing else remains to be known.

Sloka 3

manuṣyāṇāṃ sahasreṣu kaścid yatati siddhaye
yatatām api siddhānāṃ kaścin māṃ vetti tattvataḥ

manusyanam = of men; sahasresu = among thousands; kascit = a rare one; yatati = strives; siddhaye = for perfection, for success or accomplishment; yatatam = of the striving ones; api = even; siddhanam = of the perfected, of the accomplished; kascit = a rare one; mam = Me; vetti = knows; tattvatah = in truth.

"Among thousands of men a rare person strives for perfection (in yoga); even among the perfected ones who strive (for liberation) a rare person knows Me in truth.

Sloka 4

bhūmir āponalo vāyuḥ khaṃ mano buddhir eva ca
ahaṃkāra itīyaṃ me bhinnā prakṛtir aṣṭadhā

bhumih = earth; apah = water; analah = fire; vayuh = air; kham = ether; manah = mind; buddhih = intelligence; eva = also; ca = and; ahankarah = ego; iti = thus; iyam = this; me = My; bhinna = different; prakrtih = Nature; astadha = eightfold.

"Earth, water, fire, air, mind, intelligence and also ego, this is the eightfold division of My Nature.

Sloka 5

apareyam itas tvanyāṃ prakṛtiṃ viddhi me parām
jīvabhūtāṃ mahābāho yayedaṃ dhāryate jagat

apara = inferior, lower; iyam = this; itah = than this; tu = but; anyam = other; prakrtim = nature; viddhi = know; me = My; param = higher, superior; jiva-bhutam = the living self consisting of all individual souls; maha-baho = O mighty-armed; yaya = by which; idam = this; dharyate = is upheld, supported; jagat = the world.

"O mighty armed one, inferior (Nature) is this; but know other than this is My higher Nature, the living Self consisting of all individual souls, by which this world is supported.

Sloka 6

etadyonīni bhūtāni sarvāṇīty upadhāraya
ahaṃ kṛtsnasya jagataḥ prabhavaḥ pralayas tathā

etat = these; yonini = source; bhutani = living beings; sarvani = all; iti = thus; upadharaya = know, understand; aham = I; krtsnasya = whole, entire; jagatah = universe; prabhavah = origin, creation; pralayah = dissolution; tatha = and, also.

"Know them thus as the source of all beings and I am (the source) of creation and dissolution of the whole universe.

Sloka 7

mattaḥ parataraṃ nānyat kiṃcid asti dhanaṃjaya
mayi sarvam idaṃ protaṃ sūtre maṇigaṇā iva

mattah = than I; para-taram = higher; na = not; anyat kincit = nothing else whatsoever; asti = there is; dhananjaya = O Dhananjaya; mayi = in Me; sarvam = all; idam = this; protam = is strung; sutre = thread; mani-ganah = a bunch of pearls; iva = like.

"There is nothing else whatsoever that is higher than I, O Dhananjaya. All this is strung upon Me like a bunch of pearls on a thread.

Sloka 8

raso.aham apsu kaunteya prabhāsmi śaśisūryayoḥ
praṇavaḥ sarvavedeṣu śabdaḥ khe pauruṣaṃ nṛṣu

rasah = taste; aham = I; apsu = in the waters; kaunteya = O son of Kunti; prabha asmi = I am the brilliance; sasi-suryayoh = in the moon and the sun; pranavah = the sacred syllable Aum; sarva vedesu = in all the Vedas; sabdah = sound ; khe = in space, ether; paurusam = virility; nrsu = in man.

"I am the taste in the waters, O son of Kunti; I am the brilliance in the sun and the moon, the sacred syllable Aum in all the Vedas, the sound in space and virility in man.

Sloka 9

puṇyo gandhaḥ pṛthivyāṃ ca tejaś cāsmi vibhāvasau
jīvanaṃ sarvabhūteṣu tapaś cāsmi tapasviṣu

punyah = pure, sacred, sweet; gandhah = fragrance; prthivyam = in the earth; ca = and; tejah = brilliance; ca = and; asmi = I am; vibhavasau = in fire; jivanam = life; sarva bhutesu = in all living beings; tapah = austerity; ca = and; asmi = I am; tapasvisu = ascetics who practice austerities.

"I am the pure fragrance in the earth and the brilliance in fire; I am the life in all living beings and the austerity of the ascetics.

Sloka 10

bījaṃ māṃ sarvabhūtānāṃ viddhi pārtha sanātanam
buddhir buddhimatām asmi tejas tejasvinām aham

bijam = the seed; mam = Me; sarva-bhutanam = of all living beings; viddhi = know; partha = O Partha; sanatanam = eternal; buddhih = intelligence; buddhi-matam = of the intelligent; asmi = I am; tejah = brightness; tejasvinam = of the brightest; aham = I am.

"Know Me, O Partha, as the eternal seed of all living beings. I am the intelligence of the intelligent, (and) I am the brightness of the brightest.

Sloka 11

balaṃ balavatāṃ cāhaṃ kāmarāgavivarjitam
dharmāviruddho bhūteṣu kāmo.asmi bharatarṣabha

balam = physical strength; bala-vatam = of the strong; ca = and; aham = I am; kama = passion; raga = attachment; vivarjitam = devoid of; dharma-aviruddhah = not against the moral obligations and religious duties; bhutesu = in all beings; kamah = desire asmi = I am; bharata-rsabha = O great among the Bharatas.

"And I am the physical strength of the strong that is devoid of passion and attachment. I am desire among all living beings, which is not contrary to the moral obligations and religious duties, O great among the Bharatas.

Sloka 12

ye caiva sātvikā bhāvā rājasās tāmasāś ca ye
matta eveti tān viddhi na tv ahaṃ teṣu te mayi

ye = these; ca = and; eva = indeed; sattvikah = sattva; bhavah = state; rajasah = rajas; tamasah = tamas; ca = and; ye = those; mattah = sprung from Me; eva = only; iti = thus; tan = them all; viddhi = know; na = not; tu = however, but; aham = I; tesu = in them; te = they; mayi = in Me.

"Indeed these having the state of sattva and those of rajas and tamas, know them all sprung from Me only. However, I am not in them. They are in Me.

Sloka 13

tribhir guṇamayair bhāvair ebhiḥ sarvam idaṃ jagat
mohitaṃ nābhijānāti mām ebhyaḥ param avyayam

tribhih = triple, three; guna-mayaih =filled with gunas; bhavaih = states or modes; ebhih = by these; sarvam = whole; idam = this; jagat = world; mohitam = deluded; na abhijanati = do not know; mam = Me; ebhyah = beyond these; param = higher; avyayam = inexhaustible.

"Deluded by these modes that are filled with the triple gunas, this whole world does not know Me who is higher and beyond them and who is inexhaustible.

Sloka 14

daivī hy eṣā guṇamayī mama māyā duratyayā
mām eva ye prapadyante māyām etāṃ taranti te

daivi = divine; hi = indeed; esa = this; guna-mayi = composed of the triple gunas; mama = My; maya = maya, enchanting or deluding power; duratyaya = difficult to overcome; mam = to Me; eva = alone; ye = those; prapadyante = surrender and take refuge, surrender; mayam etam = this delusion; taranti = transcend; te = they.

"Indeed, this My divine Maya, composed of the triple gunas, is difficult to overcome. Those who surrender and take refuge in Me, they alone transcend this delusion.

Sloka 15

na māṃ duṣkṛtino mūḍhāḥ prapadyante narādhamāḥ
māyayāpahṛtajñānā āsuraṃ bhāvam āśritāḥ

na = not; mam = to Me; duskrtinah = evil doers; mudhah = foolish, deluded; prapadyante = take refuge; nara-adhamah = most depraved human beings; mayaya = by maya; apahrta = stolen; jnanah = knowledge; asuram = demonic; bhavam = nature; asritah = abiding in, take shelter.

"The evil doers and the deluded do not take refuge in Me, who are the most deprived of the human beings, whose knowledge is stolen by my Maya, who abide in demonic nature.

Sloka 16

caturvidhā bhajante māṃ janāḥ sukṛtinorjuna
ārto jijñāsur arthārthī jñānī ca bharatarṣabha

catuh-vidhah = four types of; bhajante = worship; mam = Me; janah = people; su-krtinah = people of virtuous action; arjuna = O Arjuna; artah = the unhappy and distressed people; jijnasuh = those who are curious and inquisitive; artha-arthi = those seeking material wealth; jnani = he knowers of the Self or Brahman, the wise, the wise; ca = and; bharata-rsabha = O greatest among the Bharatas.

"Four types of people of virtuous actions worship Me, O Arjuna, the greatest among the Bharatas, the unhappy and distressed people, the curious and inquisitive ones, the seekers of material wealth and the knowers of the Self.

Sloka 17

teṣāṃ jñānī nityayukta ekabhaktir viśiṣyate
priyo hi jñāninotyartham ahaṃ sa ca mama priyaḥ

tesam = Of them; jnani = knower of the Self; nitya-yuktah = always self-absorped; eka bhakti = single minded devotion; visisyate = excels; priyah = dear; hi = surely; jnaninah = the knower of the Self; atyartham = supremely, highly; aham = I am; sah = he is; ca = and; mama = to Me; priyah = dear.

"Of them, the knower of the Self, who is always self-absorbed with single minded devotion, excels. Surely, I am supremely dear to the knower of the Self and to Me also he is dear.

Sloka 18

udārāḥ sarva evaite jñānī tv ātmaiva me matam
āsthitaḥ sa hi yuktātmā mām evānuttamāṃ gatim

udarah = generous, noble, exalted; sarve = all; eva = surely; ete = these; jnani = knower of the Self; tu = but; atma eva = like My very Self; me = My; matam = opinion; asthitah = fixed, situated; sah = he; hi = firmly; yukta-atma = absorbed in the Self; mam = to Me; eva = certainly, surely; anuttamam = the highest goal; gatim = goes, reaches.

"All these are indeed noble and exalted, but the knower of the Self, in My opinion, is like My very Self; fixed firmly, absorbed in himself, he certainly reaches Me, the highest goal

Sloka 19

bahūnāṃ janmanām ante jñānavān māṃ prapadyate
vāsudevaḥ sarvam iti sa mahātmā sudurlabhaḥ

bahunam = many; janmanam = births; ante = at the end; jnana-van = the knower of the Self; mam = to Me; prapadyate = surrender, takes refuge; vasudevah = Vasudeva; sarvam = all; iti = thus; sah = such; maha-atma = great soul; su-durlabhah = very rare.

"At the end of many births, the knower of the Self surrenders to Me, "Vasudeva is all," (thinking) thus. Such a great soul is very rare.

Sloka 20

kāmais tais tair hṛtajñānāḥ prapadyantenyadevatāḥ
taṃ taṃ niyamam āsthāya prakṛtyā niyatāḥ svayā

kamaih = by desires; taih taih = various; hrta = taken away, carried away, stripped of, deprived; jnanah = with their knowledge; prapadyante = surrender; anya = other; devatah = deities, gods; tam tam = that that, such and such, various; niyamam = observances; asthaya = following; prakrtya = by nature; niyatah = guided, propelled; svaya = by their own.

"Those, whose knowledge is carried away by various desires, worship other deities, following various observances, propelled by their own nature.

Sloka 21

yo yo yāṃ yāṃ tanuṃ bhaktaḥ śraddhayārcitum icchati
tasya tasyācalāṃ śraddhāṃ tām eva vidadhāmy aham

yah yah = whoever; yam yam = whichever; tanum = form; bhaktah = devotee; sraddhaya = with faith; arcitum = worship; icchati = desires; tasya = of his; tasya = of that; acalam = steady; sraddham = faith; tam = him; eva = surely; vidadhami = stabilize, strengthen; aham = I.

"Whoever (god), in whatever form a devotee desires to worship with faith, I strengthen that firm faith of his.

Sloka 22

sa tayā śraddhayā yuktas tasyārādhanam īhate
labhate ca tataḥ kāmān mayaivaḥ vihitān hi tān

sah = he; taya = with that; sraddhaya = faith; yuktah = endowed; tasya = that; aradhanam = worship; ihate = aspires, wishes, desires; labhate = gains, obtains; ca = and; tatah = from it; kaman = desires; maya = by Me; eva = alone; vihitan = as decreed; hi = very; tan = those.

"Endowed with that faith, he aspires to worship that form and gains from it those very desires as decreed by Me alone.

Sloka 23

antavat tu phalaṃ teṣāṃ tad bhavaty alpamedhasām
devān devayajo yānti madbhaktā yānti mām api

anta-vat tu = limited, having an end; phalam = fruit; tesam = of theirs; tat = that; bhavati = is; alpa-medhasam = who are of poor intelligence; devan = gods, divinities; deva-yajah = worshipers of gods, divinities; yanti = go; mat = My; bhaktah = devotees; yanti = come; mam = to Me; api = only.

"That fruit of theirs who are of poor intelligence is limited. The worshippers of gods go to the gods. My devotees come to Me only.

Sloka 24

avyaktaṃ vyaktim āpannaṃ manyante māmabuddhayaḥ
paraṃ bhāvam ajānanto mamāvyayam anuttamam

avyaktam = unmanifest, non-beingness; vyaktim = manifest, beingness; apannam = become, gain, obtain, reduced to; manyante = think; mam = Me; abuddhayah = ignorant people lacking in discerning intelligence; param = supreme; bhavam = state; ajanantah = without knowing; mama = of My; avyayam = immutable, inexhaustible, imperishable; anuttamam = most exalted, the best, the highest.

"Ignorant people lacking in discriminating intelligence think of Me, the Unmanifest becoming the manifest, ignorant of My supreme state, which is inexhaustible and the highest.

Sloka 25

nāhaṃ prakāśaḥ sarvasya yogamāyāsamāvṛtaḥ
mūḍhoyaṃ nābhijānāti loko mām ajam avyayam

na = not; aham = I; prakasah = illuminate, make known, visible; sarvasya = all; yoga-maya = deluding power; samavrtah = covered, eneveloped; mudhah = deluded; ayam = this; na = not; abhijanati = know; lokah =the world; mam = Me; ajam = unborn; avyayam = inexhaustible.

"I do not illuminate all. Enveloped by My deluding power, this deluded world does not know Me, who am unborn and inexhaustible.

Sloka 26

vedāhaṃ samatītāni vartamānāni cārjuna
bhaviṣyāṇi ca bhūtāni māṃ tu veda na kaścana

veda = know; aham = I; sama = equally; atitani = past; vartamanani = present; ca = and; arjuna = O Arjuna; bhavisyani = future; ca = also; bhutani = living beings; mam = Me; tu = but; veda = knows; na = not; kascana = anyone.

"I know equally the past, the present and the future of the living beings, O Arjuna, but no one knows Me.

Sloka 27

icchādveṣasamutthena dvandvamohena bhārata
sarvabhūtāni saṃmohaṃ sarge yānti paraṃtapa

iccha = attractions, like, desire; dvesa = repulsion, dislike, hatred; samutthena = arising from, produced from, born out of; dvandva = duality; mohena = by the delusion; bharata = O Bharata; sarva bhutani = all beings; sammoham = into ignorance, bewiderment; sarge = in creation; yanti = go, fall; parantapa = O destroyer of enemies.

"O Bharata, destroyer of enemies, by the delusion of duality arising from attraction and repulsion, all beings in creation fall into ignorance and bewilderment,.

Sloka 28

yeṣāṃ tv antagataṃ pāpaṃ janānāṃ puṇyakarmaṇām
te dvandvamohanirmuktā bhajante māṃ dṛḍhavratāḥ

yesam = whose; tu = however; anta-gatam = has come to an end; papam = sin; jananam = people; punya = pious; karmanam = actions; te = they; dvandva = duality; moha = delusion; nirmuktah = freed from; bhajante = worship; mam = Me; drdha-vratah = with strong resolve, determination.

"However, those of pious actions whose sin has come to an end, who are freed from delusion, worship Me with strong resolve.

Sloka 29

jarāmaraṇamokṣāya mām āśritya yatanti ye
te brahma tad viduḥ kṛtsnam adhyātmaṃ karmacākhilam

jara = old age; marana = death; moksaya = for deliverance, liberation; mam = in Me; asritya = by taking refuge; yatanti = strive, endeavor; ye = those who; te = they; brahma = Brahman; tat = that; viduh = know; krtsnam = everything; adhyatmam = concerning the Self; karma = actions; ca = and; akhilam = all.

"Those who strive for liberation from old age and death by taking refuge in Me, they know That Brahman, everything concerning the Self and all about karma.

Sloka 30

sādhibhūtādhidaivaṃ māṃ sādhiyajñaṃ ca ye viduḥ
prayāṇakālepi ca māṃ te vidur yuktacetasaḥ

sa-adhibhuta = master of the elements; adhidaivam = master of the divinities; mam = Me; sa-adhiyajnam = master of all sacrifices; ca = and; ye = those who; viduh = know; prayana kale = at the time of departing from here; api = even; ca = and; mam = Me; te = they; viduh = know; yukta-cetasah = with steadfast minds.

"Those who know me as the Master of elements, Master of divinities and Master of all sacrifices, they of steadfast minds know Me even at the time of departing from here.

Conclusion

iti srīmadbhāgavadgītāsupanisatsu brahmavidyāyām yogasāstre
srikrisnārjunasamvāde jnānavijnānayogo nāma saptamo 'dhyayah

iti = thus; srīmadbhāgavadgītā = in the sacred Bhagavadgita; upanisatsu = in the Upanishad; brahmavidyāyām = the knowledge of the absolute Brahman; yogasāstre = the scripture of yoga; srikrisnārjunasamvāde = the dialogue between Sri Krishna and Arjuna; jnānavijnānayogo nāma = by name yoga of knowledge and wisdom; saptama = seventh; adhyayah = chapter.

Thus ends the seventh chapter named Yoga of Knowledge and Wisdom in the Upanishad of the divine Bhagavadgita, the knowledge of the Absolute, the yogic scripture, and the debate between Arjuna and Lord Krishna.

8 – The Yoga of Imperishable Brahman

Sloka 1

arjuna uvāca
kiṃ tad brahma kim adhyātmaṃ kiṃ karma puruṣottama
adhibhūtaṃ ca kiṃ proktam adhidaivaṃ kim ucyate

arjunah uvaca = Arjuna said; kim = what; tat = that; brahma = Brahman; kim = what; adhyatmam = the inner Self; kim = what; karma = karma; purusa-uttama = O Supreme Person; adhibhutam = elemental self; ca = and; kim = what; proktam = is said to be; adhidaivam = divine self; kim = what; ucyate = is said to be.

Arjuna said, "O Supreme Person, what is that Brahman? What is the inner Self? What is karma, and what is said to be in the elemental Self? What is said to be in divine Self?

Sloka 2

adhiyajñaḥ kathaṃ kotra dehesmin madhusūdana
prayāṇakāle ca kathaṃ jñeyosi niyatātmabhiḥ

adhiyajnah = Lord of the sacrifices; katham = how; kah = who; atra = here; dehe = in the body; asmin = this; madhusudana = O Madhusudana; prayana-kale = at the time of departure; ca = and; katham = how; jneyah = be known; asi = You ; niyata-atmabhih = by the self-restrained.

"O Madhusudhana, how, and who is the Lord of the sacrifices in this body; and at the time departure from this world, how should You be known by self-restrained yogis?"

Sloka 3

śrībhagavān uvāca
akṣaraṃ brahma paramaṃ svabhāvodhyātmam ucyate
bhūtabhāvodbhavakaro visargaḥ karmasaṃjñitaḥ

sri-bhagavan uvaca = the Supreme Lord said; aksaram = imperishable; brahma = Brahman; paramam = transcendental; svabhavah = by nature; adhyatmam = the inner Self, related to the inner Self; ucyate = is called; bhuta-bhava = the physical state, beingness; udbhava-karah = the cause of the origin; visargah = offering, pouring, emission, giving away, oblation; karma = actions; samjnitah = is called.

"The Supreme Lord said, "Imperishable and transcendental is Brahman; by Nature it is said to be the inner Self. The sacrificial offering which is the cause of all beings and existences, is called karma

Sloka 4

adhibhūtaṃ kṣaro bhāvaḥ puruṣaś cādhidaivatam
adhiyajñoham evātra dehe dehabhṛtāṃ vara

adhibhutam = physical self or material existence; ksarah = perishable, exhaustible; bhavah = nature; purusah = Purusa, the Cosmic Person; ca = and; adhidaivatam = the adhidaivam; adhiyajnah = the Lord of the sacrifices; aham = I am; eva = certainly; atra = in this; dehe = body; deha-bhrtam vara = O best of the embodied.

"The physical self has perishable nature; the divine Self is the Cosmic Person; and O best of the embodied, in this body I am certainly the Lord of the sacrifice.

Sloka 5

antakāle ca mām eva smaran muktvā kalevaram
yaḥ prayati sa madbhāvaṃ yāti nāsty atra saṃśayaḥ

anta-kale = at the the time of death; ca = and; mam = Me; eva = only; smaran = remembering; muktva = giving up; kalevaram = the body; yah = he who; prayati = departs; sah = he; mat-bhavam = My State; yati = attains; na = not; asti = there is; atra = here; samsayah = doubt.

"And at the time of death, he who departs, giving up the body, remembering Me only, attains My State. There is no doubt about this.

Sloka 6

yaṃ yaṃ vāpi smaran bhāvaṃ tyajaty ante kalevaram
taṃ tam evaiti kaunteya sadā tadbhāvabhāvitaḥ

yam yam = whatever; va = or; api = verily; it may be; smaran = thinking or remembering bhavam = state, entity, condition; tyajati = one gives up; ante = in the end; kalevaram = the body; tam tam = that and that; eva = only; eti = it attains; kaunteya = O son of Kunti; sada = always; tat = that; bhava = state; bhavitah = absorbed, engrossed.

"Or verily, O son of Kunti, thinking of whatever state one gives up the body in the end one attains that and that only, being absorbed in that state always.

Sloka 7

tasmāt sarveṣu kāleṣu mām anusmara yudhya ca
mayy arpitamanobuddhir mām evaiṣyasy asaṃśayaḥ

tasmat = therefore; sarvesu kalesu = at all times; mam = Me; anusmara = think; yudhya = fight; ca = and; mayi = to Me; arpita = offering; manah = mind; buddhih = intelligence; mam = Me; eva = alone; esyasi = you will attain; asamsayah = undoubtedly.

"Therefore think of Me at all times and fight. Offering your mind and intelligence to Me, you will undoubtedly attain Me alone.

Sloka 8

abhyāsayogayuktena cetasā nānyagāminā
paramaṃ puruṣaṃ divyaṃ yāti pārthānucintayan

abhyasa = practice; yoga = yoga; yuktena = engaged in; cetasa = by the mind; na anya-gamina = not distracted, not moving elsewhere; paramam = the Supreme; purusam = Person, Being; divyam = divine, transcendental; yati = one achieves; partha = O Partha; anucintayan = by constantly meditating, recollecting.

"Engaged in the practice of yoga, with the mind not moving in other directions, by constantly meditating, O Partha, one attains the transcendental Supreme Purusha.

Sloka 9

kaviṃ purāṇam anuśāsitāraṃ aṇor aṇīyāṃsam anusmared yaḥ sarvasya dhātāram acintyarūpaṃ ādityavarṇaṃ tamasaḥ parastāt

kavim = omniscient; puranam = the most ancient; anusasitaram = the Lord of the universe; anoh = the smallest, atom; aniyamsam = smaller than; anusmaret = always thinks, meditates upon; yah = he who; sarvasya = of all; dhataram = the upholder; acintya = inconceivable; rupam = form; aditya-varnam = of the color of the sun, golden hued; tamasah = of the darkness; parastat = beyond.

"He who always meditates upon the Omniscient, the Most Ancient, Lord of the Universe, smaller than the smallest, upholder of all, of inconceivable form, golden hued like the Sun, and beyond darkness.

Sloka 10

prayāṇakāle manasācalena bhaktyā yukto yogabalena caiva bhruvor madhye prāṇam āveśya samyak sa taṃ paraṃ puruṣam upaiti divyam

prayana-kale = at the time of death; manasa = with mind; acalena = unwavering; bhaktya = in devotion; yuktah = engaged; yoga-balena = by the power of yoga; ca = and; eva = surely; bhruvoh = between the eyebrows; madhye = in; pranam = prana, life breath; avesya = fixing; samyak = firmly completely; sah = he; tam = that; param = Supreme; purusam = Brahman; upaiti = attains, achieves; divyam = which is divine.

"At the time of death with unwavering mind, engaged in devotion and fixing the life breath firmly between the eyebrows by the power of yoga, he attains the Supreme Brahman, which is divine.

Sloka 11

yad akṣaraṃ vedavido vadanti viśanti yad yatayo vītarāgāḥ yad icchanto brahmacaryaṃ caranti tat te padaṃ saṃgraheṇa pravakṣye

yat = that which; aksaram = imperishable; veda-vidah = knower of the Vedas; vadanti = declare; visanti = enters; yat = that which; yatayah = the self-restrained ascetics; vita-ragah = devoid of passions; yat = that which; icchantah = desiring; brahmacaryam = celibacy; caranti = practice; tat = that; te = to you; padam = word; sangrahena = in summary, briefly; pravaksye = I will explain.

"That which the knowers of the Vedas declare as imperishable, that which the self-restrained ascetics who are devoid of passions enter, desiring which (they) practice celibacy, that word I will explain to you briefly

Sloka 12

sarvadvārāṇi saṃyamya mano hṛdi nirudhya ca
mūrdhny ādhāyātmanaḥ prāṇam āsthito yogadhāraṇām

sarva-dvarani = all the openings of the body; samyamya = having controlled; manah = mind; hrdi = in the heart; nirudhya = having restrained, confined, held back; ca = and; murdhni = on the top of the head; adhaya = having fixed; atmanah = one's own; pranam = life breath; asthitah = firmly established; yoga-dharanam = in the concentration by yoga.

"Having controlled all the openings of the body, having restrained the mind within the heart, and having fixed the life breath in oneself on the top of the head, firmly established in concentration by yoga...

Sloka 13

om ity ekākṣaraṃ brahma vyāharan mām anusmaran
yaḥ prayāti tyajan dehaṃ sa yāti paramāṃ gatim

om = Aum, the sacred syllable; iti = thus; eka-aksaram = one and indestructible world; brahma = Brahman; vyaharan = chanting, reciting; mam = Me; anusmaran = remembering; yah = whoever; prayati = departs; tyajan = abandoning; deham = the body; sah = he; yati = attains; paramam = supreme; gatim = state, goal, destination.

"Reciting thus the one and indestructible word Aum, which is Brahman, (and) remembering Me, Whoever departs abandoning his body, He attains the supreme State.

Sloka 14

ananyacetāḥ satataṃ yo māṃ smarati nityaśaḥ
tasyāhaṃ sulabhaḥ pārtha nityayuktasya yoginaḥ

ananya-cetah = without thinking anything else; satatam = constantly; yah = he who; mam = Me; smarati = remembers; nityasah = uninterruptedly; tasya = for that; yogi; aham = I am; su-labhah = easy to attain; partha = O Partha; nitya = regularly; yuktasya = self-absorbed, absorbed in concentration; yoginah = reverent yogi.

"He who remembers Me constantly and uninterruptedly, without thinking anything else, for that reverent yogi who is ever absorbed in concentration, O Partha, I am easy to attain.

Sloka 15

mām upetya punarjanma duḥkhālayam aśāśvatam
nāpnuvanti mahātmānaḥ saṃsiddhiṃ paramāṃ gatāḥ

mam = to Me; upetya = having come; punarjanma = rebirth; duhkha-alayam = house of miseries; asasvatam = impermanance; na = not; apnuvanti = return to, attain; maha-atmanah = great souls; samsiddhim = to perfection; paramam = highest; gatah = attained.

"Having come to me, the great souls who have attained the highest perfection do not return to rebirth which is impermanent (and) a house of miseries.

Sloka 16

ā brahmabhuvanāl lokāḥ punarāvartinorjuna
mām upetya tu kaunteya punarjanma na vidyate

abrahma bhuvanah = including the world of Brahma; lokah = worlds; punahravartinah = recurring, recreated again and again; arjuna = O Arjuna; mam = to Me; upetya = after coming; tu = but; kaunteya = O son of Kunti; punah janma = rebirth; na = not; vidyate = there is.

"The worlds, including the world of Brahma, are recreated again and again, O Arjuna; but after coming to Me, O son of Kunti, there is no rebirth.

Sloka 17

sahasrayugaparyantam ahar yad brahmaṇo viduḥ
rātriṃ yugasahasrāntāṃ te.ahorātravido janāḥ

sahasra = thousand; yuga = yugas, great epochs; paryantam = until, up to the end; ahah = day; yat = that; brahmanah = of Brahma; viduh = they know; ratrim = night; yuga = great epochs; sahasra-antam = at the end of thousand; te = that; ahah-ratra = day and night; vidah = understand; janah = people.

"The people who know the day of Brahma lasting until a thousand great epochs, and the night lasting until a thousand great epochs, they know the Day and Night of Brahma.

Sloka 18

avyaktād vyaktayaḥ sarvāḥ prabhavanty aharāgame
rātryāgame pralīyante tatraivāvyaktasaṃjñake

avyaktat = the unmanifested; vyaktayah = manifested things; sarvah = all; prabhavanti = come into existence; ahah-agame = at the dawn of the day; ratri-agame = at the approach of night; praliyante = they all dissolve; tatra = in that ; eva = only; avyakta = the unmanifested; samjnake = which is known as.

"From the unmanifested all manifested things come into existence at the dawn of the day. At the approach of night, they all dissolve dissolved in that only which is known as the unmanifested.

Sloka 19

bhūtagrāmaḥ sa evāyaṃ bhūtvā bhūtvā pralīyate
rātryāgamevaśaḥ pārtha prabhavaty aharāgame

bhuta-gramah = the multitude of beings; sah = that; eva = very; ayam = this; bhutva bhutva = having taken birth again and again; praliyate = become dissolved; ratri = night; agame = at the approach of; avasah = helplessly, ; partha = O Partha; prabhavati = they manifest; ahah agame = upon the arrival of the day.

"That very multitude of beings, having taken birth again and again, becomes dissolved helplessly at the approach of night. O Partha, upon the arrival of the day, they manifest again.

Sloka 20

paras tasmāt tu bhāvonyovyaktovyaktāt sanātanaḥ
yaḥ sa sarveṣu bhūteṣu naśyatsu na vinaśyati

parah = distinct,; tasmat = from that; tu = but; bhavah = being, state; anyah = another; avyaktah = unmanifested; avyaktat = from the unmanifested; sanatanah = eternal; yah = who; sah = alone; sarvesu = all; bhutesu = beings; nasyatsu = being destroyed; na vinasyati = remains indestructible.

"But distinct from that unmanifested is another eternal unmanifested Being, who is alone remains indestructible when all beings are destroyed.

Sloka 21

avyaktokṣara ity uktas tam āhuḥ paramāṃ gatim
yaṃ prāpya na nivartante tad dhāma paramaṃ mama

avyaktah = unmanifested; aksarah = indestructible; iti = thus; uktah = it is described; tam = which; ahuh = they extol; paramam = the highest; gatim = Goal; yam = which; prapya = gaining; na = never; nivartante = return; tat dhama = that sacred abode; paramam = supreme; mama = Mine.

"Unmanifested, the indestructible, thus it is described, which they extol as the highest Goal, by gaining which one never returns. That supreme sacred abode is Mine.

Sloka 22

puruṣaḥ sa paraḥ pārtha bhaktyā labhyas tv ananyayā
yasyāntaḥsthāni bhūtāni yena sarvam idaṃ tatam

purusah = Purusha; sah = That; parah = the Highest, Supreme,; partha = O Partha; bhaktya = by devotion; labhyah = attained, achieved; tu = indeed; ananyaya = unwavering; yasya = whom; antah-sthani = established within; bhutani = all beings; yena = by whom; sarvam = all; idam = this; tatam = extended, spread out, pervaded.

"O Partha, indeed That Supreme Being is attained by devotion, who is without any other, in whom are established beings, by whom all this is pervaded.

Sloka 23

yatra kāle tv anāvṛttim āvṛttiṃ caiva yoginaḥ
prayātā yānti taṃ kālaṃ vakṣyāmi bharatarṣabha

yatra kale = that time when; tu = now; anavrttim = do not return; avrttim = return; ca = and; eva = also; yoginah = of yogis; prayatah = departing; yanti = after going forth; tam kalam = that time when; vaksyami = I will declare; bharatarsabha = O best of the Bharatas.

"O best of the Bharatas, I will now declare that time when departing the yogis do not return and that time when going forth they return.

Sloka 24

agnir jotir ahaḥ śuklaḥ ṣaṇmāsā uttarāyaṇam
tatra prayātā gacchanti brahma brahmavido janāḥ

agnih = fire; jyotih = light; ahah = day; suklah = the waxing period of the moon, the bright fortnight, new moon to full moon; sanmasah uttara-ayanam = the northern solastice; tatra = by that path; prayatah

= having departed; gacchanti = attain; brahma = Brahman; brahma-vidah = who are knowers of Brahman; janah = persons.

Fire, light, daytime, the waxing period of the moon, the six months when the sun is in the northern hemisphere, having departed by that Path, people who are knowers of Brahman attain Brahman.

Sloka 25

dhūmo rātris tathā kṛṣṇaḥ ṣaṇmāsā dakṣiṇāyanam
tatra cāndramasaṃ jyotir yogī prāpya nivartate

dhumah = smoke; ratrih = night; tatha = also; krsnah = the waning period of the moon, the dark fortnight from full moon to new moon; sat-masah daksina-ayanam = the southern solatice; tatra = by that path; candra-masam = the world of moon light; jyotih = light; yogi = the mystic; prapya = gained; nivartate = returns.

"Smoke, night, the waning period of the moon, the southern solstice or the six months when the sun is in the southern hemisphere, by that path the yogi attains the world of moonlight and returns.

Sloka 26

śuklakṛṣṇe gatī hy ete jagataḥ śāśvate mate
ekayā yāty anāvṛttim anyayāvartate punaḥ

sukla = white; krsne = black; gati = paths; hi = surely; ete = these two; jagatah = of the world; sasvate = eternal; mate = considered; ekaya = by the one; yati = an ascetic, the self-restrained; anavrttim = not return; anyaya = by the other; avartate = return; punah = again.

"White and black, these two are surely considered the eternal paths of the world; by the one a self-restrained ascetic does not to return and by the other returns again.

Sloka 27

naite sṛtī pārtha jānan yogī muhyati kaścana
tasmāt sarveṣu kāleṣu yogayukto bhavārjuna

na = not; ete = these two; srti = paths; partha = O Partha; janan = knowing; yogi =yogi; muhyati = deluded; kascana = whosoever; tasmat = therefore; sarvesu kalesu = at all times; yoga-yuktah = established in yoga, or absorbed in yoga; bhava = be, remain; arjuna = O Arjuna.

"Knowing these two paths, O Partha, no yogi whosoever is deluded. Therefore, at all times remain established in yoga O Arjuna.

Sloka 28

vedeṣu yajñeṣu tapaḥsu caiva dāneṣu yat puṇyaphalaṃ pradiṣṭam
atyeti tat sarvam idaṃ viditvā yogī paraṃ sthānam upaiti cādyam

vedesu = from study of the Vedas; yajnesu = the sacrificial rituals; tapahsu = the austerities; ca = and; eva = surely; danesu = giving alms, charity; yat = that; punya-phalam = the fruit of good deeds; pradistam = implied; atyeti = surpasses, goes beyond; tat = those; sarvam idam = all this; viditva = knowing; yogi = the yogi; param = supreme; sthanam = Place; upaiti = achieves; ca = also; adyam = first, foremost, primal, ancient.

"Knowing all this the yogi goes beyond the fruit of the good deeds arising from the study of the Vedas, sacrificial the rituals, austerities and charities, and attains the Highest State which is also the foremost.

Conclusion

iti srīmadbhāgavadgītāsupanisatsu brahmavidyāyām yogasāstre
srikrisnārjunasamvāde jnānavijnānayogo nāma ashtamo 'dhyayah

iti = thus; srīmadbhāgavadgītā = in the sacred Bhagavadgita; upanisatsu = in the Upanishad; brahmavidyāyām = the knowledge of the absolute Brahman; yogasāstre = the scripture of yoga; srikrisnārjunasamvāde = the dialogue between Sri Krishna and

Arjuna; akṣarabrahmayogo nāma = by name yoga of Imperishable Brahman; ashtama = eighth; adhyayah = chapter.

Thus ends the eighth chapter named Yoga of Imperishable Brahman in the Upanishad of the divine Bhagavadgita, the knowledge of the Absolute, the yogic scripture, and the debate between Arjuna and Lord Krishna.

9 – The Yoga of Sovereign Knowledge and Mystery

Sloka 1

idaṃ tu te guhyatamaṃ pravakṣyāmy anasūyave
jñānaṃ vijñānasahitaṃ yaj jñātvā mokṣyaseśubhāt

sri-bhagavan uvaca = the Lord Supreme said; idam = this; tu = however; te = to you; guhya-tamam = the utmost secret; pravaksyami = I will speak; anasuyave = who are not envious; jnanam higher knowledge; vijnana = lower knowledge; sahitam = together; yat = which; jnatva = knowing; moksyase = you will be liberated; asubhat = from the inauspicious and impure.

"The Lord Supreme said, "However, to you who is not envious of Me, I will speak about this utmost secret, the higher knowledge and the lower knowledge, knowing which you will be liberated from the inauspicious and impure (existence).

Sloka 2

rājavidyā rājaguhyaṃ pavitram idam uttamam
pratyakṣāvagamaṃ dharmyaṃ susukhaṃ kartumavyayam

raja-vidya = sovereign knowledge; raja-guhyam = sovereign secret; pavitram = sacred, sanctifying; idam = this; uttamam = supreme, the best; pratyaksa = directly; avagamam = knowable; dharmyam = righteous; su-sukham = blissful; kartum = doable, or practicable; avyayam = inexhaustible.

"This sovereign knowledge, sovereign secret, is sacred, supreme, directly knowable, righteous, blissful, practicable and inexhaustible.

Sloka 3

aśraddadhānāḥ puruṣā dharmasyāsya paraṃtapa
aprāpya māṃ nivartante mṛtyusaṃsāravartmani

asraddadhanah = insincere, devoid of faith, skeptical; purusah = people; dharmasya = in this righteous knowledge; asya = of it; parantapa = O killer of the enemies; aprapya = without attainimg; mam = Me; nivartante = return; mrtyu = mortal, death; samsara = phenomenal existence; vartmani = the path of.

"People who have no faith in this righteous knowledge of it, O destroyer of the enemies, without attaining Me, return to the path of mortal, phenomenal existence

Sloka 4

mayā tatam idaṃ sarvaṃ jagad avyaktamūrtinā
matsthāni sarvabhūtāni na cāhaṃ teṣv avasthitaḥ

maya = by Me; tatam = pervaded; idam = this; sarvam = whole; jagat = material universe; avyakta-murtina = unmanifested form; mat-sthani = exist in Me; sarva-bhutani = all beings; na = not; ca = and; aham = I; tesu = in them; avasthitah = exist.

"This whole material universe is pervaded by Me in My unmanifested form. All beings exist in Me, but I do not exist in them.

Sloka 5

na ca matsthāni bhūtāni paśya me yogam aiśvaram
bhūtabhṛn na ca bhūtastho mamātmā bhūtabhāvanaḥ

na = not; ca = and; mat-sthani = dwell in Me; bhutani = beings and things; pasya = see; me = My; yogam = yoga of action; aisvaram = majestic, supreme, royal; bhuta-bhrt = I am the upholder of all beings and things; na = not; ca = but; bhuta-sthah = present in the material things; mama = My; atma = Self; bhuta-bhavanah = the source of beings.

"The beings and things do not dwell in Me. See My Supreme Yoga! I am the Upholder of all beings and things, but I am not present in them. I Myself am the source of all beings.

Sloka 6

yathākāśasthito nityaṃ vāyuḥ sarvatrago mahān
tathā sarvāṇi bhūtāni matsthānīty upadhāraya

yatha = justas; akasa-sthitah = existing in the space; nityam = always; vayuh = wind; sarvatra-gah = travels everywhere; mahan = mighty, great; tatha = in the same manner; sarvani = all; bhutani = things and beings; mat-sthani = situated in Me; iti = thus; upadharaya = you should know.

"Just as the mighty wind travels everywhere existing in the space, in the same manner all things and beings are situated in Me. You should know thus.

Sloka 7

sarvabhūtāni kaunteya prakṛtiṃ yānti māmikām
kalpakṣaye punas tāni kalpādau visṛjāmy aham

sarva-bhutani = all things and being; kaunteya = O son of Kunti; prakrtim = Prakriti, Nature; yanti = enter, go; mamikam = My; kalpa-ksaye = at the end of the kalpa, the time cycle, the day of Brahma; punah = again; tani = them; kalpa-adau = at the beginning of the time cycle, kalpa; visrjami = I create, project, bring forth; aham = I.

"O son of Kunti, at the end of each time cycle, all things and beings enter my Nature. Again, at the beginning of each time cycle I bring them forth.

Sloka 8

prakṛtiṃ svām avaṣṭabhya visṛjāmi punaḥ punaḥ
bhūtagrāmam imaṃ kṛtsnam avaśaṃ prakṛter vaśāt

prakrtim = Nature; svam = My; avastabhya = under control; visrjami = I bring forth; punah punah = repeatedly again, again; bhuta-gramam = the mulitude of things and beings; imam = this; krtsnam = the whole; avasam = helplessly; prakrteh = by Nature; vasat = held under its control.

"Holding My Nature under Control I bring forth repeatedly the whole multitude of things and beings, who are powerlessly held by Nature under its control

Sloka 9

na ca māṃ tāni karmāṇi nibadhnanti dhanaṃjaya
udāsīnavad āsīnam asaktaṃ teṣu karmasu

na = not; ca = and; mam = Me; tani = these; karmani = actions; nibadhnanti = bind; dhananjaya = O conqueror of riches; udasina-vat = indifferent, unconcerned, passive; asinam = remaining; asaktam = disinterested, unattached; tesu = in those; karmasu = actions

"And these actions do not bind Me, O conqueror of riches, (as I am) indifferent and unattached to those actions.

Sloka 10

mayādhyakṣeṇa prakṛtiḥ sūyate sacarācaram
hetunānena kaunteya jagad viparivartate

maya = under My; adhyaksena = supervision, watchful observation; prakrtih = Nature; suyate = manifests; sa = with; cara-acaram = moving and the nonmoving things; hetuna = because anena = of this; kaunteya = O son of Kunti; jagat = the whole world, manifest universe; viparivartate = revolves.

"Under my watchful observation, Nature brings forth both the moving and the nonmoving things. Because of this only the whole world revolves

Sloka 11

avajānanti māṃ mūḍhā mānuṣīṃ tanum āśritam
paraṃ bhāvam ajānanto mama bhūtamaheśvaram

avajananti = disregard, disrespect; mam = Me; mudhah manusim = foolish people lacking in intelligence; tanum = body; asritam = residing; param = supreme, transcendental; bhavam = state, nature; ajanantah = not knowing; mama = My; bhuta = beings; maha-isvaram = the supreme Lord of.

"Foolish people who lack intelligence disrespect Me when I reside in the physical body, not knowing My Supreme State as the Supreme Lord of all beings.

Sloka 12

moghāśā moghakarmāṇo moghajñānā vicetasaḥ
rākṣasīm āsurīṃ caiva prakṛtiṃ mohinīṃ śritāḥ

mogha-asah = vain hopes; mogha-karmanah = useless rites; mogha-jnanah = purposeless knowledge; vicetasah = senseless, mindless; raksasim = demonic; asurim = evil; ca = and; eva = surely; prakrtim = nature; mohinim = deceitful; sritah = take shelter.

"With vain hopes, useless rites, purposeless knowledge, they take refuge in senseless, demonic, evil and deceitful nature

Sloka 13

mahātmānas tu māṃ pārtha daivīṃ prakṛtim āśritāḥ
bhajanty ananyamanaso jñātvā bhūtādim avyayam

maha-atmanah = the great souls; tu = but; mam = o Me; partha = O Partha; daivim = divine; prakrtim = nature; asritah =taking refuge; bhajanti = worship; ananya-manasah = without any distraction; jnatva = knowing Me; bhuta adim = the source of all beings; avyayam = inexhaustible.

"But the great souls, O Partha, worship Me only without any distraction, knowing Me as the inexhaustible source of all beings.

Sloka 14

satataṃ kīrtayanto māṃ yatantaś ca dṛḍhavratāḥ
namasyantaś ca māṃ bhaktyā nityayuktā upāsate

satatam = always; kirtayantah = speaking high; mam = Me; yatantah = striving; ca = and; drdha-vratah = with firm vows; namasyantah = offering obeisance; ca = and; mam = Me; bhaktya = with devotion; nitya-yuktah = ever absorbed yogi; upasate = worship.

"Always praising Me, and striving with firm vows, also offering obeisance with devotion, the ever absorbed yogi worships Me.

Sloka 15

jñānayajñena cāpy anye yajanto mām upāsate
ekatvena pṛthaktvena bahudhā viśvatomukham

jnana = knowledge; yajnena = by the sacrifice; ca =and; api = alone; anye = others; yajantah = sacrificial worship; mam = Me; upasate = adoring, meditating; ekatvena = as one; prthaktvena = as distinct; bahudha = as many; visvatah-mukham =with faces everywhere.

"Others worship Me by the sacrifice of knowledge alone, meditating upon Me as One, as distinct, and as many with numerous faces everywhere.

Sloka 16

ahaṃ kratur ahaṃ yajñaḥ svadhāham aham auṣadham
mantro.aham aham evājyam aham agnir ahaṃ hutam

aham = I; kratuh = kratu; aham = I; yajnah = yajna; svadha = svadha; aham = I; aham = I; ausadham = medicine; mantrah = mantra, sacred chant; aham = I; aham = I; eva = certainly; ajyam = fuel, melted butter; aham = I; agnih = fire; aham = I; hutam = burnt offering.

"I am kratu, I am yajna, I am svadha, I am medicine, I am the sacred chant, I am the clarified butter, I am Agni and I am the burnt offering.

Sloka 17

pitāham asya jagato mātā dhātā pitāmahaḥ
vedyaṃ pavitram oṃkāra ṛk sāma yajur eva ca

pita = father; aham = I; asya = of this; jagatah = universe; mata = mother; dhata = supporter; pitamahah = grandfather; vedyam = to be known; pavitram = sacred, pure; om-kara = symbol of Aum; rk = the Rg Veda; sama = the Sama Veda; yajuh = the Yajur Veda; eva = certainly; ca = and.

"I am the Father this universe, the Mother, the Supporter, the Grand Father, the One to be known, the symbol of Aum, surely the Rigveda, the Sama Veda, the Yajurveda and (the Atharvaveda).

Sloka 18

gatir bhartā prabhuḥ sākṣī nivāsaḥ śaraṇaṃ suhṛt
prabhavaḥ pralayaḥ sthānaṃ nidhānaṃ bījam avyam

gatih = goal; bharta = the husband; prabhuh = Lord; saksi = the witness; nivasah = the abode; saranam = the refuge; su-hrt = the friend or lover; prabhavah = the origin or source; pralayah = dissolution; sthanam = the foundation; nidhanam = the source of abundance, treasure chest, the store house; bijam = the seed; avyayam = imperishable.

"I am the Goal, the Husband, the Lord, the Witness, the Abode, the Refuge, the Friend, the Origin, the Dissolution, the Foundation, the Source of all abundance, the Imperishable Seed.

Sloka 19

tapāmy aham ahaṃ varṣaṃ nigṛṇhāmy utsṛjāmi ca
amṛtaṃ caiva mṛtyuś ca sad asac cāham arjuna

tapami = provider of the heat; aham = I; aham = I; varsam = rain; nigrhnami = stop, restrain; utsrjami = send down; ca = and; amrtam = immortality; ca = and; eva = certainly; mrtyuh = death; ca = and; sat = existence, being; asat = nonbeing, non-existence; ca = and; aham = I; arjuna = O Arjuna.

"The source of heat I am. I restrain and release rain; O Arjuna. certainly, I am death and immortality, existence and non-existence.

Sloka 20

traividyā māṃ somapāḥ pūtapāpā yajñair iṣṭvā svargatiṃ prārthayante

te puṇyam āsādya surendralokaṃ aśnanti divyān divi devabhogān

trai-vidyah = the knowers of the triple Vedas; mam = to Me; soma-pah = drinkers of soma; puta papah = purified of sins; yajnaih = with sacrifices; istva = worshiping; svah-gatim = the goal of heaven; prarthayante = pray for; te = they; punyam = merit; asadya = having reached; sura-indra = of great god Indra; lokam = the world; asnanti = enjoy; divyan = celestial; divi = divine; deva-bhogan = heavenly pleasures.

"The knowers of the triple Vedas, drinkers of Soma, purified of their sins, worship Me with sacrifices, praying for heavenly goal. Having reached the world of the great god Indra, (by virtue of) merit, they enjoy divine and heavenly pleasures.

Sloka 21

te taṃ bhuktvā svargalokaṃ viśālaṃ kṣīṇe puṇye martyalokaṃ viśanti
evaṃ trayīdharmam anuprapannā gatāgataṃ kāmakāmā labhante

te = they; tam = that; bhuktva = having enjoyed; svarga-lokam = heavenly world; visalam = vast; ksine = being exhausted; punye = their merits; martya-lokam = mortal world; visanti = reenter, fall down; evam = thus; trayi = in the three Vedas; dharmam = religious duties; anuprapannah = following sincerely; gata-agatam = going and coming, death and rebirth; kama-kamah = desiring enjoyments; labhante – they attain.

"Having enjoyed that vast heavenly world (and) exhausted their merit, they reenter the mortal world. Thus following the religious duties prescribed in the three Vedas and seeking enjoyment, they attain the state of going and coming.

Sloka 22

ananyāś cintayanto māṃ ye janāḥ paryupāsate
teṣāṃ nityābhiyuktānāṃ yogakṣemaṃ vahāmy aham

ananyah = without any other; cintayantah = thoughts; mam = Me; ye = who; janah = people; paryupasate = worship everywhere; tesam = their; nitya = at all times, always; abhiyuktanam = absorbed in devotion; yoga-ksemam = welfare; vahami = take care; aham = I.

"The people who worship Me everywhere and at all times without any other thoughts, ever absorbed in devotion, I take care of their welfare.

Sloka 23

yepy anyadevatābhaktā yajante śraddhayānvitāḥ
tepi mām eva kaunteya yajanty avidhipūrvakam

ye = those; api = even; anya = of other; devata = dinvinities; bhaktah = devotees; yajante = worship; sraddhaya anvitah = endowed with faith; te = they; api = also; mam = Me; eva = only; kauntey a = O son of Kunti; yajanti = worship; avidhi-purvakam = ignorantly or in an inappropriate manner.

"Even the devotees who worship other divinities endowed with faith, they also worship Me only, O son of Kunti, (although) in an inappropriate manner.

Sloka 24

ahaṃ hi sarvayajñānāṃ bhoktā ca prabhur eva ca
na tu mām abhijānanti tattvenātaś cyavanti te

aham = I am; hi = indeed; sarva = of all; yajnanam = sacrifices; bhokta = enjoyer; ca = and; prabhuh = the Lord; eva = even; ca = and; na = not; tu = but; mam = Me; abhijananti = know; tattvena = in eternal aspect, in reality; atah = therefore; cyavanti = fall; te = they.

"I am indeed the enjoyer and the Lord of all sacrifices; but they do not know Me in My eternal aspect. Therefore, they fall.

Sloka 25

yānti devavratā devān pitṛn yānti pitṛvratāḥ
bhūtāni yānti bhūtejyā yānti madyājinopi mām

yanti = achieve; deva-vratah = the worshipers of divinities; devan = to the divinities; pitrn = to ancestors; yanti = go; pitr-vratah = worshipers of the ancestors; bhutani = to spirit world; yanti = go; bhuta-ijyah = worshipers of spirits; yanti = go; mat = My; yajinah = devotees; api = only; mam = to Me.

"The worshippers of the divinities go to the divinities; the worshippers of the ancestors go to the ancestors; the worshippers of spirits go to the spirit world. My devotees come to Me only.

Sloka 26

patraṃ puṣpaṃ phalaṃ toyaṃ yo me bhaktyāprayacchati
tad ahaṃ bhaktyupahṛtam aśnāmi prayatātmanaḥ

patram = a leaf; puspam = a flower; phalam = a fruit; toyam = water; yah = whoever; me = to Me; bhaktya = with devotion; prayacchati = offers; tat = that; aham = I; bhakti-upahrtam = offer made in devotion; asnami = accept; prayata = pious, holy, pure ; atmanah = of the soul.

"Whoever offers Me with devotion a leaf, a flower, a fruit, water, I accept that offer of the pure soul made in devotion

Sloka 27

yat karoṣi yad aśnāsi yaj juhoṣi dadāsi yat
yat tapasyasi kaunteya tat kuruṣva madarpaṇam

yat = whatever; karosi = you do; yat = whatever; asnasi = you eat; yat = whatever; juhosi = sacrificial offering you make; dadasi = you give as charity; yat = whatever; yat = whatever; tapasyasi = austerities you perform; kaunteya = O son of Kunti; tat = that; kurusva = do; mat = to Me; arpanam = offer.

"Whatever you do, whatever you eat, whatever sacrificial offering you make, whatever you give as charity, whatever austerities you perform, O son of Kunti, offer that to Me.

Sloka 28

śubhāśubhaphalair evaṃ mokṣyase karmabandhanaiḥ
saṃnyāsayogayuktātmā vimukto mām upaiṣyasi

subha = good, auspicious; asubha = evil, inauspicious; phalaih = fruit; evam = thus; moksyase = you become liberated; karma bandhanaih = bondage caused by actions; sannyasa = renunciation; yoga = yoga; yukta-atma = with the mind established; vimuktah = liberated; mam = to Me; upaisyasi = will attain, come.

"Thus you become liberated from the bondage caused by the fruit of both good and bad actions. With your mind established in the yoga of renunciation and becoming liberated, you will come to Me.

Sloka 29

samohaṃ sarvabhūteṣu na me dveṣyosti na priyaḥ
ye bhajanti tu māṃ bhaktyā mayi te teṣu cāpy aham

samah = equal; aham = I am; sarva-bhutesu = to all being; na = none; me = to Me; dvesyah = hateful; asti = is; na = none; priyah = dear; ye = those; bhajanti = worship; tu = yet; mam = to Me; bhaktya = in devotion; mayi =exist in Me; te = they; tesu = in them; ca = also; api = certainly; aham = I.

"I am equal to all beings. None is hateful to Me, none is dear. Those who worship Me with devotion, they exist in Me and I exist in them.

Sloka 30

api cet sudurācāro bhajate mām ananyabhāk
sādhur eva sa mantavyaḥ samyag vyavasito hi saḥ

api = even; cet = if; su-duracarah = a person of very evil conduct; bhajate = worship; mam = Me; ananya-bhak = without distraction; sadhuh = good, pious; eva = surely; sah = he; mantavyah = to be considered; samyak = rightly; vyavasitah = positioned in life; hi =for; sah = he.

"Even if a person of very evil conduct worships Me with single minded devotion, surely he is to be considered pious because he has rightly positioned himself in life.

Sloka 31

kṣipraṃ bhavati dharmātmā śaśvacchāntiṃnigacchhati
kaunteya pratijānīhi na me bhaktaḥ praṇaśyati

ksipram = promptly, quickly; bhavati = becomes; dharma-atma = pious soul, a person of righteous conduct; sasvat-santim = everlasting peace; nigacchati = attains; kaunteya = O son of Kunti; pratijanihi = know for certain; na = never; me = My; bhaktah = devotees; pranasyati = perishe.

"Very quickly he becomes a person of righteous conduct and attains everlasting peace; O son of Kunti know for sure that My devotee shall never perish.

Sloka 32

māṃ hi pārtha vyapāśritya yepi syuḥ pāpayonayaḥ
striyo vaiśyās tathā śūdrās tepi yānti parāṃ gatim

mam = Me; hi = surely; partha = O Partha; vyapasritya = by taking shelter; ye = who; api = even; syuh = becomes; papa-yonayah = sinful wombs; striyah = women; vaisyah = vaisyas; tatha = and; sudrah = sudras; te api = even; yanti = go; param = highest; gatim = Goal.

"Surely O Partha, by taking shelter in Me, even those who are born from sinful wombs, women, vaisyas, and sudras, even they reach the highest Goal.

Sloka 33

kiṃ punar brāhmaṇāḥ puṇyā bhaktā rājarṣayas tathā
anityam asukhaṃ lokam imaṃ prāpya bhajasva mām

kim = how much, what to say; punah = again; brahmanah = brahmanas; punyah = meritorious, virtuous; bhaktah = devoted; raja-rsayah = saintly kings; tatha = and; anityam = transient; asukham =

sorrowful; lokam = world; imam = this; prapya = gaining; bhajasva = worship; mam = Me.

"What to say again about the virtuous brahmanas and the devoted saintly kings? Having gained this impermanent and miserable world, worship Me you should.

Sloka 34

manmanā bhava madbhakto madyājī māṃ namaskuru
mām evaiṣyasi yuktvaivam ātmānaṃ matparāyaṇaḥ

mat-manah bhava = with your mind absorbed in My state; mat = to Me; bhaktah = devoted; mat = to Me; yaji = making sacrifices; mam = to Me; namaskuru = bow with folded hands; mam = to Me; eva = certainly; esyasi = come; yuktva = being absorbed; evam = thus; atmanam = within the Self; mat-parayanah = Me as the supreme Goal.

"With your mind absorbed in My thoughts, **be devoted to Me; make sacrifices to Me; (and) bow** down **to Me with folded hands. Being absorbed thus** in **your Self, you will certainly come to Me, who is your Supreme Goal.**

Conclusion

iti srīmadbhāgavadgītāsupanisatsu brahmavidyāyām yogasāstre
srikrisnārjunasamvāde rājavidyārājaguhyayogo nāma navamo 'dhyayah

iti = thus; srīmadbhāgavadgītā = in the sacred Bhagavadgita; upanisatsu = in the Upanishad; brahmavidyāyām = the knowledge of the absolute Brahman; yogasāstre = the scripture of yoga; srikrisnārjunasamvāde = the dialogue between Sri Krishna and Arjuna; rājavidyārājaguhyayogo nāma = by name yoga of sovereign knowledge and sovereign mystery; navama = ninth; adhyayah = chapter.

Thus ends the ninth chapter named Yoga of Sovereign Knowledge and Sovereign Mystery in the Upanishad of the divine Bhagavadgita, the knowledge of the Absolute, the

yogic scripture, and the debate between Arjuna and Lord Krishna.

10 – The Yoga of Divine Manifestations

Sloka 1

śrībhagavānuvāca
bhūya eva mahābāho śṛṇu me paramaṃ vacaḥ
yat tehaṃ prīyamāṇāya vakṣyāmi hitakāmyayā

sri-bhagavan uvaca = The Divine Lord said; bhuyah = again; eva = indeed; maha-baho = O mighty-armed; srnu = listen, hear; me = to My; paramam = very excellent, exalted, transcendental; vacah = words; yat = which; te = to you; aham = I; priyamanaya =who is deeply interested; vaksyami = speak; hita-kamyaya = wishing your welfare.

"Said the Supreme Lord, "O mighty armed, listen again to My very excellent words, Which I, speak to you wishing your welfare, who take delight in them.

Sloka 2

na me viduḥ suragaṇāḥ prabhavaṃ na maharṣayaḥ
aham ādir hi devānāṃ maharṣīṇāṃ ca sarvaśaḥ

na = not; me = My; viduh = know; sura-ganah = the multitude of gods; prabhavam = origin; na = not; maha-rsayah = great seers; aham = I am; adih = first, the root, the source; hi = certainly; devanam = of the gods; maha-rsinam = of the great seers; ca = and; sarvasah = in all respects.

"The gods do not know My origin, nor do the great seers. In all respects, I am certainly the first among the gods and the great seers.

Sloka 3

yo mām ajam anādiṃ ca vetti lokamaheśvaram
asaṃmūḍhaḥ sa martyeṣu sarvapāpaiḥ pramucyate

yah = who; mam = Me; ajam = unborn; anadim = without a beginning; ca = and; vetti = knows; loka maha-isvaram = Supreme Lord of the worlds; asammudhah = one who is not deluded; sah = he; martyesu =

among the mortals; sarva-papaih = from all sins; pramucyate = is freed.

"Who knows Me as unborn, without a beginning, Lord of the worlds, he is the one among the mortals who is not deluded and who is free from all sins.

Sloka 4

buddhir jñānam asaṃmohaḥ kṣamā satyaṃ damaḥśamaḥ
sukhaṃ duḥkhaṃ bhavobhāvo bhayaṃ cābhayam evaca

buddhih = intelligence; jnanam = knowledge of Brahman; asammohah = freedom from delusion; ksama = forgiveness; satyam = truthfulness; damah = control of the senses; samah = control of the mind, equanimity; sukham = pleasure; duhkham = pain, sorrow; bhavah = existence, birth; abhavah = non-existence, death; bhayam = fear; abhayam = fearlessness; eva = even; ca = and.

"Intelligence, knowledge, freedom from delusion, forgiveness, truthfulness, control of the senses, control of the mind, pleasure, pain, birth, death, and even fear and fearlessness...

Sloka 5

ahiṃsā samatā tuṣṭis tapo dānaṃ yaśoyaśaḥ
bhavanti bhāvā bhūtānāṃ matta eva pṛthagvidhāḥ

ahimsa = nonviolence; samata = equanimity; tustih = contentment; tapah = austerity; danam = charity; yasah = fame; ayasah = infamy, illrepute; bhavanti = happen; bhavah = states; bhutanam = in living beings; mattah = because of Me; eva = only; prthak-vidhah = different types.

"Non-violence, equanimity, contentment, austerity, charity, fame, infamy, these different types of states arise in beings because of Me only.

Sloka 6

maharṣayaḥ sapta pūrve catvāro manavas tathā
madbhāvā mānasā jātā yeṣāṃ loka imāḥ prajāḥ

maha-rsayah = the great seers; sapta = seven; purve = before; catvarah = four; manavah = Manus; tatha = and; mat-bhavah = born of Me; manasah = from My Mind; jatah = were born; yesam = of whom; loke = on the world; imah = these; prajah = beings.

"The seven great seers, and the four Manus before them were born out of My Mind; from them were born all these beings of the world.

Sloka 7

etāṃ vibhūtiṃ yogaṃ ca mama yo vetti tattvataḥ
sovikampena yogena yujyate nātra saṃśayaḥ

etam = this; vibhutim = power, might, manifestations; yogam = divine powers; ca = and; mama = My; yah = he who; vetti = knows; tattvatah = in truth, in reality; sah = he; avikampena = steadfast, unwavering, without wavering; yogena = in yoga; yujyate = absorbed, balanced; na = not; atra = of this, regarding this; samsayah = doubt.

"He who knows in truth My manifestations and divine powers, he becomes absorbed in steadfast yoga. Of this, there is no doubt.

Sloka 8

ahaṃ sarvasya prabhavo mattaḥ sarvaṃ pravartate
iti matvā bhajante māṃ budhā bhāvasamanvitāḥ

aham = I; sarvasya = of all; prabhavah = source, orign; mattah = because of Me; sarvam = all; pravartate = moves, issues forth; iti = thus; matva = knowing; bhajante = worship mam = Me; budhah = the wise; bhava-samanvitah = with intense fervor.

"I am the source of all; because of Me everything moves according to its nature. Knowing Me thus, the wise worship Me with intense fervor.

Sloka 9

maccittā madgataprāṇā bodhayantaḥ parasparam
kathayantaś ca māṃ nityaṃ tuṣyanti ca ramanti ca

mat-cittah = citta absorbed in Me; mat-gata-pranah = lives devoted to Me; bodhayantah = trying to know; parasparam = among themselves; kathayantah = speaking ca = and; mam = Me; nityam = always; tusyanti = contented; ca = and; ramanti = delightful, take deligh; ca = and.

"With their citta absorbed in Me, their lives devoted to Me, trying to know (about Me) from one another and always speaking about Me, they remain contented and delightful.

Sloka 10

teṣāṃ satatayuktānāṃ bhajatāṃ prītipūrvakam
dadāmi buddhiyogaṃ taṃ yena mām upayānti te 10.10

tesam = to them; satata-yuktanam = always absorbed or engaged; bhajatam = in devotional worship; priti-purvakam = with love, lovingly; dadami = I give; buddhi-yogam = state of wisdom, discriminating intelligence; tam = that; yena = by which; mam = to Me; upayanti = come; te = they.

"To them, who are ever absorbed in devotional worship with love, I give them that state of wisdom by which they come to Me.

Sloka 11

teṣām evānukampārtham aham ajñānajaṃ tamaḥ
nāśayāmy ātmabhāvastho jñānadīpena bhāsvatā

tesam = for them; eva = only; anukampa-artham = out of mercy, for the sake of compassion; aham = I; ajnana-jam = born out of ignorance; tamah = darkness; nasayami = remove, destroy; atma bhavasthah = residing in them as their own Self; jnana dipena = with the lamp of knowledge; bhasvata = instilling, shining, glowing.

"Only out of mercy for them, I remove their darkness born out of ignorance, residing in them as their own Self, shining lamp of knowledge."

Sloka 12

arjuna uvāca
paraṃ brahma paraṃ dhāma pavitraṃ paramaṃbhavān
puruṣaṃ śāśvataṃ divyam ādidevam ajaṃ vibhum

arjunah uvaca = Arjuna said; param = supreme; brahma = Brahman; param = supreme; dhama = abode, goal, light; pavitram = sacred; paramam = most; bhavan = you; purusam = person, being, purusa; sasvatam = permanent; divyam = divine; adi-devam = Primeval Lord; ajam = unborn; vibhum = the mightiest, the greatest.

"Said Arjuna, "You are the supreme Brahman, supreme Goal, the most sacred Being, who is Eternal, Divine, the Primeval God, Unborn (and) the Mightiest.

Sloka 13

āhus tvām ṛṣayaḥ sarve devarṣir nāradas tathā
asito devalo vyāsaḥ svayaṃ caiva bravīṣi me

ahuh = speak; tvam = of You; rsayah = seers; sarve = all; deva-rsih = the divine seers; naradah = Narada; tatha = also; asitah = Asita; devalah = Devala; vyasah = Vyasa; svayam = personally You; ca = and; eva = even; bravisi = speaking; me = to me.

"All the seers and the divine seers, Narada, so also Asita, Devala, and Vyasa speak of You; and even you are also personally speaking to me (the same).

Sloka 14

sarvam etad ṛtaṃ manye yan māṃ vadasi keśava
na hi te bhagavan vyaktiṃ vidur devā na dānavāḥ

sarvam = all; etat = this; rtam = true; manye = think, consider; yat = which; mam = me; vadasi = You have told; kesava = O Kesava; na = not; hi = surely; te = Your; bhagavan = blessed Lord; vyaktim =

personality, manifestation; viduh = know; devah = the gods; na = not; danavah = the danavas, demons.

"I consider true all this which you have told me, O Kesava; surely, O Blessed Lord, neither the gods nor the demons know Your manifestations.

Sloka 15

svayam evātmanātmānaṃ vettha tvaṃ puruṣottama
bhūtabhāvana bhūteśa devadeva jagatpate

svayam = Yourself; eva = alone; atmana = by Yourself; atmanam = in Yourself; vettha = know; tvam = You; purusa-uttama = O Supreme Person; bhuta-bhavana = O Creatpr of beings; bhuta-isa = O Lord of beings; deva-deva = O God of gods; jagat-pate = O Lord of the worlds.

"You alone know You by Yourself in Yourself, O Supreme Person, O Creator of beings, Lord of beings, God of gods and Lord of the worlds.

Sloka 16

vaktum arhasy aśeṣeṇa divyā hy ātmavibhūtayaḥ
yābhir vibhūtibhir lokān imāṃs tvaṃ vyāpya tiṣṭhasi

vaktum = tell; arhasi = be kind enough; asesena = in full, without any remainder; divyah = divine; hi = surely; atma = Your own; vibhutayah = manifestations; yabhih = by which; vibhutibhih = manifestations; lokan = worlds; iman = these; tvam = You; vyapya = pervading; tisthasi = being established within.

"Be kind enough to tell me in detail Your own manifestations, which are surely divine, by which manifestations you pervade these worlds, established within.

Sloka 17

kathaṃ vidyām ahaṃ yogiṃs tvāṃ sadā paricintayan
keṣu keṣu ca bhāveṣu cintyosi bhagavan mayā

katham = how; vidyam = know; aham = I shall; yogin = O supreme Yogi; tvam = You; sada = constantly; paricintayan = meditating; kesu

= in what; kesu = in what; ca = and; bhavesu = states; cintyah asi = You should be contemplated; bhagavan = O blessed Lord; maya = by me.

"How I may know you, O Supreme Yogi, constantly meditating and in which and which states You should be contemplated by me, O Blessed Lord?

Sloka 18

vistareṇātmano yogaṃ vibhūtiṃ ca janārdana
bhūyaḥ kathaya tṛptir hi śṛṇvato nāsti memṛtam

vistarena = in detail; atmanah = Your own; yogam = divine state; vibhutim = divine manifestations; ca = and; jana-ardana = O Janardana; bhuyah = again; kathaya = tell me, narrate me; trptih = satisfaction ; hi = certainly; srnvatah = listening, hearing; na asti = there is no; me = my; amrtam = immortal, sweet, liberating.

"In detail please tell me again your own divine state and manifestations, O Janardana. Certainly, for me there is no end to my satisfaction in listening to your sweet and liberating worlds."

Sloka 19

śrībhagavān uvāca
hanta te kathayiṣyāmi divyā hy ātmavibhūtayaḥ
prādhānyataḥ kuruśreṣṭha nāsty anto vistarasya me

sri-bhagavan uvaca = the Belssed Lord said; hanta = yes; te = to you; kathayisyami = I shall narrate; divyah = divine; hi = verily; atma-vibhutayah = My manifestations; pradhanyatah = important, chief, primary; kuru-srestha = O the best of the Kurus; na asti = there is no; antah = end; vistarasya = diversity, manifestations; me = My.

"The Lord Supreme said, "O best among the Kurus, I will narrate to you My most important manifestations that are truly divine. There is no end to My manifestations.

Commentary

The manifestations of the Supreme Self are infinite. Hence, Lord Krishna said that He would describe only a few. By addressing Arjuna as the best among the Kurus, He also hinted at why He decided to narrate them.

Sloka 20

aham ātmā guḍākeśa sarvabhūtāśayasthitaḥ
aham ādiś ca madhyaṃ ca bhūtānām anta eva ca

aham = I; atma = Self; gudakesa = O Gudakesa; sarva-bhuta = all beings; asaya-sthitah = situated within in the heart; aham = I am; adih = beginning; ca = and; madhyam = the middle; ca = and; bhutanam = beings; antah = end; eva = truly; ca = and.

"O Gudakesa, I am the Self residing in the heart of all beings. I am truly the beginning, the middle and the end (of them).

Sloka 21

ādityānām ahaṃ viṣṇur jyotiṣāṃ ravir aṃśumān
marīcir marutām asmi nakṣatrāṇām ahaṃ śaśī

adityanam = of the Adityas; aham = I am; visnuh = Vishnu; jyotisam = among the shining ones; ravih = the Sun; amsu-man = radiant; maricih = Marici; marutam = of the Maruts; asmi = I am; naksatranam = among stars; aham = I am; sasi = the moon.

"Among the Adityas, I am Vishnu; among the shining ones, I am the radiant Sun; among the Maruts, I am Marichi; among the starts, I am the moon.

Sloka 22

vedānāṃ sāmavedosmi devānām asmi vāsavaḥ
indriyāṇāṃ manaś cāsmi bhūtānām asmi cetanā

vedanam = among the Vedas; sama-vedah = the Sama Veda; asmi = I am; devanam = among the gods; asmi = I am; vasavah = Indra; indriyanam = among the senses; manah = the mind; ca = and; asmi = I am; bhutanam = among the beings; asmi = I am; cetana = life.

"Among the Vedas, I am the Samaveda; among the gods, I am Indra; among sense organs, I am the mind; and among the beings, I am the life.

Sloka 23

rudrāṇāṃ śaṃkaraś cāsmi vitteśo yakṣarakṣasām
vasūnāṃ pāvakaś cāsmi meruḥ śikhariṇām aham

rudranam = of the Rudras; sankarah = Lord Siva; ca = and; asmi = I am; vitta-isah = Kubera, the lord or treasures; yaksa-raksasam = among the Yaksas and Raksasas; vasunam = of the Vasus; pavakah = Pavaka; ca = and; asmi = I am; meruh = Meru; sikharinam = of the mountains; aham = I am.

"Of the Rudras, I am Siva; among the Yakshas and Rakshasas, I am Kubera, the lord of treasures; of the Vasus, I am Pavaka; and of the mountains, I am mount Meru.

Sloka 24

purodhasāṃ ca mukhyaṃ māṃ viddhi pārthabṛhaspatim
senānīnām ahaṃ skandaḥ sarasām asmi sāgaraḥ

purodhasam = of the priests; ca = and; mukhyam = foremost, renown; mam = Me; viddhi = know; partha = O Partha; brhaspatim = Brhaspati; senaninam = among commanders of the armies; aham = I am; skandah = Skanda; sarasam = among the great lakes; asmi = I am; sagarah = the ocean.

"O Partha among the chiefs priests, know that I am Brihaspati, among the commanders of armies, I am Skanda; and among the great lakes, I am the ocean.

Sloka 25

maharṣīṇāṃ bhṛgur ahaṃ girām asmy ekam akṣaram
yajñānāṃ japayajñosmi sthāvarāṇāṃ himālayaḥ

maha-rsinam = among the great seers; bhrguh = Bhrgu; aham = I am; giram = of the sounds; asmi = I am; ekam = one; aksaram = syllable Aum; yajnanam = of the sacrifices; japa-yajnah = sacrifice of chanting;

asmi = I am; sthavaranam = of the immovable things; himalayah = the Himalayas.

"Among the great seers, I am Bhrigu; among the sounds, I am the one syllable Aum; of the sacrifices, I am the sacrifice of chanting; among the immovable things, I am the Himalayas.

Sloka 26

aśvatthaḥ sarvavṛkṣāṇāṃ devarṣīṇāṃ ca nāradaḥ
gandharvāṇāṃ citrarathaḥ siddhānāṃ kapilo muniḥ

asvatthah = asvattha; sarva-vrksanam = among the trees; deva-rsinam = among the divine seers; ca = and; naradah = Narada; gandharvanam = among the gandharvas; citrarathah = Citraratha; siddhanam = among the perfect yogis; kapilah munih = Kapila Muni.

"Among the trees, I am the Asvattha tree; among the divine seers, I am sage Narada; among the gandharvas, I am Citraradha; and among the perfect yogis, I am sage Kapila.

Sloka 27

uccaiḥśravasam aśvānāṃ viddhi mām amṛtodbhavam
airāvataṃ gajendrāṇāṃ narāṇāṃ ca narādhipam

uccaihsravasam = Uccaihsrava; asvanam = among the horses; viddhi = know; mam = Me; amrtam = elixir or life; udbhavam = born from; airavatam = Airavata; gaja-indranam = kingly elephants; naranam = among human beings; ca = and; nara-adhipam = the king.

"Among the horses, Know Me as the Ucchasrva, which was born from the elixir of life; Airavata among the kingly elephants, and the ruler among the human beings

Sloka 28

āyudhānām ahaṃ vajraṃ dhenūnām asmi kāmadhuk
prajanaś cāsmi kandarpaḥ sarpāṇām asmi vāsukiḥ

ayudhanam = of the weapons; aham = I am; vajram = the thunderbolt; d hnunam = among th e cows; asmi = I am; kama-dhuk = the

Kamadhenu; prajanah = progenitors; ca = and; asmi = I am; kandarpah = Kandarpa; sarpanam = of the snakes; asmi = I am; vasukih = Vasuki.

"Of the weapons, I am the thunderbolt; among the cows, I am Kamadhenu; among the progenitors I am Kandarpa; and among the snakes, I am Vasuki.

Sloka 29

anantaś cāsmi nāgānāṃ varuṇo yādasām aham
pitṛṇām aryamā cāsmi yamaḥ saṃyamatām aham

anantah = Ananta; ca = and; asmi = I am; naganam = among the snakes; varunah = Varuna; yadasam = of the water divinities; aham = I am; pitrnam = of the ancestors; aryama = Aryama; ca = and; asmi = I am; yamah = Lord Yama; samyamatam = of the controllers; aham = I am.

"Among the snakes, I am Ananta; and Varuna among the water gods. Among the ancestors, I am Aryama; and among the controllers, I am Lord Yama.

Sloka 30

pralhādaś cāsmi daityānāṃ kālaḥ kalayatām aham
mṛgāṇāṃ ca mṛgendrohaṃ vainateyaś ca pakṣiṇām

prahladah = Prahlada; ca = and; asmi = I am; daityanam = among the demons; kalah = time; kalayatam = record keepers; aham = I am; mrganam = of the animals; ca = and; mrga-indrah = the king of animals, lion; aham = I am; vainateyah = Vainteya; ca = and; paksinam = of birds.

"I am Prahlada among the demons; and I am Time among the keepers of time; I am lion, the king of animals, among the animals; and among the birds, Vainteya.

Sloka 31

pavanaḥ pavatām asmi rāmaḥ śastrabhṛtām aham
jhaṣāṇāṃ makaraś cāsmi strotasām asmi jāhnavī

pavanah = the wind; pavatam = of the purifiers; asmi = I am; ramah = Lord Rama; sastra-bhrtam = among the wielders of weapons; aham = I am; jhasanam = among the fish; makarah = makara; ca = and; asmi = I am; srotasam = among the rivers; asmi = I am; jahnavi = Jahnavi.

"Among the purifiers, I am the wind; among the wielders of weapons, I am Lord Rama; among the fishes I am Makara; and among the rivers I am Jahnavi.

Sloka 32

sargāṇām ādir antaś ca madhyaṃ caivāham arjuna
adhyātmavidyā vidyānāṃ vādaḥ pravadatām aham

sarganam = of creations; adih = beginning; antah = end; ca = and; madhyam = middle; ca = and; eva = certainly; aham = I am; arjuna = O Arjuna; adhyatma-vidya = atma vidya, knowledge of the Self; vidyanam = of vidyas, branches of knowledge; vadah = pursuer of truth; pravadatam = debaters; aham = I am.

"O Arjuna, of the creations, I am the beginning, the middle and the end. Of the branches of knowledge, I am the knowledge of the Self. Among the debaters, I am the pursuer of truth.

Sloka 33

akṣarāṇām akārosmi dvandvaḥ sāmāsikasya ca
aham evākṣayaḥ kālo dhātāhaṃ viśvatomukhaḥ 10.33

aksaranam = among the letters; akarah = the first letter A; asmi = I am; dvandvah = dual compound, dvanda samas ; samasikasya = among the samasas, compound words; ca = and; aham = I am; eva = surely; aksayah = inexhaustible, unending; kalah = time; dhata = creator; aham = I am; visvatah-mukhah = faces in all directions..

"Among the letters, I am the first letter, a; and the dual compound among the compound words. I am surely the inexhaustible time; I am the creator, with faces in all directions

Sloka 34

mṛtyuḥ sarvaharaś cāham udbhavaś ca bhaviṣyatām
kīrtiḥ śrīr vāk ca nārīṇāṃ smṛtir medhā dhṛtiḥ kṣamā

mrtyuh = death; sarva-harah = all ending, removing; ca = and; aham = I am; udbhavah = origin; ca = and; bhavisyatam = of what happens in future; kirtih = fame; srih = beauty; vak = speech; ca = and; narinam = in women; smrtih = memory; medha = intelligence; dhrtih = fortitude; ksama = patience.

"I am the all ending death; and I am the origin of what happens in future. In women, I am fame, beauty, speech, memory intelligence, fortitude and patience.

Sloka 35

bṛhatsāma tathā sāmnāṃ gāyatrī chandasām aham
māsānāṃ mārgaśīrṣoham ṛtūnāṃ kusumākaraḥ

brhat-sama = the Brhat-sama; tatha = also; samnam = of the Sama chants; gayatri = the Gayatri; chandasam = of meters; aham = I am; masanam = of months; marga-sirsah = Margasirah, November-December; aham = I am; rtunam = of the seasons; kusuma-akarah = spring.

"I am also Brhatsama of the Sama chants; Gayatri among the meters. In the months, I am Margasirah; of the seasons, I am spring.

Sloka 36

dyutaṃ chalayatām asmi tejas tejasvinām aham
jayosmi vyavasāyosmi sattvaṃ sattvavatām aham

dyutam = dice play, gambling; chalayatam = among the deceptions; asmi = I am; tejah = brightness, glow, radiance; tejasvinam = of the radiant, glowing, bright; aham = I am; jayah = victory; asmi = I am; vyavasayah = resolve, determination; asmi = I am; sattvam = purity, sattva; sattva-vatam = of the sattvic nature; aham = I am.

"Among the deceptions, I am dice play; of the glowing, I am the glow; victory I am; resolve I am; sattva of the sattvic nature I am.

Sloka 37

vṛṣṇīnāṃ vāsudevosmi pāṇḍavānāṃ dhanaṃjayaḥ
munīnām apy ahaṃ vyāsaḥ kavīnām uśanā kaviḥ 10.37

vrsninam = of the Vrsnis; vasudevah = Vasudeva Krishna; asmi = I am; pandavanam = of the Pandavas; dhananjayah = Arjuna; muninam = of the sages; api = and; aham = I am; vyasah = sage Vyasa; kavinam = of the omniscient; usana = Usana; kavih = the omniscient.

"Of the Vrishnis I am Vasudeva Krishna.; of the Pandavas, Arjuna; among the sages, I am Vyasa; and among the omniscient ones, I am the omniscient Usanas.

Sloka 38

daṇḍo damayatām asmi nītir asmi jigīṣatām
maunaṃ caivāsmi guhyānāṃ jñānaṃ jñānavatāmaham

dandah = punishing instrument; damayatam = of the punishers; asmi = I am; nitih = moral law; asmi = I am; jigisatam = of those who seek victory; maunam = silence; ca = and; eva = verily; asmi = I am; guhyanam = of secrets; jnanam = knowledge; jnana-vatam = of the knowledgeable; aham = I am.

"Of the punishers, I am the punishing instrument. I am the moral law of those who seek victory; and verily I am the silence of the secrets. I am knowledge among the knowledgeable.

Sloka 39

yac cāpi sarvabhūtānāṃ bījaṃ tad aham arjuna
na tad asti vinā yat syān mayā bhūtaṃ carācaram

yat = whatever; ca = and; api = may be; sarva-bhutanam = of all beings; bijam = the seed; tat = that; aham = I am; arjuna = O Arjuna; na = not; tat = that; asti = there is; vina = without; yat = which; syat =

can exist; maya = by Me; bhutam = thing; cara-acaram = moving and unmoving.

"And whatever is the seed of all the beings, that I am, O Arjuna; There is nothing, moving or unmoving, which can exist without Me.

Sloka 40

nāntosti mama divyānāṃ vibhūtīnāṃ paraṃtapa
eṣa tūddeśataḥ prokto vibhūter vistaro mayā

na = nor; antah = end; asti = there is; mama = My; divyanam = divine; vibhutinam = manifestations; parantapa = O conqueror of the enemies; esah = this; tu = however; uddesatah = as an illustration; proktah = spoken; vibhuteh = manifestations; vistarah = detailed description; maya = by Me.

"There is no end to my divine manifestations, O conqueror of the enemies. However, this detailed description of (My) manifestations is spoken by Me as an illustration.

Sloka 41

yad yad vibhūtimat sattvaṃ śrīmad ūrjitam eva vā
tat tad evāvagaccha tvaṃ mama tejoṃśasaṃbhavam

yat yat = whatever; vibhuti mat= endowed with glory; sattvam = truth, object; sri-mat = beauty and prosperity; urjitam = energy; eva = for certain,; va = or; tat tat = all that; eva = only; avagaccha = know; tvam = you; mama = My; tejah = power; amsa = part of; sambhavam = manifests.

"Whatever object is endowed with beauty, prosperity and energy, know for sure that all that manifests as a part of My Power only.

Sloka 42

athavā bahunaitena kiṃ jñātena tavārjuna
viṣṭabhyāham idaṃ kṛtsnam ekāṃśena sthito jagat

athava = however; = or; bahuna = extensively; etena = this; kim = what; jnatena = knowing; tava = you; arjuna = O Arjuna; vistabhya = upholding; aham = I; idam = this; krtsnam = whole, all; eka = one; amsena = fraction; sthitah = remain; jagat = in the universe.

"However, what use it is to you knowing this extensively, O Arjuna. I am upholding all this universe established in it with a fraction (of Myself)."

Conclusion

iti srīmadbhāgavadgītāsupanisatsu brahmavidyāyām yogasāstre
srikrisnārjunasamvāde vibhūtiyogaḥ nāma dasamo 'dhyayah

iti = thus; srīmadbhāgavadgītā = in the sacred Bhagavadgita; upanisatsu = in the Upanishad; brahmavidyāyām = the knowledge of the absolute Brahman; yogasāstre = the scripture of yoga; srikrisnārjunasamvāde = the dialogue between Sri Krishna and Arjuna; vibhūtiyogo nāma = by the yoga of divine manifestations; dasama = tenth; adhyayah = chapter;

Thus ends the tenth chapter named the Yoga of Divine Manifestations in the Upanishad of the divine Bhagavadgita, the knowledge of the Absolute, the yogic scripture, and the debate between Arjuna and Lord Krishna.

11- The Yoga of the Vision of the Universal Form

Sloka 1

arjuna uvāca
madanugrahāya paramaṃ guhyam adhyātmasaṃjñitam
yat tvayoktaṃ vacas tena mohoyaṃ vigato mama

arjunah uvaca = Arjuna said; mat-anugrahaya = as a favor to me, for my sake; paramam = supreme; guhyam = secret; adhyatma = the inner Self; samjnitam = known as; yat = by which; tvaya = by You; uktam = said; vacah = words; tena = by that; mohah = delusion; ayam = this; vigatah = is gone; mama = my.

"Arjuna said, "For my sake the most supreme secret known as the inner Self was spoken by You, by which words this delusion of mine has gone.

Sloka 2

bhavāpyayau hi bhūtānāṃ śrutau vistaraśo mayā
tvattaḥ kamalapatrākṣa māhātmyam api cāvyayam

bhava = creation, existence apyayau = dissolution; hi = surely; bhutanam = of the beings; srutau = heard; vistarasah = in detail; maya = by me; tvattah = from You; kamala-patra-aksa = O lotus-eyed one; mahatmyam = greatness; api = more so; ca = and; avyayam = inexhaustible.

"The creation and dissolution of beings was heard from You by me in detail, O Lotus-eyed, and more so your inexhaustible greatness.

Sloka 3

evam etad yathāttha tvam ātmānaṃ parameśvara
draṣṭum icchāmi te rūpam aiśvaraṃ puruṣottama

evam = moreover; etat = this; yatha = just as; attha = spoken; tvam = You; atmanam = yourself; parama-isvara = Supreme Lord; drastum =

to see; icchami = I wish; te = You; rupam = form; aisvaram = supreme, sovereign; purusa-uttama = O best of purushas.

"Moreover, just as You speak about Yourself, O Supreme Lord, I wish to see Your Supreme Form, O best of the Purushas.

Sloka 4

manyase yadi tac chakyaṃ mayā draṣṭum iti prabho
yogeśvara tato me tvaṃ darśayātmānam avyayam

manyase = you think; yadi = if; tat = That; sakyam = possible; maya = by me; drastum = to be seen; iti = thus; prabho = O Lord; yoga-isvara = lord of yoga; tatah = then; me = to me; tvam = You; darsaya = show; atmanam = in myself; avyayam = inexhustible.

"O Lord If you think it is possible to be seen by me That, then O Lord of Yoga, You show me in myself the Inexhaustible."

Sloka 5

śrībhagavān uvāca
paśya me pārtha rūpāṇi śataśotha sahastraśaḥ
nānāvidhāni divyāni nānāvarṇākṛtīni ca

sri-bhagavan uvaca = the Blessed Lord said; pasya = see; me = My; partha = O Partha; rupani = forms; satasah = hundreds; atha = and; sahasrasah = thousands; nana-vidhani = numerous types; divyani = divine; nana = innumerable; varna = colors; akrtini = shapes; ca = and.

"The Supreme Lord said, "O Partha, see My divine forms in hundreds and thousands, of various types, innumerable colors and shapes.

Sloka 6

paśyādityān vasūn rudrān aśvinau marutas tathā
bahūny adṛṣṭapūrvāṇi paśyāścaryāṇi bhārata 11.6

pasya = see; adityan = the Adityas vasun = Vasus; rudran = the Rudras; asvinau = the Asvinis; marutah = the Maruts; tatha = and;

bahuni = many; adrsta = not seen; purvani = before; pasya = see; ascaryani = incredible wonders; bharata = O best of the Bharatas.

"See the Adityas, the Vasus, the Rudras, the Asvins, and the Maruts. See many incredible wonders not seen before, O best of the Bharatas.

Sloka 7

ihaikasthaṃ jagat kṛtsnaṃ paśyādya sacarācaram
mama dehe guḍākeśa yac cānyad draṣṭum icchasi

iha = here eka-stham = in one place; jagat = the universe; krtsnam = entire; pasya = see; adya = now; sa = with; cara = moving; acaram = not moving; mama = My; dehe = body; gudakesa = O gudakesa; yat ca anyat = so also anything else; drastum = to see; icchasi = you wish.

"See here now in one place the entire universe in My body, O Gudakesa, both moving and unmoving and anything else you wish to see.

Sloka 8

na tu māṃ śakyase draṣṭum anenaiva svacakṣuṣā
divyaṃ dadāmi te cakṣuḥ paśya me yogam aiśvaram

na = not; tu = but; mam = Me; sakyase = able; drastum = to see; anena = with; eva = surely; sva-caksusa = your own eyes; divyam = divine; dadami = I give; te = you; caksuh = eyes; pasya = see; me = My; yogam aisvaram = Supreme Sate.

"But surely you would not be able to see Me with your own (ordinary) eyes. I give you divine eyes to see My Supreme State."

Solka 9

sañjaya uvāca
evam uktvā tato rājan mahāyogeśvaro hariḥ
darśayām āsa pārthāya paramaṃ rūpam aiśvaram

sanjayah uvaca = Sanjaya said; evam = thus; uktva = having said; tatah = thereafter; rajan = O King; maha-yoga-isvarah = the great Lord of Yoga; harih = Hari; darsayam asa = showed; parthaya = to Arjuna; paramam = supreme; rupam = form; aisvaram = divine.

Sanjaya said, "Having said thus, O king, thereafter Hari, the great Lord of Yoga, showed Arjuna His supreme divine form.

Sloka 10

anekavaktranayanam anekādbhutadarśanam
anekadivyābharaṇaṃ divyānekodyatāyudham

aneka = innmerable; vaktra = mouths; nayanam = eyes; aneka = numerous; adbhuta = wonderful; darsanam = sights; aneka = many; divya = divine; abharanam = ornaments; divya = divine; aneka = many; udyata = uplifted state of readiness; ayudham = weapons.

"Of innumerable mouths, eyes, numerous wonderful sights, many divine ornaments, holding many weapons in a state of readiness.

Sloka 11

divyamālyāmbaradharaṃ divyagandhānulepanam
sarvāścaryamayaṃ devam anantaṃ viśvatomukham

divya = divine; malya = garlands; ambara = garments; dharam = wearing; divya = heavenly; gandha = perfumes; anulepanam = pasted with, anointed with; sarva = all kinds of; ascarya-mayam = filled with wonderful things; devam = radiant, shining; anantam = unending, infinite; visvatah-mukham = faces everywhere.

"Wearing divine garlands and garments; pasted with heavenly perfumes; filled with all kinds of wonderful things, radiant, infinite, with faces everywhere.

Sloka 12

divi sūryasahastrasya bhaved yugapad utthitā
yadi bhāḥ sadṛśī sā syād bhāsas tasya mahātmanaḥ

divi = in the sky; surya = suns; sahasrasya = thousands; bhavet = present; yugapat = simultaneously; utthita = risen, rising, born; yadi =

as if; bhah = splendor; sadrsi = similar, like; sa = that; syat = might be; bhasah = effulgence; tasya = was; maha-atmanah = the Great Self.

"As if thousands of suns have arisen simultaneously in the sky, similar to that splendor might be the effulgence of the Great Self.

Sloka 13

tatraikasthaṃ jagat kṛtsnaṃ pravibhaktam anekadhā
apaśyad devadevasya śarīre pāṇḍavas tadā

tatra = there; eka-stham = as one; jagat = universe; krtsnam = whole, entire; pravibhaktam = was divided; anekadha = into numerous things; apasyat = saw; deva-devasya = God of the gods; sarire = in the body; pandavah = Arjuna; tada = then.

"Then Arjuna then saw there, in the body of the God of gods, the entire universe that was one as divided into numerous things.

Sloka 14

tataḥ sa vismayāviṣṭo hṛṣṭaromā dhanaṃjayaḥ
praṇamya śirasā devaṃ kṛtāñjalir abhāṣata

tatah = then; sah = he; vismaya-avistah = overwhelmed with wonder; hrsta-roma = hairs standing on end due to happiness; dhananjayah = Arjuna; pranamya = bowing down; sirasa = his head; devam = to the supreme being; krta-anjalih = with folded hands; abhasata = said.

"Then overwhelmed with wonder, his hair standing on end due to immense happiness, bowing down his head to the Supreme Being, Arjuna said with folded hands.

Sloka 15

arjuna uvāca
paśyāmi devāṃs tava deva dehe sarvāṃs tathā bhūtaviśeṣasaṃghān
brahmāṇam īśaṃ kamalāsanasthaṃ ṛṣīṃś ca sarvān uragāṃś ca divyān

arjunah uvaca = Arjuna said; pasyami = I see; devan = all the gods; tava = Your; deva = O Divine Being; dehe = in the body; sarvan = all; tatha = also; bhuta = living beings; visesa-sanghan = various classes and groups of things; brahmanam = Brahma; isam = Lord; kamala-asana-stham = seated in the lotus flower; rsin = great seers; ca = and; sarvan = all; uragan = serpents; ca = and; divyan = divine.

"Said Arjuna, "O Divine Being, I see all the gods in Your body, also all living beings, various classes and groups of things, Brahma, the Lord seated in the lotus flower and all the divine serpents.

Sloka 16

anekabāhūdaravaktranetraṃ paśyāmi tvāṃ sarvatonantarūpam
nāntaṃ na madhyaṃ na punas tavādiṃ paśyāmi viśveśvara viśvarūpa

aneka = many; bahu = hands; udara = bellies; vaktra = mouths; netram = eyes; pasyami = I see; tvam = You; sarvatah = everywhere; ananta-rupam = infinite form; na antam = without an ened; na madhyam = without the middle; na punah = nor again the end; tava = Your; adim = beginning; pasyami = I see; visva-isvara = O Lord of the universe; visva-rupa = universal fomr or being.

"I see You with many hands, bellies, mouths, eyes, everywhere with infinite form, without an end without the middle nor again do I see Your beginning, O Lord of the Universe, O Universal Being.

Sloka 17

kirīṭinaṃ gadinaṃ cakriṇaṃ ca tejorāśiṃ sarvato dīptimantam
paśyāmi tvāṃ durnirīkṣyaṃ samantād dīptānalārkadyutim aprameyam

kiritinam = with a crown; gadinam = with a mace; cakrinam = with a disc; ca = and; tejah-rasim = rays of light; sarvatah = in all directions; dipti-mantam = glowing; pasyami = I see; tvam = You; durniriksyam =

difficult to see; samantat = from all sides; dipta = blazing; anala = fire; arka = sun; dyutim = radiance; aprameyam = immeasurable.

"I see You with a crown, with a mace, with a disc, and with rays of light spreading in all directions, which is difficult to see from all sides, having immeasurable light of the blazing fire (and) the sun.

Sloka 18

tvam akṣaraṃ paramaṃ veditavyaṃ tvam asya viśvasya paraṃ nidhānam
tvam avyayaḥ śāśvatadharmagoptā sanātanas tvaṃ puruṣo mato me

tvam = You; aksaram = imperishable; paramam = supreme; veditavyam = to be known; tvam = You; asya = of this; visvasya = of the universe; param = supreme; nidhanam = source of abundance; tvam = You are; avyayah = inexhaustible; sasvata-dharma-gopta = protector of the everlasting religion; sanatanah = eternal; tvam = You; purusah = Being; matah me = is my opinion.

"You are the imperishable, supreme One to be known. You are the supreme source of abundance and support for the entire universe. You are the protector of the everlasting dharma. You are the eternal Being. This is my opinion.

Sloka 19

anādimadhyāntam anantavīryam anantabāhuṃ śaśisūryanetram
paśyāmi tvāṃ dīptahutāśavaktraṃ svatejasā viśvam idaṃ tapantam

anadi = without beginning; madhya = without middle; antam = without end; ananta = infinite; viryam = valor, power, energy; ananta = unlimited; bahum = arms; sasi = moon; surya = sun; netram = eyes; pasyami = I see; tvam = You; dipta hutasa-vaktram = with a mouth like blazing fire; sva-tejasa = self-effufigence; visvam = universe; idam = this; tapantam = heating up.

"I see You without a beginning, middle and end, with infinite power, unlimited arms, with eyes like the sun and the moon, with a mouth like blazing fire, heating up this universe with your self-effulgence.

Sloka 20

dyāvāpṛthivyor idam antaraṃ hi vyāptaṃ tvayaikena diśaś ca sarvāḥ
dṛṣṭvādbhutaṃ rupam ugraṃ tavedaṃ lokatrayaṃ pravyathitaṃ mahātman

dyau = of the sky; a-prthivyoh = of the earth; idam = this; antaram = the space between; hi = surely; vyaptam = pervaded; tvaya = by You; ekena = alone, as one; disah = directions; ca = and; sarvah = all; drstva = having seen; adbhutam = marvellous, wonderful; rupam = form; ugram = terrible; tava = Your; idam = this; loka = worlds; trayam = three; pravyathitam = filled with fear; maha-atman = O Great Self.

"Surely the space between the sky and the earth and all directions are pervaded by You only; seeing this Your wonderful (and) terrible form, the three words would be filled with fear, O Great Self.

Sloka 21

amī hi tvāṃ surasaṃghā viśanti kecid bhītāḥ prāñjalayo gṛṇanti
svastīty uktvā maharṣisiddhasaṃghāḥ stuvanti tvāṃ stutibhiḥ puṣkalābhiḥ

Translatin

ami = those; hi = surely; tvam = You; sura-sanghah = groups of gods; visanti = are entering; kecit = some of them; bhitah = out of fear; pranjalayah = with palms joined; grnanti = offering you prayers; svasti = benediction; iti = thus; uktva = uttering; maha-rsi = great seers; siddha-sanghah = groups of perfect beings, siddhas; stuvanti = praise; tvam = You; stutibhih = with hymns; puskalabhih = elaborate.

"Surely those groups of gods are entering you. Some of them out of fear offering you prayers of obeisance with folded

hands. Great seers and groups of perfect beings are praising you with elaborate hymns of praise chanting benedictions.

Sloka 22

rudrādityā vasavo ye ca sādhyā viśveśvinau marutaś coṣmapāś ca
gandharvayakṣāsurasiddhasaṃghā vīkṣante tvāṃ vismitāś caiva sarve

rudra = Rudras; adityah = Adityas; vasavah = Vasus; ye = those; ca = and; sadhyah = the Sadhyas; visve = the Visvedevas; asvinau = Asvins; marutah = Maruts; ca = and; usma-pah = Usmapahs; ca = and; gandharva = Gandharvas; yaksa = Yaksas; asura-siddha = asura siddhas; sanghah = groups, congregations; viksante = behold,see; tvam = You; vismitah = with amazement; ca = and; eva = indeed; sarve = all.

"Those Rudras, Adityas,Vasus and Sadhyas, Visvadevas, Asvins, Maruts, and Usampahs, and groups of Gandharvas, Yaksas, Asura Siddhas, all indeed behold you with amazement.

Sloka 23

rūpaṃ mahat te bahuvaktranetraṃ mahābāho bahubāhūrupādam
bahūdaraṃ bahudañṣṭrākarālaṃ dṛṣṭvā lokāḥ pravyathitās tathāham

rupam = form; mahat = great; te = Your; bahu = many; vaktra = faces; netram = eyes; maha-baho = O mighty-armed one; bahu = many; bahu = arms; uru = thighs; padam = feet; bahu-udaram = many bellies; bahu-damstra = many teeth; karalam = terrifying; drstva = seeing; lokah = all the worlds; pravyathitah = disturbed tatha = and so; aham = I am.

"Seeing Your great form with many faces, eyes, many arms, thighs, feet, many bellies, and many terrifying teeth, O Mighty Armed, all the words are disturbed and So am I.

Sloka 24

nabhaḥspṛśaṃ dīptam anekavarṇaṃ vyāttānanaṃ dīptaviśāla netram
dṛṣṭvā hi tvāṃ pravyathitāntarātmā dhṛtiṃ na vindāmi śamaṃ ca viṣṇo

nabhah-sprsam = touching the heaven; diptam = glowing; aneka = with many; varnam = colors; vyatta = wide open; ananam = mouth; dipta = blazing; visala = wide; netram = eyes; drstva = seeing; hi = surely; tvam = You; pravyathita = terrified; antaratma = in my heart; dhrtim = stability; na = not; vindami = find; samam = equanimity; ca =and; visno = O Maha Visnu.

"O Vishnu, seeing You touching the heaven, glowing with many colors, with wide open mouth, blazing wide eyes, terrified in my heart, I am not finding stability and equanimity in my heart.

Sloka 25

daṃṣṭrākarālāni ca te mukhāni dṛṣṭvaiva kālānalasaṃnibhāni
diśo na jāne na labhe ca śarma prasīda deveśa jagannivāsa

damstra = with the teeth; karalani = terrible; ca = and; te = Your; mukhani = faces; drstva = having seen; eva = indeed; kala-anala = the fire of final destruction; sannibhani = resembling similar to; disah = directions; na jane = do not know; na labhe = not find; ca = and; sarma = comfort; prasida = be kind; deva-isa = O lord of the gods; jagat-nivasa = abode of the universe.

"Indeed having seen Your terrible teeth and faces resembling the fire of the final destruction, I no more know the directions, nor find any comfort, O Lord of the gods, O Abode of the Universe.

Sloka 26

amī ca tvāṃ dhṛtarāṣṭrasya putrāḥ sarve sahaivāvanipālasaṃghaiḥ
bhīṣmo droṇaḥ sūtaputras tathāsau sahāsmadīyair api yodhamukhyaiḥ

ami = those; ca = and; tvam = You; dhrtarastrasya = Dhrtarastra; putrah = sons; sarve = all; saha = along with; eva = importantly, chiefly; avani-pala = kings, rulers of the earth; sanghaih = multitude; bhismah = Bhisma; dronah = Dronacarya; suta-putrah = Karna, son of Suta; tatha = and; asau = that; saha = including; asmadiyaih = our; api = even; yodha-mukhyaih = warrior chiefs.

"And into You all those sons of Dhritarashtra, along with multitudes of kings, importantly Bhishma, Drona, and that son of Suta, including even our own warrior chiefs...

Sloka 27

vaktrāṇi te tvaramāṇā viśanti daṃṣṭrākarālāni bhayānakāni
kecid vilagnā daśanāntareṣu saṃdṛśyante cūrṇitair uttamāṅgaiḥ

vaktrani = mouths; te = Your; tvaramanah = in great speed; visanti = entering; damstra = teeth; karalani = blood curdling; bhayanakani = very fearsome, terrible; kecit = some; vilagnah = being stuck; dasana-antaresu = between the teeth; sandrsyante = are seen; curnitaih = crushed; uttama-angaih = with their head.

"In great haste (they) are entering Your mouths that have very fearsome blood curdling teeth. Some are seen being stuck in between the teeth, with their heads crushed.

Sloka 28

yathā nadīnāṃ bahavombuvegāḥ samudram evābhimukhā dravanti
tathā tavāmī naralokavīrā viśanti vaktrāṇy abhivijvalanti

yatha = as; nadinam = of the rivers; bahavah = many; ambu-vegah = swift currents of waters; samudram = ocean; eva = only; abhimukhah = towards in the direction of; dravanti = flow; tatha = so does, in the same manner; tava = Your; ami = all those; nara-loka-virah = heroes of the human world; visanti = passing, entering; vaktrani = mouths; abhivijvalanti = blazing, glowing.

"As the swift currents of the waters from many rivers flow towards the ocean only, so does all those heroes of the human world are passing into Your blazing mouth.

Sloka 29

yathā pradīptaṃ jvalanaṃ pataṅgā viśanti nāśāya samṛddhavegāḥ
tathaiva nāśāya viśanti lokās tavāpi vaktrāṇi samṛddhavegāḥ

yatha = as; pradiptam = blazing; jvalanam = fire; patangah = moths; visanti = enter; nasaya = for destruction; samrddha = with great; vegah = speed; tatha eva = in the same manner; nasaya = for destruction; visanti = entering; lokah = all people; tava = Your; api = and; vaktrani = mouths; samrddha-vegah = with great speed.

"As moths enter into a blazing fire with great speed for their destruction, in the same manner all the people are entering into Your mouths with great speed for their destruction.

Sloka 30

lelihyase grasamānaḥ samantāl lokān samagrān vadanair jvaladbhiḥ
tejobhir āpūrya jagat samagraṃ bhāsas tavogrāḥ pratapanti viṣṇo

lelihyase = licking lips; grasamanah = devouring; samantat = from all sides; lokan = people; samagran = all; vadanaih = by mouthfuls; jvaladbhih = with flaming, blazing; tejobhih = with vigorous heat; apurya = filled; jagat = the universe; samagram = enitre; bhasah = with effulgent rays; tava = Your; ugrah = terrible; pratapanti = scorched; visno = O Vishnu.

"Licking your lips, with flaming mouths, You are devouring all the people from all sides. The entire universe is scorched by the effulgent rays of Your vigorous heat, O Vishnu.

Sloka 31

ākhyāhi me ko bhavān ugrarūpo namostu te devavara prasīda vijñātum icchāmi bhavantam ādyaṃ na hi prajānāmi tava pravṛttim

akhyahi = please explain; me = to me; kah = who; bhavan = are You; ugra-rupah = in this fierce form; namah astu = my salutations; te = to You; deva-vara = best of the gods; prasida = be gracious; vijnatum = to know; icchami = I wish; bhavantam = You; adyam = Primal, First; na = never; hi = certainly; prajanami = I know; tava = Your; pravrttim = actions, basic nature.

"Please explain to me who You are in this fierce form. My salutations to You, O Best of the Gods, be gracious to me. I want to know You, the First among all. Surely, I do not know Your actions."

Sloka 32

śrībhagavān uvāca
kālosmi lokakṣayakṛt pravṛddho lokān samāhartum iha pravṛttaḥ
ṛtepi tvāṃ na bhaviṣyanti sarve yevasthitāḥ pratyanīkeṣu yodhāḥ

sri-bhagavan uvaca = the Blessed Lord said; kalah = Time; asmi = I am; loka = the worlds; ksaya-krt = destroyer; pravrddhah = vast and mighty; lokan = the worlds; samahartum = to destroy; iha = in this world; pravrttah =manifest; rte = without; api = even; tvam = you; na bhavisyanti = will not exist; sarve = all; ye = who; avasthitah = standing; prati-anikesu = on the other side; yodhah = the warriors.

"Said the Lord Supreme,"I am Time, the Destroyer of the worlds, vast and mighty, who manifests to destroy the worlds. Even without you, all the warriors who are standing on the other side will cease to exist.

Sloka 33

tasmāt tvam uttiṣṭha yaśo labhasva jitvā śatrūn bhuṅkṣva rājyaṃ samṛddham

mayaivaite nihatāḥ pūrvam eva nimittamātraṃ bhava savyasācin.

tasmat = therefore; tvam = you; uttistha = stand up; yasah = fame; labhasva = to gain; jitva = conquering; satrun = enemies; bhunksva = enjoy; rajyam = kingdom; samrddham = vast and prosperous, flourishing; maya = by Me; eva = surely; ete = these; nihatah = killed; purvam = already, before, eva = for sure; nimitta-matram = mere instrument, cause; bhava = are; savya-sacin = O skilful archer.

"Therefore, you should stand up to gain fame, conquering the enemies, to enjoy a vast and prosperous kingdom. They are already killed by Me for sure. You are but a mere instrument, O skilful archer.

Sloka 34

droṇaṃ ca bhīṣmaṃ ca jayadrathaṃ ca karṇaṃ tathānyān api yodhavīrān
mayā hatāṃs tvaṃ jahi mā vyathiṣṭhā yudhyasva jetāsi raṇe sapatnān

dronam ca = and Drona; bhismam ca = and Bhisma; jayadratham ca = and Jayadratha; karnam = and Karna; tatha = so also; anyan = other; api = more over; yodha-viran = heroic warriors; maya = by Me; hatan = killed; tvam = you; jahi = slay; ma = never; vyathisthah = feel disturbed; yudhyasva = fight; jeta asi = you should be victorious; rane = in the battle; sapatnan = enemies.

"Drona and Bhishma and Jayadratha and Karna and so also other heroic warriors are already killed by Me. You should therefore fight, without feeling distressed, and emerge victorious in the battle against your enemies."

Sloka 35

sañjaya uvāca
etac chrutvā vacanaṃ keśavasya kṛtāñjalir vepamānaḥ kirīṭī
namaskṛtvā bhūya evāha kṛṣṇaṃ sagadgadaṃ bhītabhītaḥ praṇamya

sanjayah uvaca = Sanjaya said; etat = thus; srutva = having heard; vacanam = the words; kesavasya = of Kesava; krta-anjalih = with hands folded; vepamanah = trembling; kiriti = Arjuna; namaskrtva = offering obeissance, bowing down; bhuyah = again; eva = and; aha krsnam = spoke to Krsna; sa-gadgadam = in a choked voice; bhita-bhitah = fearfully; pranamya = with reverence.

"Said Sanjaya, "Having heard the words of Kesava, Arjuna with hands folded, trembling, and bowing down, spoke again to Krishna, in a voice choked with fear and reverence."

Sloka 36

arjuna uvāca
sthāne hṛṣīkeśa tava prakīrtyā jagat prahṛṣyaty anurajyate ca
rakṣāṃsi bhītāni diśo dravanti sarve namasyanti ca siddhasaṃghāḥ

arjunah uvaca = Arjuna said; sthane = rightly; hrsika-isa = O Hrisikesa, Master of the senses; tava = Your; prakirtya = supreme glory; jagat = the world; prahrsyati = exultation, rapture; anurajyate = drawn, attracted; ca = and; raksamsi = the demons; bhitani = with fear; disah = directions; dravanti = fleeing; sarve = all; namasyanti = offering obeisances; ca = and; siddha-sanghah = the perfect human beings.

"Said Arjuna, " O Master of the senses, the world is enraptured and attracted by Your supreme glory. The demons are fleeing in all directions; and all the perfect ones are offering you their obeisance with great reverence.

Sloka 37

kasmāc ca te na nameran mahātman garīyase brahmaṇopy ādikartre
ananta deveśa jagannivāsa tvam akṣaraṃ sad asat tatparaṃ yat

kasmat = why; ca = and; te = to You; na = not; nameran = offer obeissances; maha-atman = O Great Self; gariyase = far superior to; brahmanah = Brahma; api = even; adi-kartre = the first creator; ananta = infinite; deva-isa = God of the gods; jagat-nivasa = abode of the universe; tvam = You are; aksaram = imperishable; sat-asat = both existence and non-existence; tat = That; param = highest; yat = which is.

"Why should not they offer obeisance to You, O Great Self, who is far superior to even Brahma? You are the First Creator, infinite, God of the gods, Abode of the Universe, imperishable, both existence and non-existence, (and) That which is the Highest.

Sloka 38

tvam ādidevaḥ puruṣaḥ purāṇas tvam asya viśvasya paraṃ nidhānam
vettāsi vedyaṃ ca paraṃ ca dhāma tvayā tataṃ viśvam anantarūpa

tvam = You; adi-devah = First God; purusah = person, Purusah; puranah = ancient; tvam = You; asya = this; visvasya = universe; param = supreme, transcendental; nidhanam = abundance; vetta = knower; asi = You are; vedyam ca = and the knowable; param ca = and supreme; dhama = abode, place; tvaya = by You; tatam = is pervaded; visvam = universe; ananta-rupa = infinite forms.

"You are the First God, the Most Ancient Purusha, the supreme Abundance of this universe, the knower and the knowable, and the Supreme Abode. The entire universe is pervaded by You, O Being of infinite forms.

Sloka 39

vāyur yamognir varuṇaḥ śaśāṅkaḥ prajāpatis tvaṃ prapitāmahaś ca
namo namas testu sahastrakṛtvaḥ punaś ca bhūyopi namo namas te

vayuh = Vayu; yamah = Lord Yama; agnih = Agni; varunah = Varuna; sasa-ankah = Sasanka; prajapatih = Prajapati; tvam = You; prapitamahah = great grandfather; ca = and; namah = salutations; namah = salutations; te = to You; astu = are; sahasra-krtvah = a thousand times; punah ca = and again; bhuyah = again; api = also; namah = salutations; namah te = salutations to You.

"Vayu, Yama, Agni, Varuna, Sasanka, Prajapati, and the Great Grandfather You are. I offer salutations and salutations to You a thousand times. Salutations and Salutations to You again and again.

Sloka 40

**namaḥ purastād atha pṛṣṭhatas te namostu te sarvata eva sarva
anantavīryāmitavikramas tvaṃ sarvaṃ samāpnoṣi tatosi
sarvaḥ**

namah = salutations; purastat = from the front; atha = and; prsthatah = from behind; te = You; namah astu = salutations; te = to You; sarvatah = from all sides; eva = indeed; sarva = O All; ananta-virya = infinite power; amita-vikramah = infinite valor; tvam = You; sarvam = everything; samapnosi = envelop; tatah = therefore; asi = are; sarvah = everything.

"My salutations to You from the front side and the back side; O All, I offer my salutations from all sides indeed. You are infinite in power, infinite in valor. You envelop everything, therefore You are everything.

Sloka 41

**sakheti matvā prasabhaṃ yad uktaṃ he kṛṣṇa he yādava he
sakheti
ajānatā mahimānaṃ tavedaṃ mayā pramādāt praṇayena vāpi**

sakha = friend; iti = thus; matva = thinking; prasabham = impetuously; yat = whatever; uktam = said; he krsna = O Krsna; he yadava = O Yadava; he sakhe iti = O my dear friend; ajanata = without knowing; mahimanam = greatness; tava = Your; idam = this; maya = by me; pramadat = carelessly; pranayena = out of love; va api = either or.

"Thinking thus you as a friend whatever was said by me impetuously, O Krishna, O Yadava, O my dear Friend,

without knowing Your greatness, out of either carelessness or love ...

Sloka 42

yac cāvahāsārtham asatkṛtosi vihāraśayyāsanabhojaneṣu ekothavāpy acyuta tatsamakṣaṃ tat kṣāmaye tvām aham aprameyam

yat = whatever; ca = and; avahasa-artham = in jest; asat-krtah = disrespect; asi = done to You; vihara = during recreation, walking for pleasure; sayya = while resting; asana = sitting; bhojanesu = while eating ; ekah = along in private; atha va = or; api = even; acyuta = O infallible one; tat-samaksam = in public in front of others; tat = that; ksamaye = seek forgiveness; tvam = from You; aham = I; aprameyam = incomprehensible.

"Whatever was done to You either in jest or in disrespect, during recreation, while resting, while sitting, while eating, alone or in front of others, for that I seek your forgiveness, O incomprehensible One.

Sloka 43

pitāsi lokasya carācarasya tvam asya pūjyaś ca gurur garīyān na tvatsamosty abhyadhikaḥ kutonyo lokatrayepy apratimaprabhāva

pita = father; asi = You are; lokasya = of all; cara = moving; acarasya = nonmoving; tvam = You are; asya = of this; pujyah = venerable; ca = and; guruh = master; gariyan = still greater; na = not; tvat-samah = equal to You; asti = there is; abhyadhikah = greater than; kutah = how can there be; anyah = other; loka-traye = in the three worlds; api = even; apratima = immeasurable; prabhava = power.

"You are the Father of all things both moving and non-moving. You are greater than any teacher of this world who is venerable. There is nothing equal to You in the three worlds. How can there be, O Immeasurable Power?

Sloka 44

tasmāt praṇamya praṇidhāya kāyaṃ prasādaye tvām aham īśam īḍyam
piteva putrasya sakheva sakhyuḥ priyaḥ priyāyārhasi deva soḍhum.

tasmat = therefore; pranamya = bowing down; pranidhaya = laying down completely; kayam = the body; prasadaye = to seek; tvam = to You; aham = I; isam = God, the Lord; idyam = venerable; pita iva = like a father; putrasya = of a son; sakha iva = like a friend; sakhyuh = of a friend; priyah = lover; priyayah = of the beloved; arhasi = You should; deva = O God; sodhum = forgive, bear with, tolerate.

"Therefore, bowing down and laying down my body completely, I seek to worship You, who is the Lord and venerable. O Lord, You should forgive me the way a father (forgives) his son, a friend his friend, (and) a lover his beloved.

Sloka 45

adṛṣṭapūrvaṃ hṛṣitosmi dṛṣṭvā bhayena ca pravyathitaṃ mano me
tad eva me darśaya deva rūpaṃ prasīda deveśa jagannivāsa

adrsta = not seen; purvam = before, in the past; hrsitah = happy, delighted; asmi = I am; drstva = having seen; bhayena = with fear; ca = and, but; pravyathitam = disturbed, agitated; manah = mind; me = my; tat = that; eva = very; me = to me; darsaya = show; deva = O God; rupam = form; prasida = be gracious; deva-isa = O God of the gods; jagat-nivasa = Abode of the universe.

"Having seen what was never seen before. I am happy and delighted; but my mind is agitated with fear. Please show me that very form, O God of the gods and the Abode of the Universe.

Sloka 46

kirīṭinaṃ gadinaṃ cakrahastaṃ icchāmi tvāṃ draṣṭum ahaṃ tathaiva
tenaiva rūpeṇa caturbhujena sahastrabāho bhava viśvamūrte

kiritinam = with crown; gadinam = with mace; cakra-hastam = disc in hand; icchami = I wish; tvam = You; drastum = to see; aham = I; tatha eva = verily as before; tena eva = that very; rupena = form; catuh-bhujena = with four hands; sahasra-baho = he who has a thhousand arms; bhava = appear, become, manifest; visva-murte = O Universal Being.

"I wish to se e You very much as before, wearing a crown, carrying a mace and holding a disc in (Your) hand. O the One with a thousand arms, O the Universal Being, manifest before me in that very form with four arms.

Sloka 47

śrībhagavān uvāca
mayā prasannena tavārjunedaṃ rūpaṃ paraṃ darśitam ātmayogāt
tejomayaṃ viśvam anantam ādyaṃ yan me tvadanyena na dṛṣṭapūrvam

sri-bhagavan uvaca = the Supreme Lord said; maya = by Me; prasannena = pleased; tava = with you; arjuna = O Arjuna; idam = this; rupam = form; param = supreme; darsitam = shown; atma-yogat = by my yoga ; tejah-mayam = full of brilliance; visvam = the universal; anantam = infinite; adyam = the first; yat me = of Mine; tvat anyena = none other than you; na drsta-purvam = saw previously.

"The Supreme Lord said, "Having been pleased with you, O Arjuna, this Supreme Form, which is full of brilliance, universal, infinite, the first, that (form) of Mine, which none other than you saw previously, was shown by Me to you with My yoga.

Sloka 48

na veda yajñādhyayanair na dānaiḥ na ca kriyābhir na tapobhir ugraiḥ
evaṃrūpaḥ śakya ahaṃ nṛloke draṣṭuṃ tvadanyena kurupravīra

na = not; veda = knowledge of the Vedas; yajna = sacrifice; adhyayanaih = study; na danaih = by charity; na = not; ca = and; kriyabhih = by actions; na = not; tapobhih = even by austerities; ugraih = severe; evam = thus; rupah = form; sakyah = can be seen; aham = I; nr-loke = human world; drastum = see; tvat = you; anyena = by another; kuru-pravira = O best among the Kurus.

"Neither by the study of the Vedas and sacrifices nor by acts of charity, and not even by rituals and severe austerities I can thus be seen in this form in the human world by anyone other than you, O most valiant among the Kurus.

Sloka 49

mā te vyathā mā ca vimūḍhabhāvo dṛṣṭvā rūpaṃ ghoram īdṛṅ mamedam
vyapetabhīḥ prītamanāḥ punas tvaṃ tad eva me rūpam idaṃ prapaśya

ma = not; te = you; vyatha = worry, suffer; ma = not; ca = and; vimudha-bhavah = become deluded; drstva = seeing; rupam = form; ghoram = terrible; idrk = such as; mama = My; idam = this; vyapeta-bhih = becoming free from fear; prita-manah = cheerful mind punah = again; tvam = you; tat = that; eva = even; me = of Mine; rupam = form; idam = this; prapasya = see.

"Do not be worried or deluded seeing this form of Mine which is so terrible as this; becoming free from fear, with a cheerful mind, see again that (earlier) form of Mine."

Sloka 50

sañjaya uvāca
ity arjunaṃ vāsudevas tathoktvā svakaṃ rūpaṃ darśayām āsa bhūyaḥ

āśvāsayām āsa ca bhītam enaṃ bhūtvā punaḥ saumyavapur mahātmā

sanjayah uvaca = Sanjaya said; iti = thus; arjunam = to Arjuna; vasudevah = Vasudeva; tatha = thus; uktva = speaking, saying; svakam = His own; rupam = form; darsayamasa = showed; bhuyah = again; asvasayamasa = pacified, revived the spirits; ca = and; bhitam = fearful; enam = this; bhutva punah = returning, becoming again; saumya-vapuh = pleasant form; maha-atma = the Great Self.

"Said Sanjaya, "Thus speaking to Arjuna, Vasudeva showed His own form again; returning to His pleasant form, the Great Self revived the spirits of the fearful one."

Sloka 51

arjuna uvāca
dṛṣṭvedaṃ mānuṣaṃ rūpaṃ tava saumyaṃ janārdana
idānīm asmi saṃvṛttaḥ sacetāḥ prakṛtiṃ gataḥ

arjunah uvaca = Arjuna said; drstva = seeing; idam = this; manusam = human; rupam = form; tava = Your; saumyam = plesant; janardana = O chastiser of the enemies; idanim = now; asmi = I have; samvrttah = become sa-cetah = mindful, with mind; prakrtim = nature; gatah = returned.

Said Arjuna, "Seeing this Your pleasant human form, O Janardana, I have become mindful. My original nature is restored.

Sloka 52

śrībhagavān uvāca
sudurdarśam idaṃ rūpaṃ dṛṣṭvān asi yan mama
devā apy asya rūpasya nityaṃ darśanakāṅkṣiṇaḥ

sri-bhagavan uvaca = the supreme lord said; su-durdarsam = very difficult to see; idam = this; rupam = form; drstavan asi = you have seen; yat = which; mama = of Mine; devah = the divinities; api = indeed, even; asya = of this; rupasya = form; nityam = always, daily; darsana-kanksinah = yearn to see.

"The Supreme Lord said, "This form of Mine which you have seen is very difficult to see. Even the divinities are always eager to see this form.

Sloka 53

nāhaṃ vedair na tapasā na dānena na cejyayā
śakya evaṃvidho draṣṭuṃ dṛṣṭavān asi māṃ yathā 11.53

Translatin

na = not; aham = I; vedaih = through the Vedas; na = not; tapasa = by austerity; na = not; danena = by gifts, charity; na = not; ca = and; ijyaya = by sacrifices; sakyah = possible; evam-vidhah = in this manner; drastum = to see; drstavan = have seen; asi = you; mam = Me; yatha = as.

"Neither through the Vedas nor by austerity nor by gifts nor by sacrifices can I be seen in this manner as you have seen Me.

Sloka 54

bhaktyā tv ananyayā śakya aham evaṃvidhorjuna
jñātuṃ draṣṭuṃ ca tattvena praveṣṭuṃ ca paraṃtapa

bhaktya = by devotion; tu = but; ananyaya = not by other means; sakyah = can be; aham = I; evam-vidhah = in this manner; arjuna = O Arjuna; jnatum = known; drastum = seen; ca = and; tattvena = in reality; pravestum = entered into; ca = and; parantapa = O destroyer of foes.

"But by devotion, not by any other means, can I be known or seen in this manner, and can be entered into reality, O destroyer of foes.

Sloka 55

matkarmakṛn matparamo madbhaktaḥ saṅgavarjitaḥ
nirvairaḥ sarvabhūteṣu yaḥ sa mām eti pāṇḍava

mat = for me; karma = actions; krt = perform; mat-paramah = Me as the Supreme; mat-bhaktah = with devotion to Me; sanga-varjitah =

abandoning attachment; nirvairah = without enemity; sarva-bhutesu = all living beings; yah = who; sah = he; mam = to Me; eti = comes; pandava = O son of Pandu.

" O son of Pandu, he who performs actions for Me, accepting Me as the Supreme (Goal), with devotion to Me, abandoning all attachment, without enmity towards all living beings, he comes to Me."

Conclusion

iti srīmadbhāgavadgītāsupanisatsu brahmavidyāyām yogasāstre srikrisnārjunasamvāde visvarupadarsana yogo nāmaikadasopa 'dhyayah

iti = thus; srīmadbhāgavadgītā = in the sacred Bhagavadgita; upanisatsu = in the Upanishad; brahmavidyāyām = the knowledge of the absolute Brahman; yogasāstre = the scripture of yoga; srikrisnārjunasamvāde = the dialogue between Sri Krishna and Arjuna; visvarupadarsana yogo nāma = by name yoga of the vision of the universal form; nāmaikadasopah = eleventt; adhyayah = chapter;

Thus ends the eleventh chapter named the Yoga of the Vision of the Universal Form in the Upanishad of the divine Bhagavadgita, the knowledge of the Absolute, the yogic scripture, and the debate between Arjuna and Lord Krishna.

12 – The Yoga of Devotion

Sloka 1

Arjuna uvāca
evaṃ satatayuktā ye bhaktās tvāṃ paryupāsate
ye cāpy akṣaram avyaktaṃ teṣāṃ ke yogavittamāḥ

arjunah uvaca = Arjuna said; evam = thus; satata = always; yuktah = engaged; ye = those; bhaktah = devotees; tvam = You; paryupasate = devotional service, religious meditation; ye = those; ca = and; api = others; aksaram = imperishable; avyaktam = unmanifested; tesam = of them; ke = who; yoga-vit-tamah = the most perfect in yoga.

"Arjuna said, "Thus always engaged those devotees who worship You and others the imperishable and the inexhaustible, of them who is the most perfect in yoga?"

Sloka 2

mayy āveśya mano ye māṃ nityayuktā upāsate
śraddhayā parayopetāḥ te me yuktatamā matāḥ

sri-bhagavan uvaca = the Blessed Lord said; mayi = to Me; avesya = by fixing, concentrating; manah = the mind; ye = those who; mam = Me; nitya = always; yuktah = absorbed; upasate = worship; sraddhaya = with faith; paraya = supreme upetah = endowed; te = they; me = Me; yukta-tamah = most balancedt; matah = opinion, thinking.

"Said Lord Supreme, "By fixing their minds upon Me, ever absorbed in Me, those who worship Me endowed with supreme faith, in My opinion they are the most balanced.

Sloka 3

ye tv akṣaram anirdeśyaṃ avyaktaṃ paryupāsate
sarvatragam acintyaṃ ca kūṭasthaṃ acalaṃ dhruvam

ye = those; tu = but; aksaram = imperishable; anirdesyam = indefinable, indescribable, indeterminate; avyaktam = unmanifested; paryupasate = worship; sarvatra-gam = omnipresent; acintyam = inconceivable, beyond thought; ca = and; kuta-stham = the highest, standing at the top, occupying the highest place; acalam = immovable, constant; dhruvam = fixed.

"But those who worship the Imperishable, the Indefinable, the Unmanifested, the Omnipresent, the Inconceivable and the Highest, the Immovable, the Fixed...

Sloka 4

saṃniyamyendriyagrāmaṃ sarvatra samabuddhayāḥ
te prāpnuvanti mām eva sarvabhūtahite ratāḥ

sanniyamya = restraining; indriya-gramam = all the senses; sarvatra = everywhere; sama-buddhayah = with equanimity, even minded; te = they; prapnuvanti = attain; mam = Me; eva = surely; sarva-bhuta-hite = in the welfare of all beings; ratah = devoted to, takes delight.

"Restraining all the senses, remaining the same everywhere, taking delight in the welfare of all beings, the surely attain Me only.

Sloka 5

kleśodhikataras teṣāṃ avyaktāsaktacetasām
avyaktā hi gatir duḥkhaṃ dehavadbhir avāpyate

klesah = obstacles, afflictions; adhika-tarah = very, greater, excessive; tesam = for them; avyakta = unmanifested; asakta = is drawn to; cetasam = mind; avyakta = unmanifested; hi = indeed; gatih = goal; duhkham = struggle, pain, sorrow,; deha-vadbhih = by the embodied souls; avapyate = attained.

"Obstacles and afflictions are greater for them whose minds are drawn to the Unmanifested. Indeed, the Unmanifested as the Goal is attained with great struggle by the embodied souls.

Sloka 6

ye tu sarvāṇi karmāṇi mayi saṃnyasya matparaḥ
ananyenaiva yogena māṃ dhyāyanta upāsate

ye = those who; tu = but; sarvani = all; karmani = actions; mayi = to Me; sannyasya = renouncing; mat-parah = having accepted Me; ananyena = without any distraction; eva = only, alone; yogena = by practising yoga; mam = to Me; dhyayantah = meditating; upasate = worship;.

"But those who worship Me only renouncing all actions, accepting Me only without any other thought, meditating upon Me by practicing yoga...

Sloka 7

teṣāṃ ahaṃ samuddhartā mṛtyusaṃsārasāgarāt
bhavāmi na cirāt pārtha mayy āveśitacetasām

tesam = them; aham = I; samuddharta = liberator; mrtyu = death; samsara = phenomenal world; sagarat = ocean ocean; bhavami = become; na cirat = without delay; partha = O Partha; mayi = in Me; avesita = absorbed; cetasam = mind.

"For them whose minds are absorbed in Me, O Partha, I become, without delay, the Liberator from the death ridden ocean of the phenomenal world

Sloka 8

mayy eva mana ādhatsva mayi buddhiṃ niveśaya
nivasiṣyasi mayy eva ata ūrdhvaṃ na saṃśayaḥ

mayi = on Me; eva = alone; manah = mind; adhatsva = fix; mayi = in Me; buddhim = intelligence; nivesaya = rest, respose, establish; nivasisyasi = you live; mayi = in Me; eva = alone; atah urdhvam = After that; na samsayah = without any doubt.

"Fix your mind on Me only; rest your intelligence in Me. After that, without any doubt you will live in Me alone.

Sloka 9

atha cittaṃ samādhātuṃ na śaknoṣi mayi sthiram
abhyāsayogena tato mām ichāptuṃ dhanaṃjaya

atha = now; cittam = mind; samadhatum = stabilize, fix; na = not; saknosi = able; mayi = upon Me; sthiram = steadily, firmly; abhyasa = regular practice; yogena = by yoga; tatah = then; mam = Me; iccha = seek, wish, desire; aptum = to attain; dhanam-jaya = O Dhananjaya.

"Now, if you are not able to fix your mind upon Me steadily, then, O Dhananjaya, try to attain Me by the yoga of constant practice.

Sloka 10

abhyāsepy asamarthosi matkarmaparamo bhava
madartham api karmāṇi kurvan siddhim avāpsyasi

abhyase = to practice; api = even; asamarthah = unable; asi = you are; mat-karma = My actions; paramah = supremely devoted; bhava = produce, cause; mat-artham = for Me; api = also; karmani = actions; kurvan = by performing; siddhim = perfection; avapsyasi = attain.

"If you are unable to practice even (this), be the cause of My Supreme actions. By performing actions for Me, also, you will attain perfection.

Sloka 11

athaitad apy aśaktosi kartuṃ madyogam āśritaḥ
sarvakarmaphalatyāgaṃ tataḥ kuru yatātmavān

atha = again; etat = this; api = even; asaktah = not interested; asi = you are; kartum = doing; mat = My; yogam = divine state; asritah =taking refuge; sarva-karma = all actions; phala = fruit; tyagam = renunciation; tatah = thereafter; kuru = do; yata-atma-van = keeping mind under control

"Again if you are not interested in doing even this, taking refuge in My Divine State, thereafter renounce the fruit of all actions, keeping your mind under control.

Sloka 12

śreyo hi jñānam abhyāsāj jñānād dhyānaṃ viśiṣyate
dhyānāt karmaphalatyāgas tyāgāc chāntir anantaram

sreyah = better; hi = surely; jnanam = knowledge; abhyasat = than practice; jnanat = than knowledge; dhyanam = meditation; visisyate = excel; dhyanat = than meditation; karma-phala-tyagah = renunciation of the results of actions; tyagat = by renunciation; santih = peace; anantaram = follows, subsequent to.

"Surely knowledge is better than practice; better than knowledge is meditation; better than meditation is renunciation of the fruit of action. From renunciation, peace follows next.

Sloka 13

adveṣṭā sarvabhūtānāṃ maitraḥ karuṇa eva ca
nirmamo nirahaṃkāraḥ samaduḥkhasukhaḥ kṣamī

advesta =without hatred; sarva-bhutanam = for all the living beings; maitrah = friendly; karunah = compassionate; eva = even; ca = and; nirmamah = without the feeling of mine; nirahankarah = without egoism; sama = same; duhkha = sorrow; sukhah = happness; ksami = forgiving.

"Without hatred, with friendliness and compassion for all living beings, also without the feeling of mine, without egoism, remaining same in sorrow and happiness, forgiving...

Sloka 14

saṃtuṣṭaḥ satataṃ yogī yatātmā dṛḍhaniścayaḥ
mayy arpitamanobuddhir yo madbhaktaḥ sa mepriyaḥ

santustah = satisfied, contended; satatam = ever, always; yogi = yogi; yata-atma = self-controlled; drdha-niscayah = strongly determine; mayi = Me; arpita = offered; manah = mind; buddhih = intelligence; yah = he who; mat-bhaktah = devotee of Mine; sah me priyah = is very dear to Me.

"The yogi who is ever contented, self-controlled, strongly determined, who has offered his mind and intelligence, that devotee of Mine is very dear to Me.

Sloka 15

yasmān nodvijate loko lokān nodvijate ca yaḥ
harṣāmarṣabhayodvegair mukto yaḥ sa ca me priyaḥ

yasmat = by whom; na = not; udvijate = disturbed; lokah = the world; lokat = by the world; na = not; udvijate = disturbed; ca = and; yah = he who is; harsa = joy; amarsa = impatience; bhaya = fear; udvegaih = distress; muktah = freed; yah = who; sah = he; ca = also; me = Mine; priyah = very dear.

"By whom the world is not disturbed and he who is not disturbed by the world, who is free from joy, impatience, fear and distress, he is also dear to Me.

Sloka 16

anapekṣaḥ śucir dakṣa udāsīno gatavyathaḥ
sarvārambhaparityāgī yo madbhaktaḥ sa me priyaḥ

anapeksah = without expectation; sucih = pure; daksah = skilful, capable; udasinah = impartial; gata-vyathah = free from sorrow; sarva-arambha = all undertakings; parityagi = who has renounced; yah = he who; mat-bhaktah = that devotee of Mine; sah = he; me = to Me; priyah = very dear.

"He who is without expectations, pure, skilful, impartial, without sorrow, who has renounced all undertakings, that devotee of Mine is very dear to Me.

Sloka 17

yo na hṛṣyati na dveṣṭi na śocati na kāṅkṣati
śubhāśubhaparityāgī bhaktimān yaḥ sa me priyaḥ

yah = he who; na = not; hrsyati = rejoices; na = not; dvesti = hates; na = not; socati = laments; na = not; kanksati = desires; subha = good, auspicious; asubha = bad, inauspicious; parityagi = he who renounces; bhakti-man = filled with devotion; yah = who; sah = he is; me = Me; priyah = dear.

"He who does not rejoice, does not hate, does not lament, does not desire, who renounces both the auspicious and the inauspicious, who is a filled with devotion, He is dear to Me.

Sloka 18

samaḥ śatrau ca mitre ca tathā mānāpamānayoḥ
śītoṣṇasukhaduḥkheṣu samaḥ saṅgavivarjitaḥ

samah = equal, same; satrau = to foe; ca = and; mitre = to friend; ca = also; tatha = so; mana = in honor; apamanayoh = dishonor; sita = cold; usna = heat; sukha = happiness; duhkhesu = sorrow; samah = eaual; sanga-vivarjitah = giving up attachment, association, contact, relationships.

"Equal to friend and foe, so also in honor and dishonor, equal to cold, heat, happiness (and) sorrow, free from attachment

Sloka 19

tulyanindāstutir maunī saṃtuṣṭo yena kenacit
aniketaḥ sthiramatir bhaktimān me priyo naraḥ

tulya = equal; ninda = blame, accusation; stutih = praise, adulation; mauni = silent; santustah = satisfied, contended; yena kena cit = with anything, whatever; aniketah = without fixed abode, homeless; sthira = stable, fixed; matih = mind; bhakti-man = full of devotion; me = Me; priyah = dear; narah = the person.

"Equal to blame and praise, silent, satisfied with anything; without a fixed abode, with stable mind, full of devotion, the person (of such qualities) is dear to Me.

Sloka 20

ye tu dharmyāmṛtam idaṃ yathoktaṃ paryupāsate
śraddadhānā matparamā bhaktās tetīva me priyāḥ

ye = those; tu = however, but; dharma = dharma, religious practice; amrtam = liberating; idam = this; yatha = as; uktam = stated paryupasate = worship; sraddadhanah = with faith; mat-paramah = Me as the Supreme; Goal bhaktah = devotee; te = such; ativa = extremely; me = Me; priyah = dear.

"However, those who practice this liberating dharma as stated (by Me before), worship Me with intense faith as the Supreme Goal, such devotees are extremely dear to Me.

Conclusion

iti srīmadbhāgavadgītāsupanisatsu brahmavidyāyām
yogasāstre
srikrisnārjunasamvāde bhaktiyogo nāma dvādaśo 'dhyayah.

iti = thus; srīmadbhāgavadgītā = in the sacred Bhagavadgita; upanisatsu = in the Upanishad; brahmavidyāyām = the knowledge of the absolute Brahman; yogasāstre = the scripture of yoga; srikrisnārjunasamvāde = the dialogue between Sri Krishna and Arjuna; bhakti yogo nāma = by name yoga of devotion; dvādaśah = twelfth; adhyayah = chapter.

Thus ends the twelfth chapter named the Yoga of Devotion in the Upanishad of the divine Bhagavad-Gita, the knowledge of the Absolute, the yogic scripture, and the debate between Arjuna and Lord Krishna.

13 – The Yoga of the Field and the Knower of the Field

Sloka 1

arjuna uvāca
prakṛtiṃ puruṣaṃ caiva kṣetraṃ kṣetrajñam eva ca
etad veditum icchāmi jñānaṃ jñeyaṃ ca keśava

arjunah uvaca = Arjuna said; prakrtim = Nature; purusam = Purusa; ca = and; eva = also; ksetram = the field; ksetra-jnam = knower of the field; eva = so also; ca = and; etat = these; veditum = to know; icchami = wish; jnanam = knowledge; jneyam = what is to be known; ca = and; kesava = O Kesava.

"Said Arjuna, "Prakriti and Purusa, also the Field and the Knower of the Field, and so also knowledge and what is to be known, these I wish to know, O Kesava."

Sloka 2

śrībhagavān uvāca
idaṃ śarīraṃ kaunteya kṣetram ity abhidhīyate
etad yo vetti taṃ prāhuḥ kṣetrajña iti tadvidaḥ

sri-bhagavan uvaca = the Blessed Lord said; idam = this; sariram = bod y ;kauntey a = O son of Kunti; ksetram = the field ; iti = th us; abhidhiyate = is called; etat = this; yah = who; vetti = knows; tam = he; prahuh = call; ksetra-jnah = knower of the field; iti = thus; tat-vidah = the learned.

"Said the Lord Supreme, "This body, O son of Kunti, is called 'the field'. He who knows it thus, the wise call him 'the knower of the field.'

Sloka 3

kṣetrajñaṃ cāpi māṃ viddhi sarvakṣetreṣu bhārata
kṣetrakṣetrajñayor jñānaṃ yat taj jñānaṃ mataṃmama

ksetra-jnam = the knower of the field; ca = and; api = and; mam = Me; viddhi = know; sarva = all; ksetresu = in the fields; bharata = O descendent of Bharata; ksetra = the field; ksetra-jnayoh = the knower of the field; jnanam = knowledge; yat = which; tat = that; jnanam = knowledge; matam = opinion; mama = that.

"And know Me, O descendent of Bharata, as the Knower of the Field in all the fields. In my opinion, that is knowledge, which is the knowledge of the field and of the knower of the field.

Sloka 4

tat kṣetraṃ yac ca yādṛk ca yadvikāri yataś ca yat
sa ca yo yatprabhāvaś ca tat samāsena me śṛṇu

tat = that; ksetram = field; yat = what; ca = and; yadrk = how it is; ca = and; yat = what; vikari = changes; yatah = from which cause; ca = also; yat = which; sah = he; ca = and; yah = who; yat = what; prabhavah = powers; ca = and; tat = that (body); samasena = briefly, in brief; me = from Me; srnu = hear, listen.

"What that field is and how it is, and what changes (arise) from which causes, who (He is) and what (His) powers are, hear all that from Me in brief.

Sloka 5

ṛṣibhir bahudhā gītaṃ chandobhir vividhaiḥ pṛthak
brahmasūtrapadaiś caiva hetumadbhir viniścitaiḥ

rsibhih = by the seers; bahudha = variously; gitam = sung, extolled; chandobhih =by Vedic meters; vividhaih = numerous; prthak = distinct separate; brahma-sutra = Brahma sutras; padaih = statement; ca = and; eva = surely; hetu-madbhih = by the followers of reason; viniscitaih = ascertain conclusively.

"Sung variously by the seers in numerous, distinct Vedic meters, and even ascertained conclusively by the followers of reason in the statements of the Brahmasutras.

Sloka 6

mahābhūtāny ahaṃkāro buddhir avyaktam eva ca
indriyāṇi daśaikaṃ ca pañca cendriyagocarāḥ

maha-bhutani = the five great elements; ahankarah = ego; buddhih = intelligence; avyaktam = the unmanifested; eva = very, itself; ca = and; indriyani = the senses; dasa-ekam = eleven; ca = and; panca = five; ca = and; indriya-go-carah = objects of the senses.

"The five great elements, the ego, intelligence, and the Unmanifested itself, the senses and the eleventh and the five sense objects...

Sloka 7

icchā dveṣaḥ sukhaṃ duḥkhaṃ saṃghātaś cetanādhṛtiḥ
etat kṣetraṃ samāsena savikāram udāhṛtam

iccha = desire; dvesah = repulsion; sukham = happiness; duhkham = sorrow; sanghatah = the aggregate; cetana = animatedness, liveliness; dhrtih = resolve, determination, firmness; etat = this; ksetram = field; samasena = briefly; sa-vikaram = along with modication; udahrtam = is said.

"Desire, repulsion, happiness, sorrow, the aggregate, liveliness, determination, briefly spoken, this is the field with its modifications.

Sloka 8

amānitvam adambhitvam ahiṃsā kṣāntir ārjavam
ācāryopāsanaṃ śaucaṃ sthairyam ātmavinigrahaḥ

amanitvam = humility, absence of pride; adambhitvam = without vanity, unpretentiousness; ahimsa = nonviolence, non-injury, without cruelty; ksantih = tolerance, forgiveness; arjavam = sincerity, straightforwardness; acarya-upasanam = service to teacher; saucam = cleanliness; sthairyam = stability; atma-vinigrahah = self-control.

"Absence of pride, humbleness, non-violence, tolerance, sincerity, service to teacher, cleanliness, stability, self-control...

Sloka 9

indriyārtheṣu vairāgyam anahaṃkāra eva ca
janmamṛtyujarāvyādhiduḥkhadoṣānudarśanam

indriya-arthesu = with regard to the sense objects; vairagyam = dispassion; anahankarah = egolessness; eva ca = so also; janma = birth; mrtyu = death; jara = old age; vyadhi = disease; duhkha = sorrow; dosa = blemish, fault, harm, injury, evil; anudarsanam = seeing;.

"Dispassion with regard to the sense objects, egolessness, so also seeing the blemish in birth, death, old age, disease, (and) sorrow...

Solka 10

asaktir anabhiṣvaṅgaḥ putradāragṛhādiṣu
nityaṃ ca samacittatvam iṣṭāniṣṭopapattiṣu 13.10

asaktih = without attachment or interest; anabhisvangah = without mental attachment, without clinging; putra = sons; dara = wife; grha-adisu = home and the like.; nityam = always; ca = and; sama-cittatvam = equanimity; ista = like, desirable; anista = dislike, undesirable; upapattisu = attainmemt.

"Without attachment, without clinging to sons, wife, home and the like, with equanimity towards the attainment of the desirable and the undesirable...

Sloka 11

mayi cānanyayogena bhaktir avyabhicāriṇī
viviktadeśasevitvam aratir janasaṃsadi

mayi = to Me; ca = and; ananya-yogena = not by other means; bhaktih = devotion; avyabhicarini = unwavering, undistracted, constant; vivikta desa sevitvam = inclined to retreat into solirary places; aratih = without taking delight; jana = people; samsadi = company.

"By unwavering devotion to Me without any other means, inclined to retreat into solitary places, without taking delight in the company of people...

Sloka 12

adhyātmajñānanityatvaṃ tattvajñānārthadarśanam
etaj jñānam iti proktam ajñānaṃ yad atonyathā

adhyatma = the Self; jnana = knowledge; nityatvam = everlasting; tattva-jnana = knowledge of reality; artha = object, purpose, goal; darsanam = insight; etat = his; jnanam = knowledge; iti = thus; proktam = declared; ajnanam = ignorance; yat = that which is; atah = from this; anyatha = others.

"Everlasting knowledge of the Self, insight into the purpose of the knowledge of reality, this is declared to be knowledge. Ignorance is that which is other than this.

Sloka 13

jñeyaṃ yat tat pravakṣyāmi yaj jñātvāmṛtam aśnute
anādimat paraṃ brahma na sat tan nāsad ucyate

jneyam = what is to be known, knowable; yat = that; tat = which; pravaksyami = I shall now speak; yat = which; jnatva = knowing; amrtam = immortatlity; asnute = tastes, attains; anadi = without beginning; mat= considered, thought of, believed; param = Supreme; brahma = Brahman; na = not; sat = being; tat = that; na = nor; asat = non-being; ucyate = is said.

"That which is to be known I shall now speak to you, knowing which immortality is attained. The Supreme Brahman, who is believed to be without beginning, is said to be neither Being nor Non-Being.

Sloka 14

sarvataḥ pāṇipādaṃ tat sarvatokṣiśiromukham
sarvataḥ śrutimal loke sarvam āvṛtya tiṣṭhati

sarvatah = everywhere; pani = hands; padam = legs; tat = that which; sarvatah = everywhere; aksi = eyes; sirah = head; mukham = mouths; sarvatah = everywhere; sruti-mat = ears; loke = in the world; sarvam = everything; avrtya = pervading, enveloping; tisthati = exists.

"That which has hands (and) feet, everywhere, which has eyes, head, (and) mouths everywhere, which has ears everywhere; exists in the world enveloping everything.

Sloka 15

sarvendriyaguṇābhāsaṃ sarvendriyavivarjitam
asaktaṃ sarvabhṛc caiva nirguṇaṃ guṇabhoktṛ ca

sarva = all; indriya = senses; guna = gunas, qualities; abhasam = endowed with power or radiance; sarva = all; indriya = senses; vivarjitam = devoid of , without; asaktam = unattached, without attachment; sarva-bhrt = upholding all; ca = and; eva = surely; nirgunam = without gunas or qualities; guna-bhoktr = devourer of the gunas; ca = but.

"Endowed with the radiance of all senses and their qualities, (yet) devoid of all senses, unattached, (but) upholding all; and surely without qualities, but enjoyer of the qualities...

Sloka 16

bahir antaś ca bhūtānām acaraṃ caram eva ca
sūkṣmatvāt tad avijñeyaṃ dūrasthaṃ cāntike ca tat

bahih - without; antah = within; ca =and; bhutanam = of the living being; acaram = unmoving; caram = moving; eva = similarly; ca = and; suksmatvat = because of subtle nature; tat = that, It; avijneyam = unknowable; durastham = far away; ca = and; antike = near; ca = and; tat = that.

"Without and within all beings, unmoving and similarly moving, It is unknowable because of Its subtle nature. That is also far away and near.

Sloka 17

avibhaktaṃ ca bhūteṣu vibhaktam iva ca sthitam
bhūtabhartṛ ca taj jñeyaṃ grasiṣṇu prabhaviṣṇu ca

avibhaktam = undivided, indivisible; ca = and, yet; bhutesu = in living beings; vibhaktam = divided; iva = similarly; ca = and; sthitam = remains, exists, seated; bhuta-bhartr = supporter or upholder of beings; ca = and; tat = that; jneyam = known grasisnu = absorbing, devouring; prabhavisnu = creator, originator; ca = and.

"Undivided, yet (It) exists in the beings as divided. Similarly, That Upholder of the beings is also known to be the Devourer and the Creator

Sloka 18

jyotiṣām api taj jyotis tamasaḥ param ucyate
jñānaṃ jñeyaṃ jñānagamyaṃ hṛdi sarvasya viṣṭhitam

jyotisam = of the radiant objects; api = verily; tat = that; jyotih = the light; tamasah = darkness; param = beyond; ucyate = said to be; jnanam = knowledge; jneyam = knowable; jnana-gamyam = the end of knowledge; hrdi = in the heart; sarvasya = of all; visthitam = situated.

"That Light of the radiant objects is said to be beyond darkness. Knowledge, the Knowable and the end of all knowledge is situated in the heart of all.

Sloka 19

iti kṣetraṃ tathā jñānaṃ jñeyaṃ coktaṃ sanāsataḥ
madbhakta etad vijñāya madbhāvāyopapadyate 13.19

iti = thus; ksetram = the field; tatha = also; jnanam = knowledge; jneyam = the knowable; ca = and; uktam = explained; samasatah = briefly; mat-bhaktah = My devotee; etat = this; vijnaya = By knowing; mat-bhavaya = My state; upapadyate = qualify to attain.

"Thus the field, also knowledge and the knowable are explained briefly. By knowing this My devotee is qualified to attain My state.

Sloka 20

prakṛtiṃ puruṣaṃ caiva viddhy anādi ubhāv api
vikārāñś ca guṇāṃś caiva viddhi prakṛtisaṃbhavān 13.20

prakrtim = Prakriti, Nature; purusam = Purusha, Cosmic Person; ca = and; eva = surely; viddhi =know; anadi = without beginning; ubhau = both; api = also; vikaran = modifications, changes; ca = and; gunan = gunas; ca = and; eva = surely; viddhi = know; prakrti = Nature; sambhavan = profrom.

"Know that both Purusha and Prakriti are surely without a beginning; also know that modifications and gunas surely arise from Nature.

Sloka 21

kārya kāraṇa kartṛtve hetuḥ prakṛtir ucyate
puruṣaḥ sukhaduḥkhānāṃ bhoktṛtve hetur ucyate

karya = actions; karana = means of action, instruments; kartrtve = agent of action; hetuh = the cause; prakrtih = Nature; ucyate = is said to be; purusah = purusha; sukha = of happiness; duhkhanam = sorrow; bhoktrtve = enjoyment; hetuh = the means; ucyate = is said to be.

"With regard to action, the means of action, the agent of action, Nature is said to be the cause. With regard to happiness and sorrow, Purusha is the cause for enjoyment.

Sloka 22

puruṣaḥ prakṛtistho hi bhuṅkte prakṛtijān guṇān
kāraṇaṃ guṇasaṅgosya sadasadyonijanmasu

purusah = purusa; prakrti-sthah = established in Prakriti; hi = indeed; bhunkte = enjoys; prakrti-jan = arising, produced from Nature; gunan = gunas, qualities; karanam = cause; guna-sangah = attachment with the qualities; asya = of his; sat-asat = good and evil; yoni = womb; janmasu = birth.

"Established in Prakriti indeed Purusha enjoys the qualities arising from Nature. Attachment with qualities is the cause of his birth in good and evil wombs.

Sloka 23

upadraṣṭānumantā ca bhartā bhoktā maheśvaraḥ
paramātmeti cāpyukto dehesmin puruṣaḥ paraḥ

upadrasta = overseer, witness; anumanta = permitter, giver of permissions, ; ca = and; bharta = supporter; bhokta = enjoyer; maha-isvarah = great lord; parama-atma = supreme self; iti = thus; ca = and; api uktah = is described, spoken of; dehe = in the body; asmin = this; purusah = purusa; parah = highest, supreme.

"The Overseer, Permitter, Supporter, Enjoyer, Great Lord, who is described as the Supreme Self is in the body, Purusa, the Highest.

Soka 24

ya evaṃ vetti puruṣaṃ prakṛtiṃ ca guṇaiḥ saha
sarvathā vartamānopi na sa bhūyobhijāyate

yah = he who; evam = thus; vetti = knows; purusam = purusa; prakrtim = prakriti, nature; ca = and; gunaih = gunas; saha = with; sarvatha = in all ways; vartamanah = in the present; api = even; na = not; sah = he; bhuyah = again; abhijayate = is born.

"He who knows thus Purusha and Prakriti along with the gunas, will not be born again whatever may be his present (way of life).

Sloka 25

dhyānenātmani paśyanti kecid ātmānam ātmanā
anye sāṃkhyena yogena karmayogena cāpare

dhyanena = by meditation; atmani = in oneself; pasyanti = see; kecit = some; atmanam = the Self; atmana = by oneself; anye = others; sankhyena = by Samkhya; yogena = yoga; karma-yogena = by karma yoga; ca = and; apare = others.

"Some by meditation see the Self in oneself by oneself; others by Samkhya Yoga; and other by Karma yoga.

Sloka 26

anye tv evam ajānantaḥ śrutvānyebhya upāsate
tepi cātitaranty eva mṛtyuṃ śrutiparāyaṇāḥ

anye = others; tu = however, but; evam = thus; ajanantah = without knowing, not knowing; srutva = by hearing; anyebhyah = from others; upasate = worship; te = they; api = also; ca = and; atitaranti = transcend, overcome; eva = surely; mrtyum = death; sruti-parayanah = constantly hearing the Vedas.

"Others, however, who do not know thus, may worship Me by hearing (about Me) from others. They also will surely transcend death by constantly hearing the Vedas.

Sloka 27

yāvat saṃjāyate kiṃcit sattvaṃ sthāvarajaṅgamam
kṣetrakṣetrajñasaṃyogāt tad viddhi bharatarṣabha

yavat = whatever; sanjayate = takes birth; kincit = any; sattvam = living being, existence; sthavara = unmoving; jangamam = moving; ksetra = the field; ksetra-jna = knower of the field; samyogat = union; tat viddhi = know that; bharata-rsabha = O chief among the Bharatas.

"Whatever thing, moving or unmoving, comes into existence, know that because of the union between the field and the knower of the field, O chief among the clan of Bharatas.

Sloka 28

samaṃ sarveṣu bhūteṣu tiṣṭhantaṃ parameśvaram
vinaśyatsv avinaśyantaṃ yaḥ paśyati sa paśyati

samam = equally; sarvesu = in all; bhutesu = living beings; tisthantam = established, ensconced; parama-isvaram = the Supreme Lord; vinasyatsu = in the destructible; avinasyantam = indestructible; yah = who; pasyati = sees; sah = he; pasyati = sees really.

"He who sees the Supreme Lord established in all living beings equally as the Indestructible in the destructible, he sees really.

Sloka 29

samaṃ paśyan hi sarvatra samavasthitam īśvaram
na hinasty ātmanātmānaṃ tato yāti parāṃ gatim

samam = equally; pasyan = seeing; hi = indeed; sarvatra = everywhere; samavasthitam = established alike or similarly; isvaram = the Lord; na = not; hinasti = harm or injure; atmana = by the self; atmanam = the Self; tatah = therefore; yati = attains, goes; param = the highest; gatim = goal.

"Indeed seeing equally the Lord who is established alike everywhere, he does not harm the Self by the Self. Therefore, he attains the Highest Goal.

Sloka 30

prakṛtyaiva ca karmāṇi kriyamāṇāni sarvaśaḥ
yaḥ paśyati tathātmānam akartāraṃ sa paśyati

prakrtya = by Nature; eva = alone; ca = and; karmani = actions; kriyamanani = being done; sarvasah = in all respects; yah = he who; pasyati = sees; tatha = and; atmanam = the Self; akartaram = non-doer; sah = he; pasyati = sees.

"He who sees that actions are performed by Nature only in all respects and the Self is the non-doer, he (really) sees.

Sloka 31

yadā bhūtapṛthagbhāvam ekastham anupaśyati
tata eva ca vistāraṃ brahma saṃpadyate tadā

yada = when; bhuta = living beings; prthak= different, separate; bhavam = existences, states; eka-stham = situated or rooted in one; anupasyati = knows with certainty; tatah = from there or that; eva = also; ca = and; vistaram = manifested; brahma = Brahman; sampadyate = attains; tada = then.

"When one knows with certainty that the different states of living beings are established in One and that their manifestation is also (seen arising) from That, then one attains Brahman.

Sloka 32

anāditvān nirguṇatvāt paramātmāyam avyayaḥ
śarīrasthopi kaunteya na karoti na lipyate

anaditvat = because without beginning; nirgunatvat = because without qualities; parama = supreme; atma = Self; ayam = this; avyayah = inexhaustible; sarira-sthah = situated in the body; api = although; kaunteya = O son of Kunti; na = not; karoti = does, perform; na = not; lipyate = touched or affected.

"Being without a beginning, being without qualities, this Supreme Self is inexhaustible. Although He is present in the body, O son of Kunti He does not act and He is not tainted.

Sloka 33

yathā sarvagataṃ saukṣmyād ākāśaṃ nopalipyate
sarvatrāvasthito dehe tathātmā nopalipyate

yatha = as; sarva-gatam = all-pervading; sauksmyat = because of subtlety; akasam = the sky; na = not; upalipyate = touched, tained; sarvatra = everywhere; avasthitah = present, situated; dehe = in the body; tatha = similarly; atma = the Self; na = does not; upalipyate = touched, entangled.

"Just as the all pervading sky is not touched or tainted because of its subtlety, so is the Self, which is present everywhere in the body, is not touched or tainted.

Sloka 34

yathā prakāśayaty ekaḥ kṛtsnaṃ lokam imaṃ raviḥ
kṣetraṃ kṣetrī tathā kṛtsnaṃ prakāśayati bhārata

yatha = just as; prakasayati = illuminates; ekah = one, single; krtsnam = the whole; lokam = world; imam = this; ravih = the sun; ksetram =

the field; ksetri = the knower of the field; tatha = similarly; krtsnam = all; prakasayati = illuminates; bharata = O descenden of Bharata.

"Just as the one sun illuminates this whole world, so does the Knower of the field illuminates the field, O descendent of Bharata.

Sloka 35

kṣetrakṣetrajñayor evam antaraṃ jñānacakṣuṣā
bhūtaprakṛtimokṣaṃ ca ye vidur yānti te param

ksetra = of the field; ksetra-jnayoh = of the knower of the field; evam = thus; antaram = difference; jnana-caksusa = through the eyes of knowledge; bhuta = living beings; prakrti =Nature; moksam = liberation; ca = and; ye = those who; viduh = know; yanti = go; te = they; param = Supreme.

"Those who know thus through the eyes of knowledge the difference between the field and the Knower of the field and the liberation of beings from Prakriti, they go to the Supreme.

Conclusion

iti srīmadbhāgavadgītāsupanisatsu brahmavidyāyām
yogasāstre
srikrisnārjunasamvāde kṣetrakṣetrajñavibhāgayogo nāma
trayodaśo 'dhyayah.

iti = thus; srīmadbhāgavadgītā = in the sacred Bhagavadgita; upanisatsu = in the Upanishad; brahmavidyāyām = the knowledge of the absolute Brahman; yogasāstre = the scripture of yoga; srikrisnārjunasamvāde = the dialogue between Sri Krishna and Arjuna; kṣetrakṣetrajñavibhāgayogo nāma = by name the yoga of the distinction between the Field and the Knower of the Field; trayodasah = thirteen; adhyayah = chapter.

Thus ends the thirteenth chapter named the Yoga of the Distinction Between the Field and the Knower of the Field in the Upanishad of the divine Bhagavadgita, the knowledge of

the Absolute, the yogic scripture, and the debate between Arjuna and Lord Krishna.

14 – The Yoga of the Division of the Triple Gunas

Sloka 1

paraṃ bhūyaḥ pravakṣyāmi jñānānāṃ jñānamuttamam
yaj jñātvā munayaḥ sarve parāṃ siddhim ito gatāḥ

sri-bhagavan uvaca = the Supreme Lord said; param = supreme; bhuyah = again; pravaksyami = I shall speak; jnananam = of all types of knowledge; jnanam = knowledge; uttamam = superior, the best; yat = which; jnatva = knowing; munayah = the meditating sages; sarve = all; param = the highest; siddhim = attaining; itah = here; gatah = departed, gone.

"The Supreme Lord said, "I shall speak again about the supreme knowledge, the best of all types of knowledge, knowing which the meditating sages attained the highest perfection when they departed from here.

Sloka 2

idaṃ jñānam upāśritya mama sādharmyam āgatāḥ
sargepi nopajāyante pralaye na vyathanti ca

idam = this; jnanam = knowledge; upasritya = taking refuge, following; mama = My; sadharmyam = essential nature, state; agatah = attain; sarge api = even during creation; na = never; upajayante = reborn; pralaye = during dissolution; na = not; vyathanti = suffer; ca = and.

"By taking refuge in this knowledge those who attain My essential Nature are not reborn at the time of creation nor do they suffer during dissolution.

Sloka 3

mama yonir mahad brahma tasmin garbhaṃ dadhāmyaham
saṃbhavaḥ sarvabhūtānāṃ tato bhavati bhārata

mama = My; yonih = womb; mahat brahma = the great expansive Prakriti; tasmin = in this; garbham = the seed, embryo; dadhami = place, offer; aham = I; sambhavah = ensues; sarva-bhutanam = of all living beings; tatah = from that; bhavati = arise; bharata = O descendent of Bharata.

"My womb is the great expansive Prakriti. In that I place the seed. From that ensues the birth of all living beings.

Sloka 4

sarvayoniṣu kaunteya mūrtayaḥ saṃbhavanti yāḥ
tāsāṃ brahma mahad yonir ahaṃ bījapradaḥ pitā

sarva-yonisu = of all the wombs; kaunteya = O son of Kunti; murtayah = forms; sambhavanti = are born; yah = which; tasam =of them; brahma = Brahma; mahat = great yonih = the womb; aham = I am; bija-pradah = the giver of seed; pita = father.

"Of all the wombs in which forms are born, O son of Kunti, Brahma is the great womb; I am the Seed Giving Father.

Sloka 5

sattvaṃ rajas tama iti guṇāḥ prakṛtisambhavāḥ
nibadhnanti mahābāho dehe dehinam avyayam

sattvam = sattva; rajah = rajas; tamah = tamas; iti = thus; gunah = qualities, modes of nature; prakrti = nature; sambhavah = arise, are born; nibadhnanti = bind; maha-baho = O mighty-armed one; dehe = in this body; dehinam = embodied self; avyayam = inexhuastible, imperishable.

"Sattva, rajas, tamas, thus the qualities are born of Nature, which bind the inexhaustible embodied Self in the body, O might armed one.

Sloka 6

tatra sattvaṃ nirmalatvāt prakāśakam anāmayam
sukhasaṅgena badhnāti jñānasaṅgena cānagha

tatra = of them; sattvam = the quality of sattva, purity; nirmalatvat = being pure and tranquail in nature; prakasakam = illuminating, reflector of light; anamayam = healthy, sound; sukha = pleasure, happiness; sangena = through attachment, association; badhnati = binds; jnana = knowledge; sangena = through attachment ca = and; anagha = O sinless one.

"Of them, being pure and tranquil in nature, sattva is illuminating, (and) healthy; it binds through attachment to pleasure and through attachment to knowledge, O sinless one.

Sloka 7

rajo rāgātmakaṃ viddhi tṛṣṇāsaṅgasamudbhavam
tan nibadhnāti kaunteya karmasaṅgena dehinam

Translation

rajah = the quality of rajas; raga-atmakam = nature of passion; viddhi = know; trsna = thirst for things, hunger; sanga = attachment; samudbhavam = born of, produced from; tat = that; nibadhnati = binds; kaunteya = O son of Kunti; karma-sangena = through attachment to action; dehinam = the embodied beings.

"Know that rajas has the nature of passion, born of attachment and thirst for things. It binds the embodied beings, O son of Kunti, through attachment to action.

Sloka 8

tamas tv ajñānajaṃ viddhi mohanaṃ sarvadehinām
pramādālasyanidrābhis tan nibadhnāti bhārata

tamah = tamas; tu = but; ajnana-jam = born of ignorance; viddhi = know; mohanam = delusion; sarva-dehinam = of the embodied beings; pramada = negligence; alasya =sloth, laziness; nidrabhih = sleep; tat = that; nibadhnati = binds; bharata = O descendent of Bharata.

"But know that tamas is born of ignorance, which deludes the embodied beings. That binds, O descendent of Bharata, through negligence, sloth and sleep.

Sloka 9

sattvaṃ sukhe saṃjayati rajaḥ karmaṇi bhārata
jñānam āvṛtya tu tamaḥ pramāde saṃjayaty uta

sattvam = sattva; sukhe = through pleasure, happiness; sanjayati = binds; rajah = rajas; karmani = through actions; bharata = O descendent of Bharata; jnanam = knowledge; avrtya = enveloped; tu = but; tamah = tamas; pramade = through negligence; sanjayati = binds; uta = it is said.

"Sattva binds through pleasure; rajas binds through actions; but O descendent of Bharata, it said that tamas binds through negligence by enveloping knowledge.

Sloka 10

rajas tamaś cābhibhūya sattvaṃ bhavati bhārata
rajaḥ sattvaṃ tamaś caiva tamaḥ sattvaṃ rajas tathā

rajah = rajas; tamah = tamas; ca = and; abhibhuya = by subduing; sattvam = mode of goodness; bhavati = increases, prevails, predominates; bharata = O descendent of Bharata; rajah = rajas; sattvam = sattva; tamah = tamas; ca = and; eva = similarly; tamah = tamas; sattvam = sattva; rajah = rajas; tatha = thus.

"Sattva prevails by subduing rajas and tamas, O descendent of Bharata; rajas by (subduing) sattva and tamas; and similarly, tamas (by subduing) sattva and rajas

Sloka 11

sarvadvāreṣu dehesmin prakāśa upajāyate
jñānaṃ yadā tadā vidyād vivṛddhaṃ sattvam ity uta

sarva-dvaresu = through all the doors; dehe asmin = in the body; prakasah = illumination; upajayate = radiate; jnanam = knowledge; yada = when; tada = then; vidyat = one should know; vivrddham = increased; sattvam = sattva; iti = thus; uta = said, declared.

"When through all the doors in the body, the illumination of knowledge radiates, then one should know that the sattva has increased profusely. Thus, it is declared.

Sloka 12

lobhaḥ pravṛttir ārambhaḥ karmaṇām aśamaḥ spṛhā
rajasy etāni jāyante vivṛddhe bharatarṣabha 14.12

lobhah pravrttih = greediness, propensity to greed; arambhah = beginning, initiating; karmanam = in actions; asamah = unrest, restlessness; sprha = hankering, seeking; rajasi = in rajas; etani = all tthese; jayante = develop, manifest, arise; vivrddhe = becomes predominant; bharata-rsabha = O chief among the the Bharatas.

"Greediness in beginning actions, restlessness, hankering, these (qualities) manifest when rajas becomes predominant, O chief among the Bharatas.

Sloka 13

aprakāśopravṛttiś ca pramādo moha eva ca
tamasy etāni jāyante vivṛddhe kurunandana

aprakasah = darkness; apravrttih = inactivity; ca = and; pramadah = carelessness, negligence; mohah = delusion; eva = even; ca =and; tamasi = of tamasa; etani = these; jayante = manifest, prevail; vivrddhe = predominate; kuru-nandana = O son of Kuru.

"Darkness, inactivity, carelessness, and delusion, these surely manifest when tamas predominates, O son of Kuru.

Sloka 14

yadā sattve pravṛddhe tu pralayaṃ yāti dehabhṛt
tadottamavidāṃ lokān amalān pratipadyate

yada = when; sattve = sattva; pravrddhe =increases, predominates; tu = completely; pralayam = death, dissolution; yati = goes, journeys; deha-bhrt = embodied self; tada = then; uttama-vidam = those who know the highest; lokan = the worlds; amalan = pure, without impurites; pratipadyate = attains.

"When an embodied being enters death, with sattva predominating in him greatly, then he attains the pure worlds of those who know the highest.

Sloka 15

**rajasi pralayaṃ gatvā karmasaṅgiṣu jāyate
tathā pralīnas tamasi mūḍhayoniṣu jāyate**

rajasi = he who is predominantly rajasic; pralayam = death, dissolution; gatva = journeying; karma-sangisu = those attached to action; jayate = takes birth, is born; tatha = thsu, in the same manner pralinah = upon death, dissolution; tamasi = he who is predominantly tamasic; mudha = deluded, ignorant; yonisu = wombs; jayate = take birth.

"He who is predominantly rajasic, upon journeying into death , is born among those who are attached to actions; in the same manner he who is predominantly tamasic takes birth in the wombs of the deluded.

Sloka 16

**karmaṇaḥ sukṛtasyāhuḥ sāttvikaṃ nirmalaṃ phalam
rajasas tu phalaṃ duḥkham ajñānaṃ tamasaḥ phalam**

karmanah = actions; su-krtasya = of good; ahuh = they say; sattvikam = born of sattva; nirmalam = pure; phalam = fruit; rajasah = of rajas; tu = but; phalam = fruit; duhkham = sorrow; ajnanam = ignorance; tamasah = of tamas; phalam = fruit.

"They say that the fruit of good actions is pure and born of sattva; but the fruit of rajas is sorrow; the fruit of tamas is ignorance.

Sloka 17

**sattvāt saṃjāyate jñānaṃ rajaso lobha eva ca
pramādamohau tamaso bhavatojñānam eva ca**

sattvat = from sattva sanjayate = is born; jnanam = knowledge; rajasah = from rajas; lobhah = greed; eva = verily; ca = and; pramada =

negligence; mohau = delusion; tamasah = from tamas; bhavatah = arises; ajnanam = ignorance; eva = surely; ca = and.

"From sattva is born knowledge; and from rajas surely greed; from tamas arise negligence, delusion and surely ignorance.

Sloka 18

ūrdhvaṃ gacchanti sattvasthā madhye tiṣṭhantirājasāḥ
jaghanyaguṇavṛttisthā adho gacchhanti tāmasāḥ

urdhvam = upwards; gacchanti = go; sattva-sthah = who are established in sattva; madhye = in the middle; tisthanti = sit, remain, reside; rajasah = who are rajasic; jaghanya = lowest; guna = kind, quality; vrtti-sthah = settled, occupied; adhah = down; gacchanti = go; tamasah = tamasic people.

"Those who are established in sattva go upward; those who are rajasic remain in the middle; tamasic people who indulge in the activities of the lowest kind go downwards.

Sloka 19

inānyaṃ guṇebhyaḥ kartāraṃ yadā draṣṭānupaśyati
guṇebhyaś ca paraṃ vetti madbhāvaṃ sodhigacchhati

na anyam = none other; gunebhyah = than the qualities; kartaram = doer,; yada = when; drasta = the seer; anupasyati = sees, perceives; gunebhyah = than the guans; ca = and; param = higher, superior; vetti = knows; mat-bhavam = My State, essential nature; sah = he; adhigacchati = goes, attains.

"When the seer sees none other than the gunas as the doer and knows That which is higher than the guans, he attain My State.

Sloka 20

guṇān etān atītya trīn dehī dehasamudbhavān
janmamṛtyujarāduḥkhair vimuktomṛtam aśnute

gunan = gunas; etan = these; atitya = by transcending; trin = three; dehi = the embodied self; deha = body; samudbhavan = origin, birth;

janma = birth; mrtyu = death; jara = old age; duhkhaih = sorrow; vimuktah = freed from; amrtam = immortality; asnute = attains.

"Going beyond these three qualities, which are (responsible for) the origin of the body, the embodied Self, becoming free from birth, death, old age and sorrow, attain immortality."

Sloka 21

arjuna uvāca
kair liṅgais trīn guṇān etān atīto bhavati prabho
kimācāraḥ kathaṃ caitāṃs trīn guṇān ativartate

arjunah uvaca = Arjuna said; kaih = by what; lingaih = signs, marks; trin = three; gunan = qualities; etan = theses; atitah = transcendence, going beyond; bhavati = manifest, become; prabho = O Lord; kim = what; acarah = behavior; katham = how; ca = and; etan = these; trin = three; gunan = qualities; ativartate = transcend.

"Asked Arjuna, "O Lord, by what signs the transcendence of these triple gunas manifests (in a person)? What is his behavior and how does he transcend these three gunas?"

Sloka 22

Śrībhagavān uvāca
prakāśaṃ ca pravṛttiṃ ca moham eva ca pāṇḍava
na dveṣṭi saṃpravṛttāni na nivṛttāni kāṅkṣati

sri-bhagavan uvaca = the Supreme Lord said; prakasam = light, radiance, illuminating; ca = and, pravrttim = passion; ca = and; moham = illusion; eva = even; ca = and; pandava = O son of Pandu; na = not; dvesti = hates, resents, dislines; sampravrttani = when they exist, prevail; na nivrttani = do not exist, do not prevail; kanksati = desires, seeks.

"The Supreme Lord replied, "Light, passion and delusion, O son of Pandu, (he) neither dislikes when they exit nor desires when they do not exist.

Sloka 23

udāsīnavad āsīno guṇair yo na vicālyate
guṇā vartanta ity eva yovatiṣṭhati neṅgate

udasina-vat =as if indifferent; asinah = seated; gunaih = by the gunas; yah = one who; na = not; vicalyate = is disturbed or distracted; gunah = the gunas; vartante = act; iti evam = knowing thus; yah = one who; avatisthati = remains firmly established; na = not; ingate = flickering.

"Seated as if indifferent, undisturbed by the gunas, knowing that the gunas alone act, he remains firmly established and does not waver.

Sloka 24

samaduḥkhasukhaḥ svasthaḥ samaloṣṭāśmakāñcanaḥ
tulyapriyāpriyo dhīras tulyanindātmasaṃstutiḥ

sama = same, equal; duhkha = in sorrow; sukhah = in happiness; sva-sthah = self-reliant; sama = same, equal; losta = a lump of earth; asma = stone; kancanah = gold; tulya = same; priya = pleasant; apriyah = unpleasant; dhirah = steady; tulya = balanced; ninda = in censure, blame, criticism; atma-samstutih = self-adulation.

"Same in sorrow and happiness, self-reliant, equal to a lump of earth, stone and gold, equal to the pleasant and the unpleasant, steady, balanced in censure and self-adulation...

Sloka 25

mānāpamānayos tulyas tulyo mitrāripakṣayoḥ
sarvārambhaparityāgī guṇātītaḥ sa ucyate

mana = in honor; apamanayoh = in dishonor; tulyah = equal; tulyah = equal; mitra = friend; ari = enemy; paksayoh = in association, taking sides; sarva = all; arambha = taking initiative; parityagi = who has renounced; guna-atitah = transcended the gunas; sah = he; ucyate = said to be.

"Equal in honor and dishonor, equal to friend and foe in taking sides, who has renounced taking all initiative is said to be the one who has transcended the gunas.

Sloka 26

māṃ ca yovyabhicāreṇa bhaktiyogena sevate
sa guṇān samatītyaitān brahmabhūyāya kalpate

mam = Me; ca = and; yah = who; avyabhicarena = without distraction; bhakti-yogena = by the yoga of devotion; sevate = serves; sah = he; gunan = gunas; samatitya = transcends; etan = these; brahma-bhuyaya = the Self or the State of Brahman; kalpate = is qualified.

"Whoever servers Me without distraction and by the yoga of devotion, he transcends these qualities and he is qualified for the State of Brahman.

Sloka 27

brahmaṇo hi pratiṣṭhāham amṛtasyāvyayasya ca
śāśvatasya ca dharmasya sukhasyaikāntikasya ca.

brahmanah = in Brahman; hi = surely; pratistha = established; aham = I am; amrtasya = immortal; avyayasya = inexhaustible; ca = and; sasvatasya = eternal, permanent; ca = and; dharmasya = Dharma; sukhasya = bliss; aikantikasya = highest and absolute; ca = and.

"Surely I am established here as Brahman, the immortal, inexhaustible, and eternal, the Dharma and the highest bliss.

Conclusion

iti srīmadbhāgavadgītāsupanisatsu brahmavidyāyām
yogasāstre
srikrisnārjunasamvāde guṇatrayavibhāgayogo nāma
caturdaśo 'dhyayah.

iti = thus; srīmadbhāgavadgītā = in the sacred Bhagavadgita; upanisatsu = in the Upanishad; brahmavidyāyām = the knowledge of the absolute Brahman; yogasāstre = the scripture of yoga; srikrisnārjunasamvāde = the dialogue between Sri Krishna and

Arjuna; guṇatrayavibhāgayogo nāma = by name th e y ɑg a of the division of the triple gunas; caturdasah = fourteen; adhyayah = chapter.

Thus ends the fourteenth chapter named the Yoga of the Division of the Triple Gunas in the Upanishad of the divine Bhagavadgita, the knowledge of the Absolute, the yogic scripture, and the debate between Arjuna and Lord Krishna.

15 – The Yoga of the Supreme Person

Sloka 1

śrībhagavān uvāca
ūrdhvamūlam adhaḥśākham aśvatthaṃ prāhur avyam
chandāṃsi yasya parṇāni yas taṃ veda sa vedavit 15.1

sri-bhagavan = the supreme lord; uvaca = said; urdhva-mulam = roots above, upwards; adhah = below, downwards; sakham = branches; asvattham = asvattha tree; prahuh = said; avyayam = unending; chandamsi = Vedic hymns; yasya = of which; parnani = the leaves; yah = who; tam = that; veda = knows; sah = he; veda-vit = the knower of the Brahman.

"Said the Supreme Lord, "With roots above, branches below, the Asvattha tree is said to be unending, of which the Vedic hymns are the leaves. He who knows that is a knower of Brahman.

Sloka 2

adhaś cordhvaṃ prasṛtāstasya śākhā guṇapravṛddhā viṣayapravālāḥ
adhaś ca mūlāny anusaṃtatāni karmānubandhīni manuṣyaloke

adhah = downward; ca = and; urdhvam = upward; prasrtah = spread, extending; tasya = of its; sakhah = branches; guna = gunas; pravrddhah = nourished, strengthened; visaya = sense objects; pravalah = buds, sprouts; adhah = downward; ca = and; mulani = roots; anusantatani = extended, spread; karma anubandhini = following the actions; manusya-loke = in the world of human beings.

"Downward and upward are spread the branches of that (Tree), nourished by the gunas. The sense objects are its sprouts. Downward are spread (its) roots, following the actions in the world of human beings.

Sloka 3

na rūpam asyeha tathopalabhyate nānto na cādir na ca saṃpratiṣṭhā
aśvattham enaṃ suvirūḍhamūlaṃ asaṅgaśastreṇa dṛḍhena chittvā

na = not; rupam = form; asya = of this; iha = here, this; tatha = also; upalabhyate = seen, available, found; na = not; antah = end; na = not; ca = and; adih = beginning; na = not; ca = and; sampratistha = foundation; asvattham = asvattha tree; enam = this; su-virudha = well developed; mulam = roots; asanga-sastrena = by the sword or weapon of detachment; drdhena = strong; chittva = by cutting.

"The form of this is not seen here; so also neither its end nor its beginning nor its foundation. By cutting the well developed roots of this Asvattha tree with the sword of detachment...

Sloka 4

tataḥ padaṃ tatparimārgitavyaṃ yasmin gatā na nivartanti bhūyaḥ
tameva cādyaṃ puruṣaṃ prapadye yataḥ pravṛttiḥ prasṛtā purāṇī

tatah = thereafter; padam = place; tat = that; parimargitavyam = has to be sought; yasmin = where; gatah = going; na = no; nivartanti = returns; bhuyah = again; tam = in That; eva = only; ca = and; adyam = the first, primeval; purusam = purusa, person; prapadye = take refuge; yatah = from whom; pravrttih = nature; prasrta = issued forth, spread out, extended; purani = remote past.

"Thereafter, that Place has to be sought by going where there is no return again, (thinking),' I take refuge in that Primeval Purusha only from whom Nature issued forth in the remote past.'

Sloka 5

nirmānamohā jitasaṅgadoṣā adhyātmanityā vinivṛttakāmāḥ dvandvair vimuktāḥ sukhaduḥkhasaṃjñaiḥ gacchhanty amūḍhāḥ padam avyayaṃ tat

nih = without; mana = pride, egoism; mohah = delusion; jita = victorious; sanga = attachment; dosah = impurity; adhyatma = absorbed in the Self; nityah = always; vinivrtta = disengaged; kamah = lust; dvandvaih = dualities; vimuktah = free from; sukha-duhkha = pleasure and pain; samjnaih = such as; gacchanti = attains; amudhah = one without delusion; padam = state; avyayam = indestructible; tat = that.

"Without pride (and) delusion, victorious over the impurity of attachment, always absorbed in the Self, disengaged from lust, free from the dualities such as pleasure and pain, the one who is without delusion attains that indestructible State.

Sloka 6

na tad bhāsayate sūryo na śaśāṅko na pāvakaḥ
yad gatvā na nivartante tad dhāma paramaṃ mama

na = not; tat = that; bhasayate =illuminates; suryah = the sun; na = not; sasankah = the moon; na = nor; pavakah = fire; yat = where; gatva = going; na = not, never; nivartante = return; tat = that; dhama = abode; paramam = supreme; mama = My.

"Neither the sun nor the moon nor the fire illuminates That. By going where one never returns, That is My Abode.

Commentary

The Abode of Brahman is the highest and the most supreme. It is self-luminous unlike our world, which depends upon the sun and the moon. It is also free from the duality and limitations of the manifested worlds. Since it is eternal, it is also free from influence of time and the process of renewal and regeneration. Hence, those who reach it never return to the mortal world or suffer from the modifications of Nature.

Sloka 7

mamaivāṃśo jīvaloke jīvabhūtaḥ sanātanaḥ
manaḥṣaṣṭhānīndriyāṇi prakṛtisthāni karṣati

mama = My; eva = only; amsah = aspects, portion, part; jiva-loke = world of beings; jiva-bhutah = living Self, embodied Self; sanatanah = eternal; manah = mind; sasthani = six; indriyani = senses; prakrti = nature; sthani = established; karsati = draws, attracts.

"The eternal embodied Self in the world of beings is My aspect only. Established in Prarkriti, it attracts the the senses of which the mind is the sixth.

Sloka 8

śarīraṃ yad avāpnoti yac cāpy utkrāmatīśvaraḥ
gṛhitvaitāni saṃyāti vāyur gandhān ivāśayāt

sariram = body; yat = when; avapnoti = acquired; yat = when; ca = and; api = even; utkramati = departs; isvarah = the Lord, the Self; grhitva = taking; etani = these; samyati = goes away; vayuh = air; gandhan = fragrance; iva = like; asayat = from the flower.

"When the Lord departs and even when He acquires the body, He goes away taking these, like the wind (carries away) the fragrance from the flower.

Sloka 9

śrotraṃ cakṣuḥ sparśanaṃ ca rasanaṃ ghrāṇam eva ca
adhiṣṭhāya manaś cāyaṃ viṣayān upasevate

srotram = ears; caksuh = eyes; sparsanam = skin; ca = and; rasanam = tongue ghranam = nose; eva = even; ca = also; adhisthaya = presiding over; manah = mind; ca = and; ayam = this; visayan = sense objects; upasevate = enjoys.

"Presiding over the ears, the eyes and the skin, also the nose and the tongue, and even the mind, This (Self) enjoys the sense objects.

Sloka 10

utkrāmantaṃ sthitaṃ vāpi bhuñjānaṃ vā guṇānvitam
vimūḍhā nānupaśyanti paśyanti jñānacakṣuṣaḥ

utkramantam = in the end; sthitam = present, situated, located; va = or; api = also; bhunjanam = enjoying; va = or; guna-anvitam = adorned with qualities; vimudhah = deluded people; na = not; anupasyanti = see; pasyanti = see; jnana-caksusah = eyes of knowledge.

"Deluded people do not see it when it departs in the end or when it is present (in the body), enjoying or adorned with qualities. Those with the eyes of wisdom see.

Sloka 11

yatanto yoginaś cainaṃ paśyanty ātmany avasthitam
yatantopy akṛtātmāno nainaṃ paśyanty acetasaḥ

yatantah = with intense effort, striving,; yoginah = yogis; ca = and; enam = this; pasyanti = see; atmani = in themselves avasthitam = present, established; yatantah = striving; api = but; akrta-atmanah = imperfect or incomplete beings; na = not; enam = this; pasyanti =see; acetasah = indiscriminate ones, those who lack discrimination.

"And with intense effort the yogis see this established in themselves; but the imperfect beings and the indiscriminate ones cannot see this even with striving.

Sloka 12

yad ādityagataṃ tejo jagad bhāsayatekhilam
yac candramasi yac cāgnau tat tejo viddhi māmakam

yat = that; aditya-gatam = in the sun; tejah = brilliance, light; jagat = the world; bhasayate = illuminates; akhilam = whole; yat = that which; candramasi = in the moon; yat = that which; ca = and; agnau = in the fire; tat = that; tejah = splendor; viddhi = know; mamakam = Mine.

"That brilliance in the sun which illuminates the whole world; that which is in the moon and that which is in the fire, know that brilliance (also) is Mine.

Sloka 13

gām āviśya ca bhūtāni dhārayāmy aham ojasā
puṣṇāmi cauṣadhīḥ sarvāḥ somo bhūtvā rasātmakaḥ

gam = the earth; avisya = entering; ca = and; bhutani = living beings; dharayami = support, sustain; aham = I; ojasa = by My vigor, energy; pusnami = nourish; ca = and; ausadhih = herbs, plants; sarvah = all; somah = soma; bhutva = becoming; rasa-atmakah = filled with juice, juicy, succulent.

"And entering the earth I sustain all beings with My vigor and nourish all the plants by becoming the juicy Soma.

Sloka 14

ahaṃ vaiśvānaro bhūtvā prāṇināṃ deham āśritaḥ
prāṇāpānasamāyuktaḥ pacāmy annaṃ caturvidham

aham = I; vaisvanarah = Vaisvanarah, the digestive fire; bhutva = becoming; praninam = in the living beings; deham = body; asritah = residing, taking refuge; prana = prana, upward breath; apana = apana, downward breath; samayuktah = union, association; pacami = digest; annam = food; catuh-vidham = four kinds of.

"Residing in the body of living beings (and) becoming the digestive fire, together with upward and downward breath I digest four kinds of food.

Sloka 15

sarvasya cāhaṃ hṛdi saṃniviṣṭomattaḥ smṛtir jñānam apohanaṃ ca
vedaiś ca sarvair aham eva vedyo vedāntakṛd vedavid eva cāham

sarvasya = of all; ca = and; aham = I; hrdi = in the heart; sannivistah = seated, situated; mattah = from Me; smrtih = memory; jnanam = knowledge; apohanam loss, removal; ca = and; vedaih = from the Vedas; ca = and; sarvaih = all; aham = I am; eva = alone; vedyah = which is to be known, knowable; vedanta-krt = the creator of the

Vedanta; veda-vit = knower of the Vedas; eva = even; ca = and; aham = I ;

"And I am seated in the heart of all. From me only are memory, knowledge and even their loss. I alone am the object to be known from the Vedas. I Myself am the Creator of the Vedanta and the Knower of the Vedas.

Sloka 16

dvāv imau puruṣau loke kṣaraś cākṣara eva ca
kṣaraḥ sarvāṇi bhūtāni kūṭasthokṣara ucyate 15.16

dvau = two; imau =these; purusau = purusas; loke = in the world; ksarah = perishable; ca = and; aksarah = imperishable; eva = indeed; ca = and; ksarah = the perishable; sarvani = all; bhutani = living beings; kuta-sthah = standing at the top, occupying the highest place, the ancestor of all; aksarah =indestructible; ucyate = is said.

"Indeed these Purushas in the world are two, the perishable and the imperishable. All the living beings are the perishable, but the highest of all is said to be the imperishable.

Sloka 17

uttamaḥ puruṣas tv anyaḥ paramātmety udāhṛtaḥ
yo lokatrayam āviśya bibharty avyaya īśvaraḥ

uttamah = the highest, supreme; purusah = purusha; tu = but, however; anyah = different, another; parama = supreme; atma = self; iti = thus; udahrtah =said to; yah = who; loka = worlds; trayam = three; avisya = pervading; bibharti = upholds; avyayah = inexhaustible; isvarah = the Lord.

"However, different is the highest Purusha, who is said to be the Supreme Self, the imperishable Lord who upholds the three worlds, pervading them,.

Sloka 18

yasmāt kṣaram atītoham akṣarād api cottamaḥ
atosmi loke vede ca prathitaḥ puruṣottamaḥ

yasmat = since; ksaram = the perishable; atitah = higher, beyond; aham = I; aksarat = the imperishable; api = even; ca = and; uttamah = above or better than; atah = thereby; asmi = I am; loke = in the world; vede = in the Vedas; ca = and; prathitah = known; purusa-uttamah = as the Supreme Person.

"Since I am beyond the perishable and above even the imperishable, therefore I am well known in the world and in the Vedas as the Supreme Person.

Sloka 19

yo mām evam asaṃmūḍho jānāti puruṣottamam
sa sarvavid bhajati māṃ sarvabhāvena bhārata

yah = he who; mam = Me; evam = thus; asammudhah = without delusion; janati = knows; purusa-uttamam = the Supreme Person; sah = he; sarva-vit = all knowing; bhajati = worships; mam = Me; sarva-bhavena = with complete devotion; bharata = O descendent of Bharata.

"He who knows Me thus without delusion as the Supreme Person, he, the all knowing, worships Me with complete devotion, O descendent of Bharata.

Sloka 20

iti guhyatamaṃ śāstram idam uktaṃ mayānagha
etat buddhvā buddhimān syāt kṛtakṛtyaś ca bhārata

iti = thus; guhya-tamam = the most secretive; sastram = scripture; idam = this; uktam = described, revealed; maya = by Me; anagha = O sinless one; etat = this; buddhva = understanding; buddhi-man = wise; syat = one becomes; krta-krtyah = accomplished in duty; ca = and; bharata = O descendent of Bharata.

"Thus, this most secretive scripture has been revealed by Me, O sinless one; understanding this, the wise one becomes accomplished in duty, O descendent of Bharata!

Conclusion

iti srīmadbhāgavadgītāsupanisatsu brahmavidyāyām yogasāstre srikrisnārjunasamvāde puruṣottamayogo nāma pañcadaśo 'dhyayah.

iti = thus; srīmadbhāgavadgītā = in the sacred Bhagavadgita; upanisatsu = in the Upanishad; brahmavidyāyām = the knowledge of the absolute Brahman; yogasāstre = the scripture of yoga; srikrisnārjunasamvāde = the dialogue between Sri Krishna and Arjuna; puruṣottamayogo nāma = by name the yoga of the supreme person; pancadasah = fifteen; adhyayah = chapter.

Thus ends the fifteenth chapter named the the Yoga of the Supreme Person in the Upanishad of the divine Bhagavadgita, the knowledge of the Absolute, the yogic scripture, and the debate between Arjuna and Lord Krishna.

16 – The Division of the Divine and Demonic Properties

Sloka 1

śrībhagavān uvāca
abhayaṃ sattvasaṃśuddhir jñānayogavyavasthitiḥ
dānaṃ damaś ca yajñaś ca svādhyāyas tapa ārjavam

sri-bhagavan uvaca = the supreme lord said; abhayam = fearlessness; sattva-samsuddhih = with predominance of sattva; jnana = knowledge; yoga = yoga; vyavasthitih = established in; danam = charity; damah = self-restraint; ca = and; yajnah = sacrifice; ca = and; svadhyayah = self-study of the scriptures; tapah = austerity; arjavam = simplicity.

"The Supreme Lord said, "Fearlessness, predominance of sattva, well established in the yoga of knowledge, (engaged in) charity, self-restraint, self-study of the scriptures, austerity and simplicity...

Sloka 2

ahiṃsā satyam akrodhas tyāgaḥ śāntir apaiśunam
dayā bhūteṣv aloluptvaṃ mārdavaṃ hrīr acāpalam

ahimsa = non-injury; satyam = truthfulness; akrodhah = freedom from anger; tyagah = self-sacrificing, renunciation; santih = peace; apaisunam = non-slandering, aversion to backbiting; daya = compassion; bhutesu = living being; aloluptvam = non-covetousness; mardavam = gentleness; hrih = modesty; acapalam =unwavering.

Meaninig

"Non-injury, truthfulness, freedom from anger, self-sacrificing, peaceful, non-slandering, compassion towards all beings, non-covetousness, gentleness, modesty, unwaveringness...

Sloka 3

tejaḥ kṣamā dhṛtiḥ śaucam adroho nātimānitā
bhavanti saṃpadaṃ daivīm abhijātasya bhārata

tejah = vigor; ksama = forgiveness; dhrtih = fortitude; saucam = cleanliness; adrohah = freedom from treachery; na = not; ati-manita = self-importance; bhavanti = manifest; sampadam = properties, qualities; daivim =divine; nature abhijatasya = born in consequences of, out of; bharata = O descendent of Bharata.

"Vigor, forgiveness, fortitude, cleanliness, freedom from treachery, absence of self-importance, (these) are the qualities of those who are born as a result of divine nature, O descendent of Bharata!

Sloka 4

dambho darpobhimānaś ca krodhaḥ pāruṣyam eva ca
ajñānaṃ cābhijātasya pārtha saṃpadam āsurīm

dambhah = vanity; darpah = arrogance; abhimanah = self-pride; ca = and; krodhah = anger; parusyam = harshness; eva = even; ca = and; ajnanam = ignorance; ca = and; abhijatasya = born out of or in consequence of; partha = O Partha; sampadam = possessions, qualities, endowments; asurim = demoniac nature.

"Vanity, arrogance, self-pride, anger, harshness and even ignorance are the qualities of those who are born as a result of demonic nature.

Sloka 5

daivī saṃpad vimokṣāya nibandhāyāsurī matā
mā śucaḥ saṃpadaṃ daivīm abhijātosi pāṇḍava

daivi = divine; sumpat = qualities, virtures; vimoksaya = for liberation; nibandhaya = for bondage; asuri = demonic qualities; mata = opined to be, considered to be; ma = do not; sucah = worry; sampadam = nature; daivim = divine; abhijatah = born as a result of; asi = you are; pandava = O son of Pandu.

"Divine qualities are for liberation; demonic qualities are considered to be binding. Do not worry, O son of Pandu, you are born in consequence of divine nature.

Sloka 6

dvau bhūtasargau lokesmin daiva āsura eva ca
daivo vistaraśaḥ prokta āsuraṃ pārtha me śṛṇu

dvau = twofold; bhuta-sargau = creation of beings; loke = in the world; asmin = this; daivah = divine; asurah = demonic; eva = surely; ca = and; daivah = divine; vistarasah = in detail; proktah = described; asuram = demonic; partha = O Partha; me = from Me; srnu =hear.

"Twofold is the creation of beings in this world, the divine and the demonic. The divine has been described in detail; O Partha, (now) hear from Me about the demonic (nature).

Sloka 7

pravṛttiṃ ca nivṛttiṃ ca janā na vidur āsurāḥ
na śaucaṃ nāpi cācāro na satyaṃ teṣu vidyate

pravrttim = what should be done; ca = and; nivrttim = what should not be done; ca = and; janah = people; na = not viduh = know; asurah = demonic; na = not; saucam = cleanliness; na = not; api = also; ca = and; acarah = customary or formal behavior; na = not; satyam = truth; tesu = in them; vidyate = there is.

"The demonic people do not know what should be done or what should not be done. They do not know about cleanliness and customary behavior. There is no truthfulness in them.

Sloka 8

asatyam apratiṣṭhaṃ te jagad āhur anīśvaram
aparasparasaṃbhūtaṃ kim anyat kāmahaitukam

asatyam = unreal, false; apratistham = without support or foundation; te = they; jagat = the world; ahuh = they say; anisvaram = without Isvara; aparaspara = by mutual union; sambhutam = comes into existence; kim anyat = what else; kama-haitukam = because of sexual passion.

"They say, 'The world is unreal, has no foundation, (and) has no Lord. It comes into existence because of mutual union arising from sexual passion. What else can there be?'

Sloka 9

etāṃ dṛṣṭim avaṣṭabhya naṣṭātmānolpabuddhayaḥ
prabhavanty ugrakarmāṇaḥ kṣayāya jagatohitāḥ

etam = this; drstim = perspective, view, opinion; avastabhya = accepting, holding; nasta = depraved, lost; atmanah = souls; alpa-buddhayah = of poor intelligence; prabhavanti = flourish, prevail; ugra-karmanah = in terrible activities; ksayaya = for the destruction; jagatah = of the world; ahitah = ill, harm.

"Holding on to this perspective, the depraved souls of poor intelligence prevail by (indulging in) terrible and destructive actions for the ill of the world

Sloka 10

kāmam āśritya duṣpūraṃ dambhamānamadānvitāḥ
mohād gṛhītvāsadgrāhān pravartanteśucivratāḥ

kamam = lust; asritya = yielding, taking refuge, surrendering; duspuram = insatiable; dambha = vanity; mana = pride; mada = arrogance; anvitah = filled with; mohat = because of delusion; grhitva = seeking, grasping, recoursing; asat = illusory, false; grahan = things; pravartante = engage or indulge in actions, behave; asuci vratah = the worshippers of the unclean.

"Yielding to insatiable lust, filled with vanity, pride, (and) arrogance, seeking illusory things because of delusion, the worshippers of the unclean engage in actions.

Sloka 11

cintām aparimeyāṃ ca pralayāntām upāśritāḥ
kāmopabhogaparamā etāvad iti niścitāḥ

cintam = worries; aparimeyam = countless; ca = and; pralaya-antam = until the end; upasritah = taking refuge; kama-upabhoga = enjoyment of desires; paramah = the highest; etavat = this is all; iti = thus; niscitah = concluding.

"With countless worries, and taking refuge in the enjoyment of desires until the end as the highest goal, concluding thus that it is all...

Sloka 12

āśāpāśaśatair baddhāḥ kāmakrodhaparāyaṇāḥ
īhante kāmabhogārtham anyāyenārthasaṃcayān

asa-pasa = the bonds of hope; sataih = innumerable, many, hundreds; baddhah = caught, bound; kama = lust; krodha = anger; parayanah = given to the thoughts of; ihante = strive; kama = lust; bhoga = enjoyment of material objects; artham = for the sake of; anyayena = unjust or unlawful means; artha = wealth; sancayan = amass, accumulate.

"Caught in innumerable bonds of hope, given to the thoughts of lust and anger, they strive to amass wealth by unjust or unlawful means for the sake of lust and enjoyment.

Sloka 13

idam adya mayā labdham imaṃ prāpsye manoratham
idam astīdam api me bhaviṣyati punar dhanam

idam = this; adya = today; maya = by me; labdham = gained; imam = this; prapsye = I shall gain; manah-ratham = hidden desire, wish; idam = this; asti = in my hands; idam = this; api = also; me = to me; bhavisyati = in future; punah = again; dhanam = wealth.

"This has been gained by me today; this hidden desire of mine I shall fulfill; this is in my hand; and again in future this wealth will also come to me.

Sloka 14

asau mayā hataḥ śatrur haniṣye cāparān api
īśvaro.aham ahaṃ bhogī siddhohaṃ balavān sukhī

asau = that; maya = by me; hatah = has been slain; satruh = enemy; hanisye = I shall harm; ca = and; aparan = others; api = also; isvarah = the lord; aham = I am; aham = I am; bhogi = the enjoyer; siddhah = perfect; aham = I am; bala-van = powerful; sukhi = happy.

"That enemy has been slain by me; I shall harm others also; I am the lord; I am the enjoyer; I am perfect, powerful, (and) happy..

Sloka 15

āḍhyobhijanavān asmi konyosti sadṛśo mayā
yakṣye dāsyāmi modiṣya ity ajñānavimohitāḥ

adhyah = wealthy; abhijana-van = from a superior lineage; asmi = I am; kah anyah = who else; asti = is there; sadrsah = like; maya = me; yaksye = I offer sacrifices; dasyami = I give charity; modisye = I shall rejoice; iti = thus; ajnana = by ignorance; vimohitah = deluded.

"'I am wealthy; I belong to a superior lineage; who else is there like me? I shall offer sacrifices, I shall give charity; I shall rejoice,' thus are (they) deluded by ignorance.

Sloka 16

anekacittavibhrāntā mohajālasamāvṛtāḥ
prasaktāḥ kāmabhogeṣu patanti narakeśucau

aneka = numerous; citta vibhrantah = perplexed, bewildered by thoughts; moha = delusion; jala = net; samavrtah = caught, surrounded; prasaktah = engrossed, attached; kama = desires; bhogesu = in the enjoyment; patanti = fall down; narake = into hell; asucau = those who are unclean.

"Perplexed by numerous thoughts, caught in the net of delusion, attached to the enjoyment of desires, (they) fall down into the unclean hell.

Sloka 17

ātmasaṃbhāvitāḥ stabdhā dhanamānamadānvitāḥ
yajante nāmayajñais te dambhenāvidhipūrvakam

atma-sambhavitah = self-conceited; stabdhah = arrogant, impudent; dhana-mana = wealth and pride; mada = intoxication; anvitah = filled with; yajante = perform sacrifices; nama yajnaih = namesake only; te = they; dambhena = out of vanity; avidhi-purvakam = against the established practices.

"Self-conceited, arrogant, filled with pride and the intoxication of wealth, they perform sacrifices for namesake only, out of vanity and against established practices.

Sloka 18

ahaṃkāraṃ balaṃ darpaṃ kāmaṃ krodhaṃ casaṃśritāḥ
mām ātmaparadeheṣu pradviṣantobhyasūyakāḥ

ahankaram = egoism; balam = strength; darpam = showiness, arrogance; kamam = lust; krodham = anger; ca = and; samsritah = abiding, having taken sheler, abiding in, resorting to; mam = Me; atma = own; para = other; dehesu = in bodies; pradvisantah = hating; abhyasuyakah = the excessively envious.

"Abiding in egoism, strength, showiness, lust, and anger, hateing Me in their own and other bodies, (thus prevail) the excessively envious.

Sloka 19

tān ahaṃ dviṣataḥ krurān saṃsāreṣu narādhamān
kṣipāmy ajasram aśubhān āsurīṣv eva yoniṣu

tan = these; aham = I; dvisatah = haters; kruran = cruel; samsaresu = in the phenomenal world, existence; nara-adhaman = the lowest of the humanity; ksipami = cast, throw; ajasram = forever; asubhan = inauspicious; asurisu = demonic; eva = surely; yonisu = in the wombs.

"I cast forever these cruel haters, the lowest of the humanity in the phenomenal world, into the inauspicious and demonic wombs.

Sloka 20

āsurīṃ yonim āpannā mūḍhā janmanijanmani
mām aprāpyaiva kaunteya tato yānty adhamāṃ gatim

asurim = demoniac; yonim = wombs; apannah = obtaining, acquiring; mudhah = the deluded; janmani janmani = in birth after birth; mam = Me; aprapya = without reaching, attaining; eva = ever; kaunteya = O son of Kunti; tatah = thereafter; yanti = fall, go, ; adhamam = lowest, downward, lower; gatim = world.

"Obtaining demonic wombs, the deluded beings birth after birth, without reaching Me, O son of Kunti, fall into the lowest world.

Sloka 21

trividhaṃ narakasyedaṃ dvāraṃ nāśanam ātmanaḥ
kāmaḥ krodhas tathā lobhas tasmād etat trayaṃtyajet

tri-vidham = three types; narakasya = of the hell; idam = this; dvaram = gate; nasanam = destructive; atmanah = for the being; kamah = lust; krodhah = anger; tatha = and; lobhah = greed; tasmat = therefore; etat = these; trayam = three; tyajet = must renounce.

"The door to this hell, which is destructive for the beings, is of three types, (namely) lust, anger and greed. Therefore, these (one) must renounce.

Sloka 22

etair vimuktaḥ kaunteya tamodvārais tribhir naraḥ
ācaraty ātmanaḥ śreyas tato yāti parāṃ gatim

etaih = by these; vimuktah = free; kaunteya = O son of Kunti; tamah-dvaraih = from the gates of darkness; tribhih = triple, three ; narah = a person; acarati = acts; atmanah = self; sreyah = welfare; tatah = thereafter; yati = reaches, goes; param = supreme; gatim = goal.

"A person who is free from these triple gates of darkness, O son of Kunti, acts for the welfare of his Self and reaches the highest goal.

Sloka 23

yaḥ śāstravidhim utsṛjya vartate kāmakārataḥ
na sa siddhim avāpnoti na sukhaṃ na parāṃ gatim

yah = he who; sastra-vidhim = scriptural injunctions; utsrjya = discarding, ignoring; vartate = acts; kama-karatah = under the exertion of lust; na = not; sah = he; siddhim = perfection; avapnoti = attain; na = not; sukham = happiness; na = not; param = the supreme; gatim = goal.

"Discarding scriptural injunctions, he who acts under the exertion of lust, he attains neither perfection nor happiness nor the Supreme Goal.

Sloka 24

tasmāc chāstraṃ pramāṇaṃ tekāryākāryavyavasthitau
jñātvā śāstravidhānoktaṃ karma kartum ihārhasi

Tasmat = therefore; sastram = scriptures; pramanam = the standard, basis; te = your; karya = what is to be done; akarya = what is not to be done; vyavasthitau = in ascertaining, establishing; jnatva = by knowing; sastra = of scripture; vidhana = methods, procedures; uktam = as described; karma = duty; kartum = perform; iha = here; arhasi = you should.

"Therefore, the scripture is your standard in ascertaining what is to be done and what should not be done. By knowing the methods described in the scriptures, you should perform your duty here.

Conclusion

iti srīmadbhāgavadgītāsupanisatsu brahmavidyāyām
yogasāstre
srikrisnārjunasamvāde daivāsurasaṃpadvibhāgo nāma
ṣoḍaśo 'dhyayah.

iti = thus; srīmadbhāgavadgītā = in the sacred Bhagavadgita; upanisatsu = in the Upanishad; brahmavidyāyām = the knowledge of the absolute Brahman; yogasāstre = the scripture of yoga; srikrisnārjunasamvāde = the dialogue between Sri Krishna and Arjuna; daivāsurasaṃpadvibhāgo nāma = by name the yoga of the division of the divine and demonic properties; ṣoḍaśah = sixteenth adhyayah = chapter.

Thus ends the sixteenth chapter named the Yoga of the Division of the Divine and Demonic Properties in the Upanishad of the divine Bhagavadgita, the knowledge of the Absolute, the yogic scripture, and the debate between Arjuna and Lord Krishna.

17 – The Yoga of the Threefold Division of Qualities

Sloka 1

arjuna uvāca
ye śāstravidhim utsṛjya yajante śraddhayānvitāḥ
teṣāṃ niṣṭhā tu kā kṛṣṇa sattvam āho rajas tamaḥ

arjunah uvaca = Arjuna said; ye =who; sastra-vidhim = scriptural injunctions; utsrjya = ignoring giving up; yajante = worship; sraddhaya = with faith; anvitah = endowed; tesam = of them; nistha = condition, devotion, state; tu = but; ka = what iit; krsna = O Krishna; sattvam = sattva; aho = said; rajah = rajas; tamah = tamas.

"Said Arjuna, "But, ignoring the scriptural injunctions, those who worship with full faith, what is their devotion, O Krishna? Is it of sattva, rajas or tamas?"

Sloka 2

śrībhagavān uvāca
trividhā bhavati śraddhā dehināṃ sā svabhāvajā
sāttvikī rājasī caiva tāmasī ceti tāṃ śṛṇu

sri-bhagavan uvaca = the supreme lord said; tri-vidha = three ways; bhavati = manifest; sraddha = faith; dehinam = of the embodied selves; sa = that; sva-bhava-ja = according to own nature; sattviki = sattvic; rajasi = rajasic; ca = ando; eva = certainly; tamasi = tamasic; ca = and; iti = thus; tam = about it; srnu = hear.

The Supreme Lord said, "In three ways does manifest the faith of the embodied, according to their own nature, (namely) sattva, rajas and tamas. Hear about it.

Sloka 3

sattvānurūpā sarvasya śraddhā bhavati bhārata
śraddhāmayoyaṃ puruṣo yo yacchraddhaḥ sa eva saḥ

sattva-anurupa = according to sattva; sarvasya = in everyone; sraddha = faith; bhavati = manifests; bharata = O descendent of Bharata; sraddha = faith; mayah = made up of; ayam = this; purusah = personl; yah = who; yat = that; sraddhah = faith; sah = that; eva = surely; sah = he.

"O descendent of Bharata, faith manifests in everyone (or everywhere) according to sattva. A person is made up of faith only. He is surely, what his faith is.

loka 4

yajante sāttvikā devān yakṣarakṣāṃsi rājasāḥ
pretān bhūtagaṇāñś cānye yajante tāmasā janāḥ

yajante = worship; sattvikah = sattvic people; devan = devas, gods, divinities; yaksa-raksamsi = yakshsas and rakshasas; rajasah = rajasic people; pretan = ghosts; bhuta-ganan = hosts of elemental spirits; ca = and; anye = others; yajante = worship; tamasah = tamasic; janah = people.

"Sattvic people worship devas; rajasic people worship yakshas and rakshasas; and other people of tamasic nature worship ghosts and hosts of elemental spirits.

Sloka 5

aśāstravihitaṃ ghoraṃ tapyante ye tapo janāḥ
dambhāhaṃkārasaṃyuktāḥ kāmarāgabalānvitāḥ

asastra = not by the scriptures; vihitam = instructed, approved; ghoram = severe, painful; tapyante = perform penances; ye = those; tapah = austerities, penances; janah = people; dambha = vanity, conceit; ahankara = pride, egoism; samyuktah = filled with; kama = lust; raga = passion; bala = force, power, strength; anvitah = impelled by.

"Those people, who are filled with vanity (and) egoism, perform severe penances not sanctioned in the scriptures, impelled by the force of lust and passion.

Sloka 6

karṣayantaḥ śarīrasthaṃ bhūtagrāmam acetasaḥ
māṃ caivāntaḥśarīrasthaṃ tān viddhy āsuraniścayān

karsayantah = torture, torment; sarira-stham = in the body; bhuta-gramam = organs; acetasah = without discrimination; mam = Me; ca = and; eva = surely; antah = within; sarira-stham = in the body; tan = them; viddhi = know; asura = demons; niscayan = resolve, determination.

"(Those who) torture the organs in the body without discrimination and surely Me who is in the body, know them to be of demonic resolve.

Sloka 7

āhāras tv api sarvasya trividho bhavati priyaḥ
yajñas tapas tathā dānaṃ teṣāṃ bhedam imaṃ śṛṇu

aharah = food; tu = verily; api = also; sarvasya = of all; tri-vidhah = three types; bhavati = is; priyah = dear; yajnah = sacrifice; tapah = austerity; tatha = and; danam = charity; tesam = their; bhedam = distinction; imam = thus; srnu = hear.

"Food, which is dear to all, is also verily of three types, so as sacrifice, austerity and charity. Hear now about their distinction.

Sloka 8

āyuḥsattvabalārogyasukhaprītivivardhanāḥ
rasyāḥ snigdhāḥ sthirā hṛdyā āhārāḥ sāttvikapriyāḥ

ayuh = lifespan; sattva = purity; bala = strength; arogya = health; sukha = happiness; priti = satisfaction; vivardhanah = increasing; rasyah = tasty; snigdhah = oily; sthirah = firm; hrdyah = agreeable; aharah = food; sattvika = sattvic people; priyah = dearer .

The food, which increases lifespan, purity, strength, health, happiness, (and) satisfaction, which is tasty, oily, firm, (and) agreeable, is dear to sattvic people.

Sloka 9

kaṭvamlalavaṇātyuṣṇatīkṣṇarūkṣavidāhinaḥ
āhārā rājasasyeṣṭā duḥkhaśokāmayapradāḥ

katu = bitter; amla = sour; lavana = salty; ati= very; usna = hot and spicy; tiksna = pungent; ruksa = dry; vidahinah = burning; aharah = food; rajasasya = of rajasic nature; istah = desired, liked, preferred; duhkha = pain; soka = suffering; amaya = disease; pradah = cause, produce.

"Food which is very bitter, very sour, very salty, hot and spicy, very pungent, and burning, which causes pain, suffering, (and) disease is dearer to one who is of rajasic nature.

Sloka 10

yātayāmaṃ gatarasaṃ pūti paryuṣitaṃ ca yat
ucchiṣṭam api cāmedhyaṃ bhojanaṃ tāmasapriyam

yata-yamam = not freshly cooked; gata-rasam = devoid of taste; puti = foul smelling; paryusitam = decayed; ca = and; yat = which; ucchistam = left over; api = even; ca = and; amedhyam = unfit for sacrifice; bhojanam = food; tamasa =tamsic; priyam = pleasing, dear.

"Food which is not freshly cooked, which is without taste, foul smelling, and decayed, which is left over and unfit for sacrifice, is pleasing to the people of tamasic nature.

Sloka 11

aphalāṅkṣibhir yajño vidhidṛṣṭo ya ijyate
yaṣṭavyam eveti manaḥ samādhāya sa sāttvikaḥ

aphala-akanksibhih = without the desire for the fruit; yajnah = sacrifice; vidhi drstah = dutifully according to the established practice; yah = which; ijyate = performed, offered; yastavyam = obligatory; eva = surely, certainly; iti = that; manah = mind; samadhaya = firm conviction; sah = that; sattvikah = sattvic nature.

"Without seeking the fruit, the sacrifice which is performed dutifully according to the established practice, with the firm

conviction in the mind that it is surely obligatory, it is sattvic in nature.

Sloka 12

abhisaṃdhāya tu phalaṃ dambhārtham api caiva yat
ijyate bharataśreṣṭha taṃ yajñaṃ viddhi rājasam

abhisandhaya = with an eye for; tu = but; phalam = fruit, result; dambha = vanity; artham = for the sake of; api = so also; ca = and; eva = even; yat = which; ijyate = performed; bharata-srestha = O the best among the Bharatas; tam = that; yajnam = sacrifice; viddhi = know; rajasam = of the rajasic nature.

"But that sacrifice which is performed with an eye for the fruit, so also for the sake of vanity, O the best among the Bharatas, know that to be of rajasic nature.

Sloka 13

vidhihīnam asṛṣṭānnaṃ mantrahīnam adakṣiṇam
śraddhāvirahitaṃ yajñaṃ tāmasaṃ paricakṣate

vidhi-hinam = devoid of rules; asrsta-annam = in which blessed food is not distributed or shared; mantra-hinam = devoid of mantras; adaksinam = with out offering dakshina to the priests; sraddha = faith, dedication; virahitam = without; yajnam = sacrifice; tamasam = of tamasic nature; paricaksate = they declare.

"They declare the sacrifice to be tamasic in nature, which is devoid of rules, in which blessed food is not distributed, in which mantras are not chanted, in which dakshina is given to the priests, which is devoid of faith .

Sloka 14

devadvijaguruprājñapūjanaṃ śaucam ārjavam
brahmacaryam ahiṃsā ca śārīraṃ tapa ucyate

deva = the divinities; dvija = the twice born; guru = the spiritual master; prajna = the wise; pujanam = worship, veneration; saucam = cleanliness, purity; arjavam = straightforwardness; brahmacaryam =

celibacy; ahimsa = non-injury; ca = and; sariram = of the body; tapah = austerity; ucyate = said to be.

"The Worship or veneration of gods, twice born ones, spiritual teachers, and the wise, cleanliness, straightforwardness, and non-injury are said to be the austerity of the body.

Sloka 15

anudvegakaraṃ vākyaṃ satyaṃ priyahitaṃ ca yat
svādhyāyābhyasanaṃ caiva vāṅmayaṃ tapa ucyate

anudvega = dispassion or without excitement; karam = causing; vakyam = speech; satyam = truthful; priya = pleasant; hitam = beneficial; ca = and; yat = which; svadhyaya = self-study; abhyasanam = practice; ca = and; eva = so also; van-mayam = of speech; tapah = austerity; ucyate = said to be.

"Speech which incites no passion, which is truthful and beneficial, and so also the practice of self-study - is said to be the austerity of speech.

Sloka 16

manaḥprasādaḥ saumyatvaṃ maunam ātmavinigrahaḥ
bhāvasaṃśuddhir ity etat tapo mānasam ucyate

manah-prasadah = mental peace; saumyatvam = gentleness; maunam = silence; atma vinigrahah = self-control; bhava = thoughts, feeligns; samsuddhih = purity; iti = thus; etat = this; tapah = austerity; manasam = of the mind; ucyate = said to be.

"Mental peace, gentleness, silence, self-control, purity of thoughts and feelings, this is said to be the austerity of the mind.

Sloka 17

śraddhayā parayā taptaṃ tapas tat trividhaṃ naraiḥ
aphalākāṅkṣibhir yuktaiḥ sāttvikaṃ paricakṣate

sraddhaya = with faith and sincerity; paraya = supreme, highest; taptam = performed, undertaken; tapah = austerity; tat = that; tri-vidham = three kinds; naraih = by men; aphala-akanksibhih = without the desire for the fruit; yuktaih = who are self-absorbed; sattvikam = of sattvic nature; paricaksate = they say, declare.

"When the three kinds of austerity are performed with supreme faith, by men who have no desire for the results and who are self-absorbed, they speak of it as sattvic in nature.

Sloka 18

satkāramānapūjārthaṃ tapo dambhena caiva yat
kriyate tad iha proktaṃ rājasaṃ calam adhruvam

sat-kara = fame, popularity, respect; mana = honor; puja = worship, adoration; artham = for the sake of; tapah = austerity; dambhena = ostentatious display; ca = and; eva = so alsoy; yat = which; kriyate = performed, undertakne; tat = that; iha = this worldly; proktam = said to be; rajasam = of rajasic nature, of the nature of rajas; calam = wavering; adhruvam = uncertain.

"The austerity, which is performed for the sake of fame, honor and adoration and for ostentatious display, it is said to be rajasic, this worldly, wavering and uncertain.

Sloka 19

mūḍhagrāheṇātmano yat pīḍayā kriyate tapaḥ
parasyotsādanārthaṃ vā tat tāmasam udāhṛtam

mudha = foolish; grahena = intentions, desires; atmanah = to oneself; yat = which; pidaya = pain; kriyate = performed, undertaken; tapah = austerity; parasya = another; utsadana-artham = for the destruction; va = or; tat = that; tamasam = tamasic in nature; udahrtam = said to be.

"That austerity, which is performed with a foolish intention, causing pain to oneself or for the destruction of another, is said to be of tamasic in nature.

Sloka 20

dātavyam iti yad dānaṃ dīyatenupakāriṇe
deśe kāle ca pātre ca tad dānaṃ sāttvikaṃ smṛtam

datavyam = what is to be given; iti = thus; yat = that; danam = charity; diyate = given; anupakarine = from whom no help is expected; dese = in place; kale = in time; ca = and; patre = suitability; ca = and; tat = that; danam = charity; sattvikam = of sattiv nature; smrtam = declared in the books of morality.

"That charity which is given to one from whom no help is expected, according to place, time and suitability, that charity is declared in the books of morality as sattvic in nature.

Sloka 21

yat tu prattyupakārārthaṃ phalam uddiśya vā punaḥ
dīyate ca parikliṣṭaṃ tad dānaṃ rājasaṃ smṛtam

yat = which; tu = but; prati-upakara-artham = for reciprocal help; phalam = fruit; uddisya = with the desire; va = or; punah = again; diyate = given; ca = and; pariklistam = grudgingly, with difficulty; tat = that; danam = charity; rajasam =rajasic in nature; smrtam = is declared in the books of morality.

"But the charity which is given for the sake of reciprocal help, or again with a desire for its fruit, and give grudgingly, that charity is declared in the books of morality as rajasic in nature.

Sloka 22

adeśakāle yad dānam apātrebhyaś ca dīyate
asatkṛtam avajñātaṃ tat tāmasam udāhṛtam

adesa = without consideration for place; kale = and time; yat = which; danam = charity; upatrebhyah = to undeserving persons; ca = and; diyate = is given; asat-krtam = without respect; avajnatam = with contempt; tat = that; tamasam = tmasic in nature; udahrtam = said to be.

"That charity which is given without due consideration for time and place, to undeserving persons, and given without respect and with contempt, it is said to be tamasic in nature.

Sloka 23

oṃ tat sad iti nirdeśo brahmaṇas trividhaḥ smṛtaḥ
brāhmaṇās tena vedāś ca yajñāś ca vihitāḥ purā

Om =Aum; tat = tat, that; sat = sat, truth, existence; iti = thus; nirdesah = specified; brahmanah = of Brahman; tri-vidhah = three ways, threefold; smrtah = recollecting, reciting mentally; brahmanah = Brahmanas; tena = by this; vedah = the Vedas; ca = and; yajnah = sacrifices; ca = and; vihitah = prescribed, arranged, determined; pura = in the past.

"AUM TAT SAT'- thus was specified the three ways of recollecting Brahman mentally. This is how it was prescribed in the Brahmanas, the Vedas and the sacrifices in the past.

Sloka 24

tasmād om ity udāhṛtya yajñadānatapaḥkriyāḥ
pravartante vidhānoktāḥ satataṃ brahmavādinām

tasmat = therefore; om = Aum; iti = thus; udahrtya = after uttering; yajna = sacrifice; dana = charity; tapah = austerity; kriyah = acts of; pravartante = begin, start; vidhana-uktah = in the prescribed manner; satatam = always; brahma-vadinam = those who are well versed in the knowledge of Brahman.

Therefore, those who are well versed in the knowledge of Brahman always begin the acts of sacrifice charity, (and) austerity in the prescribed manner after uttering Aum.

Sloka 25

tad ity anabhisaṃdhāya phalaṃ yajñatapaḥkriyāḥ
dānakriyāś ca vividhāḥ kriyante mokṣakāṅkṣibhiḥ

tat = that; iti = thus; anabhisandhaya = without desiring, seeking; phalam = the fruit; yajna = sacrifice; tapah = austerity; kriyah = acts;

dana = charity; kriyah = acts; ca = and; vividhah = various; kriyante = perform; moksa-kanksibhih = those who aspire for liberation.

"(Uttering) 'TAT' thus, without desiring the fruit, those who aspire for liberation perform various acts of sacrifice, austerity, and acts of charity,

Sloka 26

sadbhāve sādhubhāve ca sad ity etat prayujyate
praśaste karmaṇi tathā sacchabdaḥ pārtha yujyate

sat-bhave = reality, the state of reality; sadhu-bhave = the state of righteousness, virtuous nature; ca = and; sat = sat, Brahman, truth; iti = thus; etat = this; prayujyate = is used, is spoken; prasaste = commendable, praiseworthy; karmani = actions; tatha = so also; sat-sabdah = truthful words; partha = O Partha; yujyate = is spoken, is used.

"This world, 'Sat' is used to denote the state of reality, the state of righteousness, so also (it) is spoken, O Partha, to denote praiseworthy actions and truthful words

Sloka 27

yajñe tapasi dāne ca sthitiḥ sad iti cocyate
karma caiva tadarthīyaṃ sad ity evābhidhīyate

yajne = sacrifice; tapasi = in austerity, dane = charity; ca = and; sthitih = virtue, merit; sat = sat; iti = thus; ca = also; ucyate = referred to; karma = work; ca = and; eva = eeven; tat = that; arthiyam = for the sake of, meant for; sat = truth; iti = thus; eva = verily; abhidhiyate = is described as.

"The virtue in sacrifice, austerity and charity is also referred to as Sat and even the work done for their sake is verily described as Sat.

Sloka 28

aśraddhayā hutaṃ dattaṃ tapas taptaṃ kṛtaṃ ca yat
asad ity ucyate pārtha na ca tat pretya no iha

asraddhaya = without faith; hutam = oblation, offering made in sacrifice; dattam = given in charity; tapah = austerity; taptam =burnt; krtam = performed; ca = and; yat = that which; asat = false; iti = thus; ucyate = said to be; partha = O Partha; na = not; ca = and; tat = that; pretya = after death; no = not; iha = here.

"Without faith, whatever offering made in sacrifice, given in charity, burnt in austerity and actions performed is said to be thus false, O Partha. It is not (established) in That, neither here nor hereafter."

Conclusion

iti srīmadbhāgavadgītāsupanisatsu brahmavidyāyām yogasāstre
srikrisnārjunasamvāde śraddhātrayavibhāgayogo nama saptadaso 'dhyayah.

iti = thus; srīmadbhāgavadgītā = in the sacred Bhagavadgita; upanisatsu = in the Upanishad; brahmavidyāyām = the knowledge of the absolute Brahman; yogasāstre = the scripture of yoga; srikrisnārjunasamvāde = the dialogue between Sri Krishna and Arjuna; śraddhātrayavibhāgayogo nama = by name the yoga of the threefold division of qualities ; saptadasah = seventeenth; adhyayah = chapter.

Thus ends the seventeenth chapter named the Yoga of the Threefold Division of Qualities in the Upanishad of the divine Bhagavadgita, the knowledge of the Absolute, the yogic scripture, and the debate between Arjuna and Lord Krishna.

18 – The Yoga of Liberation by Renunciation

Sloka 1

Arjuna uvāca
saṃnyāsasya mahābāho tattvam icchāmi veditum
tyāgasya ca hṛṣīkeśa pṛthak keśiniṣūdana

arjunah uvaca = Arjuna said; sannyasasya = of renunciation; maha-baho = O mighty-armed; tattvam = truth; icchami = I want, wish; veditum = to know; tyagasya = of sacrifice; ca = ans; hrsikesa = O master of the senses; prthak = in detail, severally; kesi-nisudana = O slayer of Kesi.

Said Arjuna, "O Mighty Armed, Master of the Senses, Slayer of Kesi, I want to know in detail the truth about renunciation and sacrifice."

Sloka 2

srībhagavān uvāca
kāmyānāṃ karmaṇāṃ nyāsaṃ saṃnyāsaṃ kavayoviduḥ
sarvakarmaphalatyāgaṃ prāhus tyāgaṃ vicakṣaṇāḥ

sri-bhagavan uvaca = the Supreme Lord said; kamyanam = desires; karmanam = of actions; nyasam = resigning, giving up; sannyasam = renunciation; kavayah = the learned; viduh = know; sarva = of all; karma = actions; phala = result, fruti; tyagam = giving up; prahuh = call; tyagam = sacrifice; vicaksanah = the discriminating ones.

The Supreme Lord said, "The learned ones know that giving up the desires in the actions is renunciation. The discriminating ones call the giving up of the fruit of all actions as sacrifice.

Sloka 3

tyājyaṃ doṣavad ity eke karma prāhur manīṣiṇaḥ
yajñadānatapaḥkarma na tyājyam iti cāpare

tyajyam =should be given up; dosa-vat = because of their evil nature; iti = thus; eke = some; karma = actions; prahuh = said; manisinah = among men; yajna = sacrifice; dana = charity; tapah = austerity; karma = actions; na = not; tyajyam = to be renounced; iti = thus; ca = and; apare = others.

"Some among men say because of their evil nature actions should be given up; others say that actions such as sacrifice, charity and austerity should not be renounced.

Sloka 4

niścayaṃ śṛṇu me tatra tyāge bharatasattama
tyāgo hi puruṣavyāghra trividhaḥ saṃprakīrtitaḥ

niscayam = firm conclusion; srnu = hear; me = from Me; tatra = regarding that; tyage = renunciation; bharata-sat-tama = O best of the Bharatas; tyagah = sacrifice, renunciation; hi = surely; purusa-vyaghra = O tiger among human beings; tri-vidhah = three kinds; samprakirtitah = is stated to be.

"Hear from Me My firm conclusion regarding that sacrifice, O best of the Bharatas. Surely, O tiger among men, sacrifice is said to be of three kinds,

Sloka 5

yajñadānatapaḥkarma na tyājyaṃ kāryam eva tat
yajño dānaṃ tapaś caiva pāvanāni manīṣiṇām

yajna = sacrifice; dana = charity; tapah = austerity; karma = doing, practising; na = not; tyajyam = given up; karyam = should be performed; eva = certainly; tat = that; yajnah = sacrifice; danam = charity; tapah = austerity; ca = and; eva = even; pavanani = purifiers; manisinam = of the wise.

"Performance of sacrificial rituals, charity, (and) austerity should not be given up. They should be certainly performed. Sacrificial ritual, charity and austerity are surely purifiers of the wise.

Sloka 6

etāny api tu karmāṇi saṅgaṃ tyaktvā phalāni ca
kartavyānīti me pārtha niścitaṃ matam uttamam

etani = these; api = even; tu = however, but; karmani = actions; sangam = attachment; tyaktva = by renouncing, giving up; phalani = fruit, result; ca = and; kartavyani = to be performed; iti = thus; me = My; partha = O Partha; niscitam = firm conclusin, definite; matam = opinion; uttamam = the best.

"However, even these actions should be performed by renouncing attachment and (desire for the) fruit. O Partha, this is my firm conclusion and the best opinion.

Sloka 7

niyatasya tu saṃnyāsaḥ karmaṇo nopapadyate
mohāt tasya parityāgas tāmasaḥ parikīrtitaḥ

niyatasya = regular obligatory duties; tu = therefore; sannyasah = renunciation; karmanah = actions; na = not; apapadyate = is not justified; mohat = by delusion; tasya = of that; parityagah = giving up, renunciation; tamasah = tamas; parikirtitah = is declared.

"Therefore, renunciation of actions such as the regular obligatory duties is not justified. Giving up that due to delusion is declared tamas.

Sloka 8

duḥkham ity eva yat karma kāyakleśabhayāt tyajet
sa kṛtvā rājasaṃ tyāgaṃ naiva tyāgaphalaṃ labhet

duhkham = painful; iti = thus; eva = merely; yat = whateverm which; karma = action; kaya = bodily; klesa = suffering, affliction; bhayat = because of fear; tyajet = give up; sah = he; krtva = having done; rajasam = rajasic quality; tyagam = sacrifice; na = not; eva = certainly; tyaga = sacrifice; phalam = fruit; labhet = gain.

"Whatever action is given up as 'painful,' out of the fear of bodily afflictions, having thus performed sacrifice of rajasic quality, he will certainly not gain the fruit of sacrifice.

Sloka 9

kāryam ity eva yat karma niyataṃ kriyaterjuna
saṅgaṃ tyaktvā phalaṃ caiva sa tyāgaḥ sāttvikomataḥ

karyam = obligatory duty; iti = thus; eva = verily; yat = whatever; karma = action, duty, work; niyatam = prescribed; kriyate = is performed; arjuna = O Arjuna; sangam = attachment; tyaktva = giving up; phalam = fruit, result; ca = and; eva = even; sah = that; tyagah = sacrifice; sattvikah = sattvic nature; matah = considered.

"Whatever action is performed thus verily as obligatory duty, O Arjuna,, giving up attachment and even the fruit (of such actions), that sacrifice is considered sattvic in nature.

Sloka 10

na dveṣṭy akuśalaṃ karma kuśale nānuṣajjate
tyāgī sattvasamāviṣṭo medhāvī chinnasaṃśayaḥ

na = not; dvesti = hate; akusalam = improper, unhappy ; karma = actions; kusale = proper, happy; na = not anusajjate = becomes attached; tyagi = the person of sacrificial actions; sattva = the quality of sattva; samavistah = established in; medhavi = wise; chinna = cut asunder; samsayah = all doubts.

"The man of sacrificial actions, who is established in sattva, the wise person, who has cut asunder all doubts, neither hates improper actions nor becomes attached to proper (actions).

Sloka 11

na hi dehabhṛtā śakyaṃ tyaktuṃ karmāṇy aśeṣataḥ
yas tu karmaphalatyāgī sa tyāgīty abhidhīyate

na = not; hi = surely; deha-bhrta = an embodied being, who holds a body; sakyam = possible; tyaktum = to renounce; karmani = actions; asesatah = completely; yah = who; tu = but; karma = actions; phala =

fruit; tyagi = who renounces; sah = he; tyagi = one who is a sacrificer; iti = thus; abhidhiyate = is called.

"Surely, it not possible for an embodied being to renounce actions completely; but whoever renounces the fruit of his actions is called the one who is a sacrificer.

Sloka 12

aniṣṭam iṣṭaṃ miśraṃ ca trividhaṃ karmaṇaḥ phalam
bhavaty atyāgināṃ pretya na tu saṃnyāsināṃ kvacit

anistam = unpleasant, dislike; istam = pleasant, like; misram = mixed; ca = and; tri-vidham = three kinds; karmanah = actions; phalam = result; bhavati = manifest, happens; atyaginam = those who do not give up the fruit of their action; pretya = after death; na = not; tu = but; sannyasinam = those who practice renunciation; kvacit = at all.

"Unpleasant, pleasant and mixed, is the threefold fruit of actions manifest for those who do not renounce, but not at all for those who practice true renunciation.

Sloka 13

pañcaitāni mahābāho kāraṇāni nibodha me
sāṃkhye kṛtānte proktāni siddhaye sarvakarmaṇām

panca = five; etani = these; maha-baho = O mighty-armed; karanani = causes; nibodha = know; me = from Me; sankhye = in the Sankhya; krta-ante = the culmination of actions; proktani = declared; siddhaye = reaching success, accomplishment, excellence; sarva = all; karmanam = actions.

"Know from Me these five causes, O mighty armed one, which are declared in the Samkhya for attaining the culmination in all actions.

Sloka 14

adhiṣṭhānaṃ tathā kartā karaṇaṃ ca pṛthagvidham
vividhāś ca pṛthakceṣṭā daivaṃ caivātra pañcamam

adhisthanam = the field, the body; tatha = and; karta = the doer, the ego; karanam = causative organs; ca = and; prthak-vidham = several kinds; vividhah = numerous; ca = and; prthak = several, various; cestah = actions; daivam = the divine; ca = and; eva = surely; atra = here; pancamam = five.

"The field, so also the doer, several types and numerous causative organs, and several types of actions, and surely the divine here is the fifth...

Sloka 15

śarīravāṅmanobhir yat karma prārabhate naraḥ
nyāyyaṃ vā viparītaṃ vā pañcaite tasya hetavaḥ 18.15

sarira = body; vak = speech; mana = mind; abhih = and with; yat = whatever; karma = action; prarabhate = performs; narah = a human being; nyayyam = right; va = or; viparitam = opposite, perverse; va = or; panca = five; ete = these; tasya = of it hetavah = causes.

"Whatever action a human being performs with the body, speech and mind, whether it is right or its opposite, (for them) these five are the causes.

Sloka 16

tatraivaṃ sati kartāram ātmānaṃ kevalaṃ tu yaḥ
paśyaty akṛtabuddhitvān na sa paśyati durmatiḥ

tatra = that; evam = so; sati = being; kartaram = doer, the cause; atmanam = the self; kevalam = alone; tu = but; yah = who; pasyati = sees; akrta-buddhitvat = due to perverted intelligence; na = not; sah = he; pasyati = sees; durmatih = of evil mind.

"That being the case, due to perverted intelligence whoever sees the Self alone as the doer or the cause, he of evil mind, does not see.

Sloka 17

yasya nāhaṃkṛto bhāvo buddhir yasya na lipyate
hatvā.api sa imāṃl lokān na hanti na nibadhyate

yasya = he who; na = not; ahankrtah = egoism; bhavah = state, thoughts, feelings; buddhih = intelligence; yasya = whose; na = not; lipyate = entangled, attached; hatva api = even killing; sah = he; iman = this; lokan = world; na = not; hanti = killing; na = not; nibadhyate = becomes bound.

"He who does not have feelings of egoism, whose intelligence is not attached, he does not kill and in this world he does not become bound even by killing.

Sloka 18

jñānaṃ jñeyaṃ parijñātā trividhā karmacodanā
karaṇaṃ karma karteti trividhaḥ karmasaṃgrahaḥ

jnanam = knowledge; jneyam = object of knowledge, the knowable; parijnata = the knower; tri-vidha = three kinds, threefold; karma = action; codana = inducement, impetus; karanam = the cause; karma = actions; karta = the doer; iti = thus; tri-vidhah = three types; karma = work; sangrahah = totality.

"Knowledge, the object of knowledge and the doer: three kinds is the inducement to actions. The cause, the action and the doer, three kinds thus is the totality of actions.

Sloka 19

jñānaṃ karma ca kartā ca tridhaiva guṇabhedataḥ
procyate guṇasaṃkhyāne yathāvac chṛṇu tāny api

jnanam = knowledge; karma = action; ca = and; karta = doer; ca = and; tridha = threefold, three kinds; eva = only; guna-bhedatah = because of the differentiation of the guanas; procyate = declared said; guna-sankhyane = in the teaching about the gunas; yatha-vat = truthfully as they are; srnu = hear; tani = about them; api = and.

"In the teachings about the gunas, only three kinds of knowledge, action and doer said to arise because of the differentiation of the gunas. Hear about them truthfully, as they are.

Sloka 20

sarvabhūteṣu yenaikaṃ bhāvam avyayam īkṣate
avibhaktaṃ vibhakteṣu taj jñānaṃ viddhi sāttvikam

sarva-bhutesu = in all living being; yena = by which; ekam = one; bhavam = being, state, condition; avyayam = inexhaustible; iksate = one sees; avibhaktam = undifferentiated, indivisible; vibhaktesu = differentiated, divisible, ; tat = that; jnanam = knowledge; viddhi = know; sattvikam = of the nature of sattva.

"Know that knowledge as having the nature of sattva by which one sees the One inexhaustible Being in all living beings, the undifferentiated in the differentiated

Sloka 21

pṛthaktvena tu yaj jñānaṃ nānābhāvān pṛthagvidhān
vetti sarveṣu bhūteṣu taj jñānaṃ viddhi rājasam

prthaktvena = by separateness, distinction ; tu = but; yat = which; jnanam = knowledge; nana-bhavan = numerous entities, states; prthak-vidhan = of different kinds; vetti = perceives; sarvesu = in all; bhutesu = living beings; tat = that; jnanam = knowledge; viddhi = know; rajasam = rajasic in nature.

"But know that knowledge to be of rajasic in nature, which because of separateness perceives all beings as numerous entities of various kinds.

Sloka 22

yat tu kṛtsnavad ekasmin kārye saktam ahetukam
atattvārthavad alpaṃ ca tat tāmasam udāhṛtam

yat = which; tu = but; krtsna-vat = as if it were all; ekasmin = in one; karye = in action; saktam = interested, attached; ahaitukam = without concern for reason; atattva-artha-vat = for the sake of untruth; alpam = insignificant. little, small; ca = and; tat = that knowledge; tamasam = tamasic in nature; udahrtam = is said to be.

"But that knowledge is said to be tamasic in nature which is interested in one action only as if it were all, without concern for reason, for the sake of untruth and insignificant.

Sloka 23

niyataṃ saṅgarahitam arāgadveṣataḥ kṛtam
aphalaprepsunā karma yat tat sāttvikam ucyate

niyatam = obligatory; sanga-rahitam = without attachment; araga-dvesatah = without attraction or aversion; krtam = performed, done; aphala-prepsuna = one who does not seek the fruit ; karma = actions; yat = which; tat = that; sattvikam = sattvic in nature; ucyate = is called.

"That action is said to be sattvic in nature, which is obligatory, performed without attachment, without attraction or aversion, by one who does not seek its fruit.

Sloka 24

yat tu kāmepsunā karma sāhaṃkāreṇa vā punaḥ
kriyate bahulāyāsaṃ tad rājasam udāhṛtam

yat = that which; tu = but; kama-ipsuna = desire for the result ; karma = action; sa-ahankarena = with egoism; va = or; punah = again; kriyate = performed; bahula-ayasam = with strenuous effort; tat = that; rajasam = rajasic in nature; udahrtam = is said to be.

"But that action is said to be rajasic in nature which is performed with desire for the result, with egoism, and again with strenuous effort

Sloka 25

anubandhaṃ kṣayaṃ hiṃsām anapekṣya ca pauruṣam
mohād ārabhyate karma yat tat tāmasam ucyate

anubandham = relationship, bondage; ksayam = destruction; himsam = injury, pain; anapeksya = without consideration; ca = and; paurusam = ability, virility; mohat = delusion; arabhyate = undertaken; karma =

action; yat = which; tat = that; tamasam = tamasic in nature; ucyate = said to be.

"That action is said to be tamasic in nature which is undertaken out of delusion without consideration for relationship, destruction, injury, and ability.

Sloka 26

**muktasaṅgonahaṃvādī dhṛtyutsāhasamanvitaḥ
siddhyasiddhyor nirvikāraḥ kartā sāttvika ucyate**

mukta-sangah = free from attachment; anaham-vadi = who speaks without egoism; dhrti-utsaha = great enthusiasm; samanvitah = endowed with; siddhi = success, perfection; asiddhyoh = failure; nirvikarah = undisturbed; karta = doer; sattvikah = sattvic in nature; ucyate = is said to be.

"The doer who is free from attachment, speaks without egoism, endowed with great enthusiasm, undisturbed by success and failure is said to be sattivc in nature.

Sloka 27

**rāgī karmaphalaprepsur lubdho hiṃsātmakośuciḥ
harṣaśokānvitaḥ kartā rājasaḥ parikīrtitaḥ**

ragi = who is passionately attached; karma-p h la = th e fruit of the actions; prepsuh = who desires; lubdhah = greedy; himsa-atmakah = cruel by nature; asucih = unclean, impure; harsa-soka-anvitah = subject to joy and sorrow; karta = doer rajasah = rajasic in nature; parikirtitah = is declared to be.

"The doer who is passionately attached, who desires the fruit of his actions, who is greedy, cruel by nature, unclean, subject to joy and sorrow, is declared to be rajsic in nature.

Sloka 28

**ayuktaḥ prākṛtaḥ stabdhaḥ śaṭho naiṣkṛtikolasaḥ
viṣādī dīrghasūtrī ca kartā tāmasa ucyate**

ayuktah = who is imperfect and unskilled; prakrtah = crude; stabdhah = stubborn; sathah = deceitful; naiskrtikah = malicious, evil; alasah = lazy; visadi = depressed; dirgha-sutri = procrastinating; ca =and; karta = doer; tamasah = tamasic in nature; ucyate = said to be.

"The doer is said to be tamasic in nature, who is imperfect and unskilled, crude, stubborn, deceitful, malicious, lazy, depressed and procrastinating.

Sloka 29

buddher bhedaṃ dhṛteś caiva guṇatas trividhaṃ śṛṇu
procyamānam aśeṣeṇa pṛthaktvena dhanaṃjaya

buddheh = of intelligence; bhedam = division; dhrteh = of stability, firmness, steadiness; ca = and; eva = also; gunatah = arising from the gunas; tri-vidham = threefold, three types; srnu = hear; procyamanam = as described; asesena = in detail; prthaktvena = in different ways; dhananjaya = O Dhananjaya.

"The division of intelligence, and so also firmness is, threefold arising from the gunas; listen as it is being described in detail and in different ways.

Sloka 30

pravṛttiṃ ca nivṛttiṃ ca kāryākārye bhayābhaye
bandhaṃ mokṣaṃ ca yā vetti buddhiḥ sā pārtha sāttvikī

pravrttim = indulgence, involvement; ca = and; nivrttim = abstinence withdrawal; ca = and; karya = action; akarye = non-action; bhaya = fear; abhaye = fearlessness; bandham = bondage; moksam = liberation; ca = and; ya = that; vetti = knows; buddhih = intelligence; sa = that; partha = O Partha; sattviki = sattvic in nature.

"He who knows indulgence and abstinence, action and non-action, fear (and) fearlessness, bondage and liberation, that intelligence, O Partha, is sattvic in nature.

Sloka 31

yayā dharmam adharmaṃ ca kāryaṃ cākāryam eva ca
ayathāvat prajānāti buddhiḥ sā pārtha rājasī

yaya = by which; dharmam = dharma, righteousness; adharmam = adharma, non-righteousness; ca = and; karyam = action; ca = and; akaryam = non-action; eva = so also; ca = and; ayatha-vat = wrongly, falsely, untruthfully; prajanati = knows; buddhih = intelligence; sa = that; partha = O Partha; rajasi = rajasic in nature.

"The intelligence is rajasic in nature O Partha by which one knows wrongly dharma and adharma, and so also action and non-action

Sloka 32

adharmaṃ dharmam iti yā manyate tamasāvṛtā
sarvārthān viparītāñś ca buddhiḥ sā pārtha tāmasī

adharmam = adharma; dharmam = dharma; iti = thus; ya = which; manyate = considers; tamasa = darkness; avrta = enveloped; sarva-arthan = all things; viparitan = perverted; ca = and; buddhih = intelligence; sa = that; partha = O Partha; tamasi = tamasic in nature.

"That intelligence is tamasic in nature, O Partha, which, enveloped in darkness, considers thus adharma as dharma and all things in a perverted manner.

Sloka 33

dhṛtyā yayā dhārayate manaḥprāṇendriyakriyāḥ
yogenāvyabhicāriṇyā dhṛtiḥ sā pārtha sāttvikī

dhrtya = firmness; yaya = by which; dharayate = stabilizes; manah = mind; prana = prana; indriya = senses; kriyah = actions; yogena = through yoga; avyabhicarinya = without distractions, unwaveringly; dhrtih = such firmness; sa = that; partha = O Partha; sattviki = sattvic in nature.

"The firmness by which through yoga one stabilizes the mind, prana, the senses, (and) actions, that firmness, O Partha, is sattvic in nature.

Sloka 34

yayā tu dharmakāmārthān dhṛtyā dhārayaterjuna
prasaṅgena phalākāṅkṣī dhṛtiḥ sā pārtha rājasī

yaya = by which; tu = but; dharma-kama-arthan = duty, desires and wealth; dhrtya = by firmness; dharayate = upholds, sustains; arjuna = O Arjuna; prasangena = out of attachment; phala-akanksi = desiring the fruit of actions; dhrtih = firmness; sa = that; partha = O Partha; rajasi = rajasic in nature.

"But the firmness by which one upholds duty, desires and wealth, O Arjuna, out of attachment and desire for the fruit of actions, that firmness, O Partha, is rajasic in nature.

Sloka 35

yayā svapnaṃ bhayaṃ śokaṃ viṣādaṃ madam eva ca
na vimuñcati durmedhā dhṛtiḥ sā pārtha tāmasī

yaya = by which; svapnam = sleep; bhayam = fear; sokam = sorrow; visadam = sadness; madam = madness, intoxication; eva = so also; ca = and; na = not; vimuncati = give up; durmedha = perverted intelligence; dhrtih = firmness; sa = that; partha = O Partha; tamasi = tamasic in nature.

"That firmness is tamasic in nature by which a person of perverted intelligence does not give up sleep, fear, sorrow, sadness, and so also madness.

Sloka 36

sukhaṃ tv idānīṃ trividhaṃ śṛṇu me bharatarṣabha
abhyāsād ramate yatra duḥkhāntaṃ ca nigacchhati

sukham = pleasure, happiness; tu = about; idanim = now; tri-vidham = three types; srnu = hear; me = from Me; bharata-rsabha = O the best among the Bharatas; abhyasat = by habit, practice; ramate = enjoys;

yatra = where; duhkha = sorrow; antam = end; ca = and; nigacchati = reaches, gains.

"Now hear from Me, O the best among the Bharatas, about the three kinds of pleasure, one enjoys by habit and reaches the end of sorrow.

Sloka 37

yat tadagre viṣam iva pariṇāmemṛtopamam
tat sukhaṃ sāttvikaṃ proktam ātmabuddhiprasādajam

yat = which; tat = that; agre = in the beginning; visam iva = very much like poison; pariname = in the end; amrta = nectar; upamam = like; tat = that; sukham = pleasure; sattvikam = sattvic in nature; proktam = said to be ; atma buddhi = self-intelligence; prasada-jam = arising from.

"That which in the beginning is very much like poison, but in the end is like nectar; that pleasure is sattvic in nature and said to arise from one's own intelligence.

Sloka 38

viṣayendriyasañyogād yat tad agremṛtopamam
pariṇāme viṣam iva tat sukhaṃ rājasaṃ smṛtam

visaya = sense objects; indriya = senses; samyogat = from contact, attachment, union; yat = which; tat = that; agre = in the beginning; amrta-upamam = just like nectar; pariname = in the end; visam iva = like poison; tat = that; sukham = pleasure, happiness; rajasam = rajasic in nature; smrtam = is delcared.

"That which arises like nectar in the beginning from the contact of the senses with the sense objects but in the end is like poison, that happiness is declared as rajasic in nature.

Sloka 39

yad agre cānubandhe ca sukhaṃ mohanam ātmanaḥ
nidrālasyapramādotthaṃ tat tāmasam udāhṛtam 18.39

yat =which; agre = in the beginning; ca = and; anubandhe = subsequently; ca = also; sukham = pleasure; mohanam =delusion; atmanah = of the self; nidra = sleep; alasya = laziness; pramada = negligence; uttham = arise from; tat = that; tamasam = born of tamasic nature; udahrtam = is said to be.

"That pleasure is said to be born of tamasic nature which in the beginning and subsequently also, is delusive in nature and arises from sleep, laziness and negligence

Sloka 40

na tad asti pṛthivyāṃ vā divi deveṣu vā punaḥ
sattvaṃ prakṛtijair muktaṃ yad ebhiḥ syāt tribhirguṇaiḥ

na = not; tat = that; asti = there is; prthivyam = on earth; va = or; divi = in the heavenly worlds; devesu = among the gods; va = or; punah = again; sattvam = entity, thing; prakrti-jaih = born of Nature; muktam = free; yat = which; ebhih = from these; syat = can be; tribhih = three; gunaih = gunas.

"There is no entity born of Nature, either on earth or again among the divinities in the heavenly worlds, which is free from theses triple gunas.

Sloka 41

brāhmaṇakṣatriyaviśāṃ śūdrāṇāṃ ca paraṃtapa
karmāṇi pravibhaktāni svabhāvaprabhavair guṇaiḥ

brahmana = the brahmanas; ksatriya = the ksatriyas; visam = the vaisyas; sudranam = the sudras; ca = and; parantapa = O subduer of the enemies; karmani = duties, actions; pravibhaktani = are divided; svabhava = essential nature; prabhavaih = born out of; gunaih = by gunas.

"O conqueror of the enemies, the duties of brahmanas, kshtriyas, vaisyas and sudras are divided according to the gunas arising from their essential nature.

Sloka 42

śamo damas tapaḥ śaucaṃ kṣāntir ārjavam eva ca
jñānaṃ vijñānam āstikyaṃ brahmakarma svabhāvajam

samah = equanimity; damah = self-control; tapah = austerity; saucam = purity; ksantih = forgiveness; arjavam = uprightness; eva = so also; ca = and; jnanam = knowledge; vijnanam = wisdom; astikyam = faith, belief; brahma = of a brahmana; karma = duty; svabhava-jam = arising from his own or essential nature.

"Equanimity, self-control, austerity, purity, forgiveness, uprightness, so also knowledge, wisdom and faith, (these) are the duties of a brahmana arising from his own nature.

Sloka 43

śauryaṃ tejo dhṛtir dākṣyaṃ yuddhe cāpy apalāyanam
dānam īśvarabhāvaś ca kṣātraṃ karma svabhāvajam

sauryam = valor; tejah = vigor; dhrtih = firmness, determination; daksyam = dexterity, ability; yuddhe = in battle; ca = and; api = also; apalayanam = not deserting; danam = generosity; isvara bhavah = lordliness; ca = and; ksatram = ksatriya; karma = duty; svabhava-jam = arising from his own nature.

"Valor, vigor, firmness, dexterity, so also not deserting in the middle of the battle, generosity, and lordliness, (these) are the duties of a kshatriya arising from his own nature.

Sloka 44

kṛṣigaurakṣyavāṇijyaṃ vaiśyakarma svabhāvajam
paricaryātmakaṃ karma śūdrasyāpi svabhāvajam

krsi = agriculture; go = cows; raksya = protection; vanijyam = trade and commerce; vaisya = vaisya; karma = duty; svabhava-jam = born out of his own nature; paricarya = service; atmakam =in the form of; karma = duty; sudrasya = of the sudra; api = and; svabhava-jam =arising from his own nature.

"Agriculture, protection of cows, trade and commerce are the duties of a vaisya born out of his own nature. Work in the form of serving others is the duty of the Sudras arising from their essential nature.

Sloka 45

sve sve karmaṇy abhirataḥ saṃsiddhiṃ labhate naraḥ
svakarmaniratah siddhiṃ yathā vindati tac chṛṇu

sve sve = one's own; karmani = duty; abhiratah = following, taking delight; samsiddhim = complete perfection, excellence, success; labhate = attains; narah = a person, human being; sva-karma = by his own duty; niratah = following; siddhim = perfection, success; yatha = how, in what manner; vindati = attains; tat = that; srnu = here listen.

"By following one's own duty a human being attains complete perfection. Hear how that perfection is achieved by following one's own duty.

Sloka 46

yataḥ pravṛttir bhūtānāṃ yena sarvam idaṃ tatam
svakarmaṇā tam abhyarcya siddhiṃ vindati mānavaḥ

yatah = from whom; pravrttih = issue forth, arise; bhutanam = of living beings; yena = by whom; sarvam = all; idam = this; tatam = is pervaded; sva-karmana = by own actions; tam = Him; abhyarcya = by worshipping; siddhim = perfection; vindati = achieves; manavah = a human being.

"From whom arise all living beings (and) by whom all this pervades, by worshipping Him through one's own actions a human being achieves the highest perfection.

Sloka 47

śreyān svadharmo viguṇaḥ paradharmot svanuṣṭhitāt
svabhāvaniyataṃ karma kurvan nāpnoti kilbiṣam

sreyan = better; sva-dharmah = one's own dharma; vigunah = devoid of merits; para-dharmat = another's duty; suanusthitat = well performed; svabhava-niyatam = according to one's nature; karma = actions; kurvan = performing; na = not; apnoti = attains; kilbisam = sin.

"Better is one's own dharma even if devoid of merits than another's dharma well performed. By performing actions according to one's own nature, one is not tainted by sin.

Sloka 48

sahajaṃ karma kaunteya sadoṣam api na tyajet
sarvārambhā hi doṣeṇa dhūmenāgnir ivāvṛtāḥ

saha-jam = which is born in oneself naturally; karma = duty; kaunteya = O son of Kunti; sa-dosam = faulty, with faultu; api = even if; na = not; tyajet = give up; sarva-arambhah = all actions, undertaking; because = surely; dosena = with fault; dhumena = with smoke; agnih = fire; iva = as; avrtah = enveloped, covered.

"One should not give up one's duty which arises in oneself naturally, O son of Kunti, even if it is faulty because all actions are enveloped by faulty just as fire is enveloped by smoke.

Sloka 49

asaktabuddhiḥ sarvatra jitātmā vigataspṛhaḥ
naiṣkarmyasiddhiṃ paramāṃ saṃnyāsenādhigacchati

asakta-buddhih = detached, disinterested intelligence; sarvatra = universally everywhere; jita-atma = conqueror of oneself ; vigata-sprhah = without desires; naiskarmya-siddhim = accomplishes perfection in obligatory actions; paramam = supreme; sannyasena = by renunciation; adhigacchati = attains.

"With his intelligence detached from everything in all manners, the conqueror of oneself, who is without desires, through renunciation accomplishes the supreme state of perfection in obligatory actions.

Sloka 50

siddhiṃ prāpto yathā brahma tathāpnoti nibodha me
samāsenaiva kaunteya niṣṭhā jñānasya yā parā

siddhim = perfection; praptah = achieved, attained; yatha = just as; brahma = Brahman; tatha = so is; apnoti = attained, reaches; nibodha = understand; me = from Me; samasena = in brief; eva = indeed; kaunteya = O son of Kunti; nistha = perfection or excellence; jnanasya = of knowledge; ya = which; para = the highest.

"Understand from Me in brief, O son of Kunti, just as perfection is achieved, how so Brahman is attained by perfection or excellence in knowledge, which is the highest.

Sloka 51

buddhyā viśuddhayā yukto dhṛtyātmānaṃ niyamya ca
śabdādīn viṣayāṃs tyaktvā rāgadveṣau vyudasya ca

buddhya = intelligence; visuddhaya = completely pure; yuktah = endowed with , filled with, united to; dhrtya = by resolve; atmanam = in oneself; niyamya = restraining; ca = and; sabda-adin = such as sound and the like.; visayan = sense objects; tyaktva = giving up; raga = attachment; dvesau = aversion; vyudasya = setting aside; ca = and.

"Endowed with intelligence that is completely pure, restraining oneself with resolve, giving up sense-objects such as sound and the like, setting aside attachment and aversion...

Sloka 52

viviktasevī laghvāśī yatavākkāyamānasaḥ
dhyānayogaparo nityaṃ vairāgyaṃ samupāśritaḥ

vivikta-sevi = dwelling in solitude; laghu-asi = eating little; yata = controlling; vak = speech; kaya = body; manasah = mind; dhyana = dhyana yoga = meditation and yoga; parah = as the highest; nityam = always; vairagyam = dispassion; samupasritah = having taken refuge.

"Dwelling in solitude, eating little, with speech, body and mind under control, practicing meditation and yoga constantly as the highest, having taken refuge in dispassion...

Sloka 53

ahaṃkāraṃ balaṃ darpaṃ kāmaṃ krodhaṃparigraham
vimucya nirmamaḥ śānto brahmabhūyāya kalpate

ahankaram = egoism; balam = strength; darpam = pride; kamam = lust; krodham = anger; parigraham = without hankering; vimucya = being delivered; nirmamah = without the thought of ownership; santah = peaceful; brahma-bhuyaya = state of Brahman; kalpate = is qualified.

"Freed from egoism, strength, pride, lust, anger, possessions, without hankering, without ownership, (he) is qualified to reach the state of Brahman.

Sloka 54

brahmabhūtaḥ prasannātmā na śocati na kāṅkṣati
samaḥ sarveṣu bhūteṣu madbhaktiṃ labhate parām

brahma-bhutah = Brahman; prasanna-atma = blissful within oneself; na = not; socati = laments; na = not; kanksati = desires; samah = same, equal; sarvesu = all; bhutesu = living beings; mat-bhaktim = devotion to Me; labhate = gains; param = supreme.

"He who has attained Brahman and become blissful within himself neither laments nor desires. Becoming equal to all beings, he gains Supreme devotion to Me.

Sloka 55

bhaktyā mām abhijānāti yāvān yaś cāsmi tattvataḥ
tato māṃ tattvato jñātvā viśate tadanantaram

bhaktya = by devotion; mam = Me; abhijanati = know; yavan = comprehensively; yah ca asmi = who I am; tattvatah = in truth; tatah = then; mam = Me; tattvatah = by truth; jnatva = knowing thus; visate = enters; tat-anantaram = afterwards.

"Through devotion he knows Me comprehensively as to who I am in truth. Then knowing Me in truth, afterwards, he enters (into My State).

Sloka 56

sarvakarmāṇy api sadā kurvāṇo madvyapāśrayaḥ
matprasādād avāpnoti śāśvataṃ padam avyayam

sarva = all; karmani = actions; api = even, although; sada = always, forever; kurvanah = engaged; mat = I am; vyapasrayah = shelter; mat = My; prasadat = grace, mercy; avapnoti = attains; sasvatam = eternal; padam = abode; avyayam = imperishable.

"Even if engaged in all actions forever, for the one to whom I am the shelter, attains the eternal, imperishable Abode through My grace.

Sloka 57

cetasā sarvakarmāṇi mayi saṃnyasya matparaḥ
buddhiyogam upāśritya maccittaḥ satataṃ bhava

cetasa = mentally, by mind; sarva-karmani = all actions; mayi = to Me; sannyasya = renouncing; mat-parah = treating Me as Supreme; buddhi-yogam = the yoga of intelligence; upasritya = taking shelter in; mat-cittah = consciousness; satatam = always; bhava = exists.

"Mentally giving up all actions to Me, treating Me as the Supreme, resorting to the concentration of your intellect, keep your mind steadily fixed.

Sloka 58

maccittaḥ sarvadurgāṇi matprasādat tariṣyasi
atha cet tvam ahaṃkārān na śroṣyasi vinaṅkṣyasi

mat = My; cittah = mind, thoughts; sarva = all; durgani = obstacles; mat = My; prasadat = kindness, mercy; tarisyasi = transcend, cross over; atha = otherwise; cet = if; tvam = you; ahankarat = because of egoism; na = not; srosyasi = do not hear; vinanksyasi = will perish.

"With your mind fixed on Me, by My grace you will transcend all obstacles. Otherwise, if you do not listen because of egoism, you will perish.

Sloka 59

yad ahaṃkāram āśritya na yotsya iti manyase
mithyaiṣa vyavasāyas te prakṛtis tvāṃ niyokṣyati

yat = if; ahankaram = egoism; asritya = taking shelter; na = not; yotsye = fight; iti = thus; manyase = think; mithya = deluded; esah = this; vyavasayah = determination, resolution; te = your ; prakrtih = nature; tvam = you; niyoksyati = force or regulate you.

"Taking shelter in egoism, if ever you think, 'I will not to fight,' deluded it will be this determination of yours. Nature will force you (to fight).

Sloka 60

svabhāvajena kaunteya nibaddhaḥ svena karmaṇā
kartuṃ necchasi yan mohāt kariṣyasy avaśopi tat

svabhava-jena = arising from one's own nature; kaunteya = O son of Kunti; nibaddhah = bound; svena = by one's own; karmana = actions, duty; kartum = to do; na = not; icchasi = like; yat = that; mohat = by delusion; karisyasi = you will do; avasah = without control, involuntarily; api = even; tat = that.

"Bound by your own actions arising from your nature, O son of Kunti, what you would not like to do out of delusion even that you will do helplessly.

Sloka 61

īśvaraḥ sarvabhūtānāṃ hṛddeśerjuna tiṣṭhati
bhrāmayan sarvabhūtāni yantrārūḍhāni māyayā

isvarah = the Supreme Lord; sarva-bhutanam = of all living beings; hrt-dese = heart region; arjuna = O Arjuna; tisthati = seated; bhramayan = move around; sarva-bhutani = all living beings; yantra =

mechanical device, machine; arudhani = mounted; mayaya = by the power of Maya.

"O Arjuna, seated in the heart region of all living beings, the Supreme Lord moves around all the beings by the power of Maya, as if they are mounted on mechanical device.

Sloka 62

tam eva śaraṇaṃ gaccha sarvabhāvena bhārata
tatprasādāt parāṃ śāntiṃ sthānaṃ prāpsyasi śāśvatam 18.62

tam = to Him; eva = only; saranam gaccha = go for shelter or protection; sarva-bhavena = entire being; bharata = O Bharata; tat-prasadat = by His mercy; param = supreme; santim = peace; sthanam = place, abode; prapsyasi = attain; sasvatam = eternal.

"Take refuge in Him only in all respects, O Bharata; by His mercy you will attain supreme peace and eternal Abode.

Sloka 63

iti te jñānam ākhyātaṃ guhyād guhyataraṃ mayā
vimṛśyaitad aśeṣeṇa yathecchasi tathā kuru

iti = thus; te = to you; jnanam = knowledge; akhyatam = revealed; guhyat = than any secret guhya-taram = more secret; maya = by Me; vimrsya = contemplating; etat = this; asesena = fully, deeply; yatha = as you; icchasi = like; tatha = so shall you; kuru = perform.

"Thus to you this knowledge has been revealed by Me, which is the secret of the secrets. Contemplating upon it fully, do whatever you like to do.

Sloka 64

sarvaguhyatamaṃ bhūyaḥ śṛṇu me paramaṃ vacaḥ
iṣṭosi me dṛḍham iti tato vakṣyāmi te hitam 18.64

sarva-guhya-tamam = the most confidential of all; bhuyah = again; srnu = listen; me = My; paramam = supreme; vacah = words; istah asi = you are dear ; me = to Me; drdham = very; iti = since; tatah = therefore; vaksyami = I speak; te = for your; hitam = benefit, wellbeing.

"Listen to Me again the most confidential and supreme words. Since you are very dear to Me, therefore I speak to you for your own good.

Sloka 65

manmanā bhava madbhakto madyājī māṃ namaskuru
mām evaiṣyasi satyaṃ te pratijāne priyosi me 18.65

mat-manah bhava =fix your mind on Me; mat-bhaktah = be My devotee; mat-yaji = My worshiper; mam = to Me namaskuru = offer your salutations; mam = to Me; eva = only, alone; esyasi = come; satyam = truth; te = to you; pratijane = I promise; priyah = dear; asi = you are; me = to Me.

Fix your mind upon Me. Be My devotee (and) My worshipper. Offer your salutations to Me. (Then) you will come to Me only. (This) truth I promise to you (since) you are very dear to Me

Sloka 66

sarvadharmān parityajya mām ekaṃ śaraṇaṃ vraja
ahaṃ tvā sarvapāpebhyo mokṣyayiṣyāmi mā śucaḥ

sarva-dharman = all obligatory duties; parityajya = giving up, renouncing; mam = to Me; ekam = alone, only; saranam = shelter, surrender; vraja = go, take; aham = I; tvam = you; sarva = all; papebhyah = from sins; moksayisyami = liberate; ma = do not; sucah = grieve, worry.

"Renouncing all obligatory duties, in Me alone take shelter. I will liberate you from all sins. Do not grieve.

Sloka 67

idaṃ te nātapaskāya nābhaktāya kadācana
na cāśuśrūṣave vācyaṃ na ca māṃ yobhyasūyati

idam = this; te = you; na = never; atapaskaya = who does not practice austerities; na = never; abhaktaya = who is not a devotee; kadacana = at any time; na = not; ca = and; asusrusave

= who does not serve; vacyam = spoken; na = not; ca = and; mam = to Me; yah = who; abhyasuyati = acts enviously.

"This should never at any time be spoken by you to one who does not practice austerities, who is not a devotee, who does not want to render service and who acts enviously towards Me.

Sloka 68

ya idaṃ paramaṃ guhyaṃ madbhakteṣv abhidhāsyati
bhaktiṃ mayi parāṃ kṛtvā mām evaiṣyaty asaṃśayaḥ

yah = he who; idam = this; paramam = supreme; guhyam = secret; mat = My; bhaktesu = to devotees; abhidhasyati = explains in detail; bhaktim = devotional service; mayi = to Me; param krtva = having performed supreme; mam = to Me; eva = only; esyati = come; asamsayah = without doubt.

"He who explains in detail this supreme secret to My devotees, having performed supreme devotion to Me will come to Me only without any doubt.

Sloka 69

na ca tasmān manuṣyeṣu kaścin me priyakṛttamaḥ
bhavitā na ca me tasmād anyaḥ priyataro bhuvi 18.69

na = not; ca = and; tasmat = than he; manusyesu = among people; kascit = even one; me = to Me; priya-krt-tamah = who performs such dearer action; bhavita = will be; na = not; ca = and; me = My; tasmat = than him; anyah = other; priya-tarah = dearer; bhuvi = in this world.

"And among all the people none whatsoever is a better performer of what is dearer to Me; Nor is there be anyone else in this world who is dearer to Me than he.

Sloka 70

adhyeṣyate ca ya imaṃ dharmyaṃ saṃvādam āvayoḥ
jñānayajñena tenāham iṣṭaḥ syām iti me matiḥ 18.70

adhyesyate = will study; ca = and; yah = he who; imam = this; dharmyam = sacred; samvadam = dialogue; avayoh = of ours; jnana = knowledge; yajnena = through sacrifice; tena = by him; aham = I; istah = worshiped; syam = shall be; iti = this; me = My; matih = opinion.

"And he who shall study this sacred dialogue of ours by the sacrifice of knowledge I will be worshipped by him. This is my opinion.

Sloka 71

śraddhāvān anasūyaś ca śṛṇuyād api yo naraḥ
sopi muktaḥ śubhāṃl lokān prāpnuyāt puṇyakarmaṇām

sraddha-van = he who is full of faith; anasuyah = without envy; ca = and; srnuyat = happens to hear; api = even; yah = any; narah = human being; sah = he; api = also; muktah = liberated from sin; subhan = auspicious; lokan = worlds; prapnuyat = attains; punya-karmanam = of those who perform meritorious actions.

"Any human being who is full of faith and without envy happens even to hear this, liberated from sin, he also attains the worlds of those who perform meritorious actions.

Sloka 72

kaccid etac chrutaṃ pārtha tvayaikāgreṇa cetasā
kaccid ajñānasaṃmohaḥ pranaṣṭas te dhanaṃjaya

kaccit = whether; etat = this; srutam = heard; partha = O Partha; tvaya = by you; eka-agrena = concentrated; cetasa = with mind; kaccit = whether; ajnana = ignorance; sammohah = delusion; pranastah = destroyed; te = of you; dhananjaya = O Dhananjaya.

"Has this been heard by you, O Partha, with concentrated mind? Has this delusion of you caused by ignorance has been destroyed, O Dhananjaya?"

Sloka 73

naṣṭo mohaḥ smṛtir labdhā tvatprasādān mayācyuta
sthitosmi gatasaṃdehaḥ kariṣye vacanaṃ tava

arjunah uvaca = Arjuna said; nastah = destroyed; mohah = delusion; smrtih = memory; labdha = regained; tvat-prasadat = by Your kindness; maya = by me; acyuta = O Acyuta; sthitah = stable; asmi = I am; gata = gone; sandehah = doubts; karisye = I shall act; vacanam = words; tava = as per Your.

Arjuna said, "My delusion has been destroyed and, O Acyuta, by your kindness I regained my memory. I am now stable, with my doubts all gone. I shall now act according to your instructions."

Sloka 74

sañjaya uvāca
ity ahaṃ vāsudevasya pārthasya ca mahātmanaḥ
saṃvādam imam aśrauṣam adbhutaṃ romaharṣaṇam

sanjayah uvaca = Sanjaya said; iti = thus; aham = I; vasudevasya = of Vasudeva; parthasya = of Partha; ca = and; maha-atmanah = great souls; samvadam = dialogue; imam = this; asrausam = heard; adbhutam = wonderful; roma-harsanam = make hair standing on end.

Sanjaya said, "Thus, I heard this dialogue of Vasudeva and the great soul, Partha, which is wonderful and makes one's hair stand on end.

Sloka 75

vyāsaprasādāc chrutavān etad guhyam ahaṃ param
yogaṃ yogeśvarāt kṛṣṇāt sākṣāt kathayataḥ svayam

vyasa-prasadat = by the blessings of the sage Vyasa; srutavan = heard; etat = this; guhyam = most secret; aham = I; param = supreme; yogam = yoga; yoga-isvarat = from the Lord of Yoga; krsnat = from Krishna; saksat = directly; kathayatah = as he was delivering; svayam = personally.

"By the grace of sage Vyasa, I heard this most secret and sacred yoga directly from the Lord of Yoga, Krishna Himself as He was delivering it personally.

Sloka 76

rājan saṃsmṛtya saṃsmṛtya saṃvādam imamadbhutam
keśavārjunayoḥ puṇyaṃ hṛṣyāmi ca muhur muhuḥ

rajan = O King; samsmrtya samsmrtya = remembering again and again; samvadam = the dialogue; imam = this; adbhutam = wonderful; kesava = Kesava; arjunayoh = and Arjuna; punyam = meritorius, pious; hrsyami = rejoice in my heart; ca = and; muhuh muhuh = minute by minute.

"O King, remembering again and again this wonderful, pious dialogue between Kesava and Arjuna I am rejoicing in my heart minute by minute

Sloka 77

tac ca saṃsmṛtya saṃsmṛtya rūpam atyadbhutaṃhareḥ
vismayo me mahān rājan hṛṣyāmi ca punaḥ punaḥ

tat = that; ca = also; samsmrtya samsmrtya = remembering again and again; rupam = form; ati adbhutam = supremely wonderful; hareh = Hari; vismayah = filled with wonder; me = my; mahan = great; rajan = O King; hrsyami = rejoicing in my heart; ca = and; punah punah = again and again.

"O king, remembering that supremely wonderful form of Hari again and again, I am filled with great wonder; I am rejoicing in my heart again and again.

Sloka 78

yatra yogeśvaraḥ kṛṣṇo yatra pārtho dhanurdharaḥ
tatra śrīr vijayo bhūtir dhruvā nītir matir mama

yatra = where; yoga-isvarah = Lord of Yoga; krsnah = Krishna; yatra = where; parthah = Partha; dhanuh-dharah = the bearer of the bow and arrows; tatra = there; srih = wealth, abundance, opulence; vijayah = victory; bhutih = happiness; dhruva = firm, certain; nitih = justice, morality; matih mama = is my opinion.

"Where there is Krishna, the Lord of Yoga, and where there is Partha, the bearer of the bow and arrows there manifest wealth, victory, happiness, and firm justice. This is my opinion.

Conclusion

iti srīmadbhāgavadgītāsupanisatsu brahmavidyāyām yogasāstre
srikrisnārjunasamvāde mokshasanyasayogo nama astadaso 'dhyayah.

iti = thus; srīmadbhāgavadgītā = in the sacred Bhagavadgita; upanisatsu = in the Upanishad; brahmavidyāyām = the knowledge of the absolute Brahman; yogasāstre = the scripture of yoga; srikrisnārjunasamvāde = the dialogue between Sri Krishna and Arjuna; mokshasanyasayogo nama = by name the yoga of liberation by renunciation ; astadasah = eighteenth; adhyayah = chapter.

Thus ends the eighteenth chapter named the the Yoga of Liberation by Renunciation in the Upanishad of the divine Bhagavadgita, the knowledge of the Absolute, the yogic scripture, and the debate between Arjuna and Lord Krishna.

The Greatness of the Bhagavadgita

The following is a free translation of the greatness of the *Bhagavadgita,* as revealed by Lord *Vishnu* to Mother Earth, and proclaimed by sage Suta in the sacred *Varahapurana.*

1. He who practices the teachings of the *Bhagavadgita* assiduously is freed from the stain of *prarabdha karma*. He lives happily in this world and upon death, becomes liberated.

2. He who studies the *Bhagavadgita* with devotion is not stained by sin, just as the lotus leaf is untouched by water.

3 & 4. Wherever the *Bhagavadgita* is kept and wherever it is read regularly, there is the holiness of all the holy places and of all gods, seers, yogis, celestial beings, and even *Narada, Uddhava* and their followers.

5. Where the *Bhagavadgita* is recited regularly, help comes swiftly from God. Where the discussion, recitation and teaching of the *Bhagavadgita* take place, there God resides doubtlessly.

6. God dwells in the Bhagavadgita. It is His best abode. With the wisdom of the *Bhagavadgita,* He protects the threes worlds.

7. The *Bhagavadgita* is God's Supreme Knowledge. It is verily Brahman Himself. It is the dot (*bindu*) in the symbol of Aum and the eternal and inexhaustible Self.

8. It is spoken by Lord Krishna, the Supreme Lord, with His own mouth to Arjuna containing the wisdom of the *Vedas* and the knowledge of the *tattvas.*

9. Whoever constantly studies the eighteen chapters of the *Bhagavadgita* with undistracted mind will gain perfect wisdom and reach the supreme goal.

10. If one cannot complete studying all the eighteen chapters of the *Bhagavadgita,* by studying even half them one gains the merit equal to that of gifting a cow.

11. By reading only one third of the *Bhagavadgita,* he obtains the merit of bathing in the waters of the *Ganga*. By reading only one sixth of it, that is three chapters, he gains the merit of performing a *soma* sacrifice.

12. He who reads daily a single chapter of the *Bhagavadgita* with devotion becomes the member of a *gana* and obtains the world of *Rudra*.

13. He who reads daily one-fourth of a chapter of the *Bhagavadgita,* he is assured of human birth in every reincarnation for the duration of a *manvantara*.

14 &15. He who reads ten, seven, five, four, two, three, one or half a verse of the *Bhagavadgita,* he securely obtains the world of moon or the ancestral world for ten thousand years. Forever reading the *Bhagavadgit*a, and having completed his stay there, when he returns to the mortal world, he would take a human birth.

16. Upon his return, if he continues to practice the *Bhagavadgita* teachings, he will attain the final liberation. At the time of dying, by uttering, "G*ita*" he reaches the immortal path.

17. By regularly listening to the wisdom of the *Bhagavadgita,* even sinners would attain the Abode of God (*Vaikuntha*) and rejoice with the Supreme Lord.

18. He who meditates upon the meaning of the *Bhagavadgita,* having performed his obligatory duties sincerely becomes a liberated soul even in the body (*jivanmukta*). Upon leaving the body, he attains the highest goal.

19. In past, great kings such as *Janaka* and others took refuge in the knowledge of the Bhagavadgita and having been cleansed of all their sins attained the immortal world.

20. Whoever completes the study of the Bhagavadgita, without reading this description of its greatness, his reading shall remain in vain and his effort shall be lost.

21. He who practices the Bhagavadgita and he who reads this eternal greatness of it, which has been declared by Lord Vishnu and proclaimed by Suta, he would gain the fruit, which has been described as above.

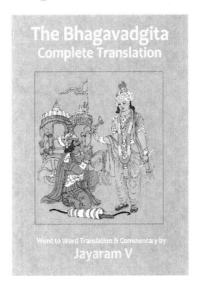

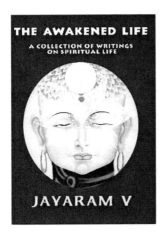

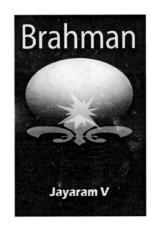

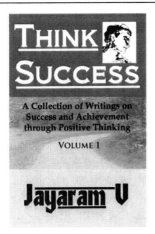

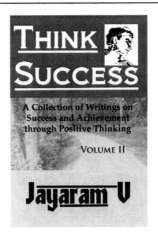

CPSIA information can be obtained at www.ICGtesting.com
Printed in the USA
LVOW12s2227180515

438926LV00009B/258/P

9 781935 760177